W9-DGT-151

SCHOOLS IN THE
GREAT DEPRESSION

STUDIES IN THE HISTORY OF EDUCATION
VOLUME 2
GARLAND REFERENCE LIBRARY OF SOCIAL SCIENCE
VOLUME 1037

STUDIES IN THE HISTORY OF EDUCATION

EDWARD R. BEAUCHAMP, *Series Editor*

SCHOOLS IN THE GREAT DEPRESSION

DOMINIC W. MOREO

GARLAND PUBLISHING, INC.
NEW YORK AND LONDON
1996

Library of Congress Cataloging-in-Publication Data

Moreo, Dominic W.
      Schools in the Great Depression / Dominic W. Moreo.
          p.   cm. — (Garland reference library of social science ; v. 1037.
    Studies in the history of education ; v. 2)
      Includes bibliographical references and index.
      ISBN 0-8153-2039-6 (alk. paper)
      1. Education—United States—History—20th century. 2. United
    States—Social conditions—1933–1945.   I. Title. II. Series: Garland
    reference library of social science ; v. 1037.   III. Series: Garland
    reference library of social science. Studies in the history of education ; vol. 2.
    LA209.M66   1996
    370'.973—dc20   95-44760
                                                         CIP

Cover illustration: Fairview Elementary School.
Courtesy of Seattle Public School Archives 223–161.

Printed on acid-free, 250-year-life paper
Manufactured in the United States of America

[In 1934] serving on the political committee of the American Workers' Party was a rewarding and humbling experience for me. I got to realize how little I knew about the nature of the country whose system I was trying to revolutionize. I acquired a sense of the nature of the difficulties of the men and women in the field. They were not glib in discussing abstractions, but they had a natural pragmatic bent of mind that led them to test large proposals by concrete applications.

—Sidney Hook, *Out of Step*, 1987

But the intellectual is tempted into a more subtle form of truancy. He has only to turn his mind in a certain direction and some unpleasant realities can disappear. He goes in search of original and sweeping ideas, and in the process may conveniently forget the humbling conditions of his own existence as a dissenter depends on the survival of the United States as a free nation in a world going increasingly totalitarian. If his thinking deliberately operates outside the paths of our common life, he complains that he has been alienated. In fact, in no age of history has the intellectual been more influential upon human affairs than in the modern world. Consider the intellectuals of the French Revolution: they have shaped the world we live in, and they were certainly truants, if we may believe Edmund Burke.

—William Barrett, *The Truants*, 1982

One of the most critical challenges to leadership is to read the signs that announce the status quo has outlived its time. Established habits of thought always tend to prevail over the candid recognition of emerging realities. What is involved is not a failure of intelligence—or even a weakness of will—but a deficiency of imagination, that rarest of faculties in any leadership. It is rare because it is not usually very important. But it becomes crucial at precisely those moments when its absence is most critical—moments that represent turning points in the evolution of policy. At such moments, innovation, not coping, is the order of the day.

—Irving Kristol, 1988

CONTENTS

Series Preface

Garland's Studies in the History of Education series includes not only volumes on the history of American and Western education, but also on the history of the development of education in non-Western societies. A major goal of this series is to provide new interpretations of educational history that are based on the best recent scholarship; each volume will provide an original analysis and interpretation of the topic under consideration. A wide variety of methodological approaches from the traditional to the innovative are used. In addition, this series especially welcomes studies that focus not only on schools but also on education as defined by Harvard historian Bernard Bailyn: "the transmission of culture across generations."

The major criteria for inclusion are (a) a manuscript of the highest quality, and (b) a topic of importance to understanding the field. The editor is open to readers' suggestions and looks forward to a long-term dialogue with them on the future direction of the series.

Edward R. Beauchamp

PREFACE

The Great Depression was not a seamless web of human experience. Disparate images of highs and lows in daily individual experiences proliferated. The lament of "Brother, can you spare a dime," of apple selling and breadlines also vied with the distractions of the decade. For many the distractions were welcome in order to avoid the daily reminders of personal failure, hunger, pain, and family hardship. At times the public watched in the press and newsreels the well-to-do cavorting in Palm Beach and Hollywood. At other times, baseball the national pastime along with the movies, radio, and picture magazines such as *Life*, *LOOK*, and the *Saturday Evening Post* brought respite for their fans, viewers, and readers as well as riches to their practitioners. In popular sports, a couple of Joes, DiMaggio and Louis, brought stylish play to baseball and boxing.

In gambling, bingo was the first form to be decriminalized in 1931, a game run by religious and charitable organizations. Although lotteries remained prohibited, contests by the thousands took their place so much so that 100 million entries were submitted for 3,000 contests. "The Depression years," as the Brenners noted, "also brought in their wake the chain-letter craze . . . and other variations of the numbers racket." Finally, "for the poor," as the Brenners added, "slot machines became the most important form of betting."[1]

As the decade opened, the weekly newsreel in movie theaters reported politicians and bankers spewing bromides: "Prosperity is just around the corner" and its refrain. But economic bust deepened and breadlines lengthened. In turn the homeless wore Hoover "blankets"—newspapers for cover or as inserts in clothing—and lived in "Hoovervilles" or shanty towns of discarded cardboard, sticks, and metal. The newsreels also revealed the march of time in breadlines, war in Manchuria, soup lines, the rise of Hitler, the 1936 Olympic games, war in Ethiopia, war in China, war in Spain, war in Poland, and eventually that "day in infamy" at Pearl Harbor.

Amid the solemnities of U.S. Senate hearings, a reporter placed a female midget on the lap of J.P. Morgan Jr. as a publicity stunt. Sadly, a few years later the woman in question would be herded into one of Hitler's death camps. Sorrow would extend to the Lindberghs over their loss of a son while the man accused of the heinous crime, Bruno Hauptmann, protested to the end his innocence. At the 1936 Olympic games, Jesse Owens' athletic victories would upset Hitler while Marian Anderson's would-be recital at Constitution Hall upset the Daughters of the American Revolution. In short, blacks who excelled disrupted for some the social status quo.

Crime disturbed the tranquility of many. To judge by the headlines of the decade, crime was on the rampage. At least robbing banks gave that impression as the sprees of John Dillinger, Bonnie and Clyde, Pretty Boy Floyd, and Willie Sutton attested. In a symbiotic embrace with these notorious figures were the G-men, the Federal Bureau of Investigation, with its shrewd head, John Edgar Hoover. Thanks to Hoover's skillful use of publicity and a selective role for his agency, the fame of the FBI grew. One offshoot of this publicity was the creation of the ten most wanted public figures, their countenances posted in every post office.

As the Depression decade drew to a close, New York City planned a fitting monument to the future as it launched a two-year world's fair. However, the guns of September 1939 curtailed this paean to hope, peace, and prosperity.

William Stott has reminded us that the genre of the documentary came of age in the thirties. In his *Documentary Expression and Thirties America*, Stott observed that "three basic techniques—direct quotation, case study, and firsthand (or participant) observation—describe the ways all written documentary works, the first two exemplifying the direct method of persuasion, and the last the vicarious."[2]

"Human documents" of the period stressed the primacy of feeling as illustrated, for example, in the photographic works of Margaret Bourke White and Walker Evans; or in case histories written for magazines; and by the voices of ordinary experience captured in varying degrees by the movies, newsreels, and radio.

In this spirit what follows is a modest attempt to delineate the effects of the Great Depression upon the schools. For the most part, the "voices" of this work are drawn from the press and periodicals of the times. On one level, this work is concerned with the coming of the Depression and its effects upon the schools. It is a tale worth telling.

Embedded in the historical narrative are three case studies. One concerns Dr. Emil Altman's penchant for drawing up lists of teachers in New York City to be dismissed. Another, the Tusher affair, delineates how parental desires to exercise school choices were stifled by New York City's school bureaucracy. Lastly, following Diane Ravitch's lead, chapter 10 explores a "school war."

On another level, the work explores how the supporters of public education responded to the retrenchment of school budgets. In short, what new institutional rationales did they proffer if any to clothe the schools?

In the introduction we postulate that the public schools as a bureaucratic system in the best of times produced what it was capable of producing, which at times coincided with the wishes of parents and the community. In the worst of times the institution muddled through. Nor did educators from the universities to the schools come forward with a new paradigm for the schools. It was a lost opportunity by the spokesmen of education as chapters 1 and 2 illustrate.

Chapter 3 recounts the Depression's depths as hard times rocked the schools across the land. The following chapter focuses on the reorganization of schools in New York City and concludes with a review of the "McCarthyite" tactics of the chief medical officer of the schools, Dr. Emil Altman, in removing "insane" teachers.

Next we turn to the Puget Sound city of Seattle in chapter 5. The following chapter presents the Tusher affair, a case study of school bureaucratic responses to parental wishes to have their children attend their neighborhood schools. The chapter concludes with a look at parental and student complaints of the schools elsewhere, including those by the Pennsylvania Amish.

Chapter 7 describes the historical albatross that teachers have labored under since the father of the public schools, Horace Mann, initiated the patriarchal tradition of expecting vestal virgins at discounted prices to man the classrooms of the land. Dr. Emil Altman reappears with his second list.

The following chapter concerns itself primarily with the increasing role of the federal government in providing "emergency" financial aid to the schools, especially the role of the Works Progress Administration.

Chapter 9 reveals that while the New Deal attempted to pump-prime the economy, the recovery was aborted by 1937, causing school districts across the land to retrench anew. The remainder of the chapter reviews parental concerns over curricula changes followed by a closing segment on black education in the decade.

While war came to Poland in September of 1939, in New York City school officials and politicians were locked in a symbiotic embrace of well-worn bromides. The final chapter explores this minor school war.

Acknowledgments

For those diligent readers who have kindly read earlier drafts of this work in whole or in part, I am greatly indebted, especially to Edward Beauchamp, David Madsen, Charles Burgess, and Diane Ravitch. Naturally they are not responsible for the errors that may remain.

To my wife, Beverly, an endless source of support in the unfolding of this work, my innumerable thanks.

SCHOOLS IN THE GREAT DEPRESSION

INTRODUCTION

A NEW PARADIGM FOR THE SCHOOLS?

We are stricken by no plague of locusts. . . . Our greatest primary task is to put people to work. . . . It can be accomplished in part by direct recruiting by the government itself, treating the task as we would treat the emergency *of war. . . . I assume unhesitatingly the leadership of this great army of our people dedicated to a disciplined attack upon our common problems.*
—Franklin D. Roosevelt, 1933[1]

In June 1934, John Maynard Keynes, the English economist, came to the United States to confer with President Franklin Delano Roosevelt. Keynes came neither to preside over the liquidation of capitalism nor to make democracy safe for politicians. Rather he came armed with a new economic paradigm with its attendant fiscal policy prescriptions in order to bail out Western economies from the slough of economic depression.

In the process, Keynes' seminal ideas redrew the contours of economic and political institutions in open societies, but more important he offered an alternative to the facile solutions tendered by closed societies such as communism and fascism. These totalitarian states banished unemployment at a price—the loss of freedom. In retrospect, Stalin, Hitler, and Mussolini were costly adventures for their respective societies.[2]

On the domestic front, the American people chose Roosevelt's New Deal call to arms. Rather than revolution, institutional tinkering and reform were the order of the day. On the local level in New York City, Fiorello H. La Guardia came to power in 1934 on a platform of reform and an end to the political corruption that plagued the preceding Jimmy Walker administration. Surrounded by talented men eager to reform city politics, the feisty and ebullient La Guardia instituted a little new deal for the city.[3]

On the labor front, John L. Lewis launched the reformation of organized labor. Dissatisfied with the reluctance of the American Federation of

Labor to organize unskilled workers, Lewis founded the Congress of Industrial Organizations to rectify this omission. The mass production industries of autos, steel, and rubber were inviting opportunities. With consummate organizing skills and verbal facility equal to Roosevelt, Lewis came, like Keynes, not to overthrow the social order but instead to gain a foothold for countless workers.[4]

By contrast, in education there were no equivalents to Roosevelt, La Guardia, Lewis, and Keynes. If anyone was capable of enunciating a new vision of the role of the schools in society, it would have been John Dewey. But it was not to be. Ironically, while Dewey had spent a lifetime calling for reconstruction of thought to keep abreast of social change, the events of the Depression outdistanced contemporary thoughts in education. There was neither a new conception of the role of the schools nor a new institutional mechanism for delivery of schooling; there was no leader of the stature and skills of John L. Lewis to lead and organize teachers; there was no local superintendent of schools akin to La Guardia. Thus bereft of ideas, vehicles, and leadership, the schools, singly and collectively, were left to drift.[5]

But in politics this was not to be the case where a Pirandellian sense of a social script in search of an author found its director. Running through the high drama of the Depression, Franklin D. Roosevelt stepped forward in the many roles of producer, director, impromptu writer, and starring player. With head cocked and cigarette holder slicing the air, Roosevelt with relish and delight rolled up his sleeves and invited the nation as well to tackle the nation's tasks. At last despair held a worthy competitor in the president at the head "of this great army of people." It was also superb theater.

From various parts of the country, they came to Washington offering their services, well wishes, and ideas to the new administration. By the end of the decade, power had passed from Wall Street to the White House. Surrounded by his own "brain-trust" of academic experts, FDR sought initially to relieve the distress among the unemployed, in turn followed by "pump-priming" of the economy. Finally attention was turned to institutional reform of the stock market and banking as well as alterations in agricultural policy and changes in the right of labor to organize.

To galvanize the American people, FDR shrewdly used language as his prime weapon to tame fears, to provide hope, and to point to avenues of actions. The historian William Leuchtenburg has observed that the New Deal owed less to the rhetoric of the Populists and Progressives at the turn of the century than to the national experience of the Wilson administration during the First World War. To the men of that administration, the emergency mobilization of the economy had been an eye-opener both in practice and in principle. In the wake of the war, mobilization had placed a premium on social control with a corresponding low tolerance for wartime dissenters such as Bill Haywood and Eugene Debs.[6]

Thus 14 years later, Roosevelt in his inaugural address, sounded the metaphors of the "emergency of war" and of the "great army of our people" to summon the nation to action. And if the Congress balked at the summons, the president announced without hesitation: "I shall not evade the clear course of duty that will then confront me. I shall ask the Congress for the one remaining instrument to meet the crisis—broad executive power *to wage a war* against the emergency, as great as the power that would be given to me if we were in fact invaded by a foreign foe."

Rather than an abstract and unseen foe, such as the vagaries of the business cycle, Roosevelt brilliantly reduced the economic crisis to the language of ordinary experience. Not only was it clearly understood by all Americans, the war motif also unified the nation and invited the unemployed to take part in surrogate battles fighting erosion of the land under the mantle of newly minted alphabet agencies such as the Civilian Conservation Corps (CCC) and the Works Progress Administration (WPA).

Yet unlike wartime experiences the economy was *not* geared up for maximum production despite various public works programs. To the contrary, various attempts had been made by the early New Deal to curtail production as the National Recovery Administration (NRA) codes and agricultural controls illustrated. Why? Ostensibly to shore up slippery prices.

Challenging this course of action, Keynes proffered unsolicited advice in December 1933 that "the United States is ready to roll toward prosperity if *a good, hard shove* can be given in the next six months." Also, despite Keynes' visit to the White House the following June, FDR's New Deal remained pragmatic and improvisational rather than coordinated and economically sophisticated. The recession of 1937 revealed that the lessons of Keynes had not been learned with dispatch. Nevertheless, the massive "shove" did come, but after Pearl Harbor when a full-scale war, not a putative one, demanded *maximum* production.[7]

After much rewriting, Keynes issued his magnum opus in 1936, *The General Theory of Employment, Interest and Money*, which redrew the landscape of economics with a new paradigm. Instead of accepting depressions as the normal expression of Adam Smith's "invisible hand" of market prices, Keynes carefully took note of the severity of the Great Depression and then delineated how an economy could come to rest at some point below the overall capacity of the economy in terms of labor and capital equipment. In short, idle men and idle equipment.

Such a statement flew in the face of Say's Law that production created its own demand with the corollary that one business firm's loss would be another's gain. In short, while a few firms might go bankrupt, the economy had a natural tendency to return to a general equilibrium. Curiously, a number of economists joined politicians in publicly denying what their senses daily revealed about idle men and plants.

After erecting an intellectual framework that summed up economic activities in three broad sectors of consumption, investment, and governmental activities, Keynes then proceeded to the policy implications of the new paradigm. For example, given the turndown in economic activity, it was essential that the federal government practice a countercyclical fiscal policy to offset the contraction of consumers and business firms. Accordingly the appropriate fiscal medicine was to reduce taxes, increase government expenditures, and incur budgetary deficits, thereby driving interest rates down. Then with workers rehired, consumer expenditures would rise, inventories of goods would increase, and business firms would invest in new plants. In tandem these actions would spur recovery.

But in the late 1930s Keynesian economics posed a challenge to the age's *cake of custom*, causing apoplexy to conservative politicians and businessmen fearful that the new fiscal policy was but a prelude to a march on socialism. With benefit of hindsight, we can see Keynes came to save capitalism with its private property and market economy, not to act as its hangman.[8]

Strangely enough, no man had come to the presidency better prepared than Herbert Hoover. But when confronted by the persistence of the Depression, he could not easily untangle himself from his principles of minimal government and the talisman of a balanced federal budget. Late in his administration when overwhelmed by the march of events, even the principle of the balanced budget was breached.

Reluctantly Hoover signed into law the creation of the Reconstruction Finance Corporation, which issued low-cost loans to banks and businesses. By itself it was too late. Also the attempt to balance the budget led to a fiscal policy by Hoover of increasing taxes and/or reducing expenditures. This was a perverse policy of fighting inflation not deflation, which when coupled with a restrictive monetary policy and the passage of the Smoot–Hawley protectionist tariff all but ensured a severe depression. As impenetrable winter cold swept across the land early in 1933, Herbert Hoover sat in the White House awaiting his dismissal.[9]

Not so easily dismissed were the public remarks of educators across the land. If the "generals" of education could not make a fresh case for the maintenance of the public schools on larger social grounds than the teaching of the three Rs, then the "troops" of teachers could only bemoan their fate of pay cuts, payless furloughs, discounted pay checks, increased student class loads, lack of textbooks and materials, a sometime deteriorating school building—all papered over by a real threat of losing one's shaky position. When teachers finally acted, they protested out of desperation, not out of strength and calculation. Splintered like a jigsaw puzzle into countless Balkanized school districts, teachers more often than not were silent in the grip of impotence. Why were teachers in this condition? Basically, the inability of teachers to be little more than "hired hands" as Howard Beale observed was attributable to historical reasons and to the fragmented structure of the public schools.[10]

A brief historical look follows in order to provide a background for what unfolds below. With the blessing of Horace Mann in the 1840s, teaching became a preserve mostly for women. By the close of the First World War, 85 percent of all teachers were women; by the onset of the 1930s the figure had declined somewhat to 80 percent. To the legal, political, and social discrimination imposed on women in teaching, they received (before the advent of the single salary schedule) approximately half the pay of their male counterparts, who were mostly high school teachers. Since women teachers who married had to resign, they were as a result cheap and docile. As marriage beckoned women teachers, turnover of staff was assured. In short, altar-bound teachers were replaced by shining new faces at a lower salary. While the perennial call for experienced "professional" teachers continued, the turnover of teachers did not dismay school boards.

Two points can be made with regard to the structure of the public schools. Although much applauded, the principle of local control of education has been abated in part by the century-old move to consolidate small school districts. Nevertheless, while local control has been politically attractive, it has reinforced the isolation of the classroom teacher, thereby hindering discourse among teachers much less pedagogical innovations. Into this breach textbook publishers and the college boards have willy-nilly introduced national norms.

The second factor restricting the public schools' ability to respond to new challenges was the birth of the bureaucratic schools, a process completed by the late 1920s in urban centers. By the turn of the century, the spread of the high school had completed the educational ladder from kindergarten to the twelfth grade. By the 1920s, the junior high had been spun off from the senior high school, thereby ushering in the 6-3-3 system. As to curricula shifts, the classical studies of the early high school gave way to multiple tracks, often implicit, of general, academic, business, and vocational courses of study. Why? To accommodate burgeoning enrollments of diverse students corralled by compulsory attendance laws.

In addition to utilitarian functions, the public schools by the time of the First World War were charged with the task of Americanizing the children of immigrants by day and their parents by night in naturalization and language classes. However, as the misfit between students and curricula, at least on the high school level, became apparent to school administrators, guidance programs were tacked onto the school's mission less to counsel students for the world of work than to adjust them to the daily school routines.

When the limits of verbal persuasion by guidance counselors of their charges were soon reached, administrative expediency demanded a policy of automatic promotion of students by the 1930s lest too many overaged and "retarded" students clog the machinery of school life.

Hence by the 1920s the urban public schools had settled into the bureaucratic routines that are all too familiar today. The birth of the bureaucratic ethos also coincided with a feverish school building program and the erection of imposing central school headquarters to house the new bureaucrats. For school officials it was a decade of growth. As for the artifacts of bureaucracy, they included the single-salary schedule, which required the wisdom of a clerk to administer. In addition, there existed a hierarchy of school administrators and staff replete with procedures, handbooks, regulations, syllabi, and endless forms in duplicate.

If, on the one hand, the superintendent was the titular head of the schools, there emerged the business manager concerned with dollar costs and the routines of the institution. Gradually the locus of power shifted into the hands of the business manager. By the time of the stock market crash of 1929, the large urban schools had largely rigidified their rituals and routines.[11]

If both school administrators and teachers were embedded in rituals and routines, this raises a question of institutional performance from another perspective. Does Thorstein Veblen's concept of "trained incapacity" apply as well to institutional performance? Do institutions, for example, respond to their clients' wishes, or are they more responsive to their own organizational needs? Generally, there are two kinds of organizations: profit and nonprofit ones. In the face of market competition, business firms that ignore their customers in favor of their executives and employees face declining sales in due course and share price and eventually bankruptcy. But this cruel taskmaster of the market does not apply so easily to nonprofit organizations from the post office and war department to the local police department and public schools. Or should they be exempt from the realm of satisfactory and unsatisfactory performance? If so, then political considerations become paramount instead of efficiency in producing goods and services.

And if society decides that some activities should enjoy the protective tariff of government provision and then coupled with a quasi-monopoly status as well, then the danger arises that such agencies may well ignore their so-called clients or customers. It is a double danger combining monopoly and political exemption from the rigors of the marketplace. The result is indifference to the quality of service offered to the public, rising yearly expenditures to the taxpayers, and an entrenched bureaucracy.[12]

The foregoing observations are applicable to the schools with an overlay of another complexity. Who are the *recipients* of what the schools offer? Is it simply the students in the classrooms? Or the community or society? More fundamentally, who pays for and who receives the benefits of schooling? Now and in the future? Such questions have generated a modest literature by economists on the subject.

Returning to the issue of institutional performance, consider the following case history. Speaking of the agencies that supply services to the blind in this country, Donald A. Schon has noted that these organizations are primarily geared to provide services toward a work-oriented purpose. Since the 1930s, however, the composition of the blind population has changed. Today they are largely composed of the aged, the multiply handicapped, those with impaired residual vision, and the blind who are poor. Yet, today, "The result is that the official blindness system provides services to only a relatively small fraction of those who are actually blind and eligible for assistance." Schon goes on to add that "since the services offered are largely education, rehabilitation and care, *only about 20 per cent of the total blind population are actually being served today.*" Why? Because of indifference or incompetence? Hardly. The answer is, as Schon chillingly observes, that "for good bureaucratic reasons, agencies tend to behave as if they believed that the blind need, or should have, *the services which happen to be offered by the agencies* rather than that agencies should modify services in response to characteristics of the blind population."[13]

Clearly, those beyond the reach of the marketplace run the risk, not unlike the penchant of generals to rerun past wars. As Kenneth Burke has reminded us, Veblen's trained incapacity "meant the state of affairs whereby *one's very abilities can function as blindness.*" What do we have here? We have, in other words, a performance ceiling on both individuals and institutions, a veritable black box. Thus both Veblen and Schon have pointed to a serious constraint in human and institutional affairs. In what follows, the above concepts will be used as heuristic devices to illuminate the past.[14]

If in the 1920s the business of America was business, then "by force of habit," Veblen has written, "men trained to a business like view of what is right and real will be irretrievably biased against any plan of production and distribution that is not drawn in terms of commercial profit and loss." However, this limitation of perspective is not restricted to businessmen alone. Aside from a liberal arts one, all specialized education leads to "trained incapacities."[15]

Given the heritage of Horace Mann and the bureaucratic ethos enveloping the schools, school officials and educators during the Depression engaged in reflex actions of opposition to budgetary cuts. But school boards and city councils across the land, as the following pages make clear, had little latitude except to slash expenditures in the face of declining revenues.

The Depression exposed another facet of the structure of the schools. The schools were rigid organizations with little or no flexibility to alter the mix of components or to offer schooling in a different mode. Schools were at their best in dealing with *routine* matters. On the other hand, slashed payrolls and school closures revealed the absence of institutional slack to meet emergencies not unlike a family bereft of a larder, savings account, and insurance. Expressed in terms that Kenneth Boulding has used, the schools were an example of an institution that *adapted* into circumscribed roles rather than remaining *adaptable*.[16]

In the absence of a new role and conception, with its attendant institutional recasting, the schools were left to minister to routine and clerical tasks. To be sure, educators since Horace Mann have not been modest in adding on new tasks to the basic mission of reading and writing. The first two chapters recount the divergent recommendations of educators as to what the schools should have delivered.

Instead of considering the limitation of the schools as an institution, a number of educators chose to place the school at the center of society with presumed Euclidian leverage to lift society. Unable to do the impossible, school officials were left with the reductive strategy of dispensing bombast and bromides while a number of schools closed and students received extended holidays. In turn, the young were left to join their elders in forming the lines of the untutored and the jobless.

Voices from the Old Guard

Middletown, like every other society, lives by a relatively small and selected group of cultural cliches, bred of its experience and emotionally heavily loaded with moral affect. These are the underlying drumbeats of life in Middletown. They make "sense" and give the security of the familiar, and in times of strain they tend to stiffen and to become obligatory behavior.

—Robert and Helen Lynd, 1937[1]

As the Depression visited the homes and classrooms of America, what advice did educators proffer the public and teachers? For the most part, we note the comments of university presidents and professors and then focus on the birth of a periodical founded by educators, the *Social Frontier*. However, we begin with John Dewey. Born in the village America of Burlington, Vermont, in 1859, John Dewey approached by the 1930s the summit of his career. With the publication of *Liberalism and Social Action* in 1935, he had turned 76. In this critical work, Dewey sought to secure a foothold for liberalism from the onslaught of the ideologues of the left and the right. He insisted that ideas preceded action in that "a liberal program has to be developed . . . and enforced upon public attention, before direct political action of a thorough-going liberal sort will follow." Yet Dewey remained disturbed because of the disjunction between knowledge and action that transpired in the public realm. "After all, our accumulated knowledge of man and his ways, furnished by anthropology, history, sociology and psychology," Dewey recounted while ignoring economics, "is vast, even though it be sparse in comparison with our knowledge of physical nature. But it is still treated as so much theoretic knowledge amassed by specialists, and at most communicated by them in books and articles to the general public." Aside from these misgivings, Dewey presented vigorously the case for democratic socialism.[2]

While Dewey's work broke no new ground, it was a work of reaffirmation of democracy, and of astute insights into the nature of thought. Dewey lampooned "those empiricists of the present day who attack every measure and policy that is new and innovating on the ground that it does not have the sanction of experience when what they really mean by 'experience' is patterns of mind that were formed in a past that no longer exists."[3]

For many economists the worldwide Depression was a chilling phenomenon that challenged the conceptions of how a market economy operated. Unable to explain the causes of the Depression, economists joined the ranks of bankers and politicians in exorcising the economic evil by jaw-boning. In this setting, John Maynard Keynes had completed "by the end of 1934 the first draft of *The General Theory of Employment, Interest and Money.*" Prior to the work's publication two years later, Keynes had sought academic comment, which after sifting and revision, he incorporated into the final draft. But to a number of economists, Keynes' mental reformulations elicited resistance by "those patterns of mind that were formed in a past that no longer existed" and whose patterns were outmoded.[4]

To the conventional wisdom of the day, Keynes quietly demurred. As noted above, he insisted instead that market economies could come to rest at a new equilibrium well below the full employment of men and machines unless countercyclical fiscal policies of expanded public expenditures and reduced taxes were enacted. Of course, budgetary deficits would ensue. For the most part, the deficits would be financed by the banking system, thus expanding the money supply and thereby driving interest rates downward. In turn, attractive credit might induce businessmen to expand and consumers to borrow for durable goods. Thus stimulated, the economy would recover.

To return to Keynes and his intellectual odyssey. For his ideas, Keynes had sought the approval of a fellow economist, D.H. Robertson in England. Instead as Roy Harrod, Keynes' biographer relates, "Robertson was frankly unsympathetic. He disliked the new concepts that Keynes employed in his analysis. He held that some of the propositions masquerading under a new guise were merely reformulations of what had been already said, reformulations which sometimes tended to allow a dangerous element of fallacy to creep in. . . . The Keynesian reconstruction was ill-judged because it made an unnecessary disturbance to well-tried modes of thought and opened the door to propositions the fallacious character of which the old terminology would have revealed." Nevertheless, the reality of the Depression intruded into the "well-tried modes of thought" in economics that were found wanting along with the bromides of bankers and politicians that the economy was fundamentally "sound." Robertson's staunch defense of the conventional wisdom led Keynes to the conclusion that Robertson had not really understood the novel aspects and the intellectual reach of the *The General Theory*.[5]

With the first draft completed, Keynes came to the United States in June 1934 eager to proffer policy recommendations. Whatever the differences of personality and position between FDR and Keynes, both welcomed the active intervention of the national government in reducing unemployment and spurring economic recovery.

On the domestic front, John Dewey did not devise a reformulation of the role of the public schools or, more broadly, of education in society. Nor did he devise a new formulation or social policy for the home allied with the school as hearth and classroom might be. Of course, Dewey shared with Keynes the belief in the efficacy of thought upon social affairs. Toward the close of the *The General Theory*, Keynes remarked of those spirits who seemed smugly secure in their self-made stances of assurance that "practical men, who believe themselves to be quite exempt from any intellectual influence, are usually the slaves of some defunct economist. Madmen in authority, who hear voices in the air, are distilling their frenzy from some academic scribbler of a few years back." He concluded that "I am sure that the power of vested interests is vastly exaggerated compared with the gradual encroachment of ideas. . . . Soon or late, it is ideas, not vested interests, which are dangerous for good or evil."[6]

If Dewey could not shed the "well-tried modes of thought" in education, then what of other educators as to the place and priority of the schools in society? To the teachers and parents of the nation, the advice that emanated from professional educators was often contradictory. To begin with, Professor George Strayer of Columbia University in 1933 took the high road by insisting that "I question whether there are any other obligations that take priority over education." Assertion, yes, but demonstration of the premise was not forthcoming. Strayer went on to add, "I confidently believe that both in our individual and our collective economy we may find it necessary to eliminate other services and luxuries in order to maintain the more fundamental service of education." Which service and luxuries were to be denied? By whom? Strayer was silent on both matters.[7]

Advice of another sort came from the president of Rutgers University, Robert C. Clothier, when he warned teachers at a state convention that the nation had "smoked economic hashish and seen economic visions, beautiful but wholly without substance . . . . The time has come to cease thinking up fine-spun webs of social and economic theory, to stop trying to find short cuts; the time is here to get back to essentials." Was Clothier the "slave of some defunct economist?" He added a host of homilies including the wish for a more enlightened citizenry, respect for law, and a "spirit of courage and initiative and self-reliance which our emergency relief measures have so tragically undermined."[8]

Taking a different tack, Dean William F. Russell of Teachers College (Columbia University) in November 1935 urged the public schools to teach about communism, religion, and other controversial subjects because "if we are to avert the dangers presented by demagogues, false prophets and pseudo socioeconomic politicians, we must have a soundly educated, well informed electorate." A month later in his annual report, Dean Russell provided a glimpse as to the target of his remarks when he took sharp issue with the New Deal's interventions into social life as a "symptom of a process of decay already in progress." Yet when his colleague Nicholas Murray Butler, president of Columbia University, praised the Little Red Schoolhouse as an "almost ideal educational instrumentality," Dean Russell challenged the simplified educational methods glorified in the nostalgic little school on the prairie. Still another educator, Harold W. Dodds of Princeton University, pleaded for a return to the ideals of colonial education. Dodds noted that "the founders of our Colonial colleges conceived them as educating individuals to play the part of leaders in a democracy. Visions of mass education came later. Can we do better than to return to this principle of individualization under programs of 'supervised freedom'?"[9]

Aside from the New Deal efforts, the plight of unorganized workers in the mass production industries of steel, auto, and rubber captured the attention of John L. Lewis. Unable to persuade the American Federation of Labor (AFL) to grant industrial charters, Lewis seceded from the AFL and brought the Congress of Industrial Organization (CIO) into existence. But in the world of education, Dean William Russell warned 600 school administrators in July of 1936 that the unionization of teachers and school employees would lead to the dominion of the schools by organized labor. Russell labeled this the "Soviet idea" in contrast to the "democratic" control of the schools exercised by the people through elected school board members. Continuing his cautionary tale, Russell advised, "We should be careful not to allow ourselves to be swept off our feet either by those unduly influenced by foreign experience or by those inadequate in their understanding of the workings of democracy and failing in their love for American ideals."[10]

Others chose to criticize the schools on strictly pedagogical grounds. Addressing Catholic educators, the Reverend Richard J. Quinlan, superintendent of Catholic schools in the archdiocese of Boston, warned educators against the "easy road to learning." Taking the measure of progressive educators, he added that "it is all very well to talk about interesting the child, but let us not confuse real education with amusing and entertaining children." Furthermore, he deplored the decline of the public schools as they neglected to stress spelling, oral reading, grammar, and arithmetic.[11]

Also inveighing against progressive education as the "rabbit-theory of education," Nicholas Murray Butler objected to "the practice and the policy of permitting the student who is a mere child to choose his own subjects of study without direction or oversight." To Butler, the result was not an education, but a rabbit turned loose much as "any infant is encouraged to roam about an enclosed field, nibbling here and there at whatever root or flower or weed may, for the moment, attract his attention or tempt his appetite." To what end? "All this is described," Butler added, "by the ludicrous term of self expression. Those who call this type of school work progressive, reveal themselves as afloat on a sea of inexperience without chart or compass . . . or even a rudder."[12]

In a similar vein, Harry M. Wriston, president of Brown University, noted that democracy was the "most dangerous from of government" that required constant vigilance by the people. Therefore he took issue with what he felt was the coddling of school children. He deplored especially the "abolition of failure by edict" in many public schools. To Wriston the greater danger to students was in "killing them by mistaken kindness than by overwork."[13]

Continuing the academic critique of education, Professor Edwin F. Carpenter, an astronomer at the University of Arizona, charged that high school and college education had degenerated into "parrot learning" for examinations. In his view the choice was an education for understanding or one for temporary memory. Carpenter hoped that the public would begin to appreciate the virtues of scholarship and non-assembly-line education, but he remained doubtful as to the outcome. On the other hand, Constance Warren, president of Sarah Lawrence College, observed that schools and colleges were too "bookish" in tone and emphasis whereas "the most valuable education comes from a practical way of living."[14]

Speaking before summer session students at Teachers College, Professor David Snedden asserted that the failure to train students for effective citizenship was the result of poor teacher training in "civic education." To remedy this deficiency, Snedden proposed that 15 percent of all school time for students between the ages of 12 to 18 be devoted to the study of civics. He also lamented that the secondary schools had failed to "fit prospective men and women to function effectively as party members, opinion makers, collective employers of public servants and judges of political policies." Long an advocate of social efficiency by the schools, Snedden included in his vocabulary the tell-tale "training," "fit" and "effective" that bespoke the school as a maze to sort out and adjust students to their niches in society.[15]

As some of the above academicians complained that an incipient Gresham's Law was at work in education, there were those who welcomed the dilution of the traditional product. L.H. Dennis, executive secretary of the American Vocational Association, for example, urged fellow educators to expand the high school curriculum in order to meet the needs of a diverse student clientele. Dennis asserted that 85 percent of high school students found little of value in the curriculum of 1935 since it was crowded with "non-essentials" or else geared to college preparation, whereas vocational education had the weight of daily reality in helping to find a job with a skill in hand. But George Strayer countered this view that the high school graduates of 1938 were "too young to get jobs in business or industry and should be *kept in school* until they reach 19 or 20 years in age." This view presented before the annual meetings of the New York State School Boards Association permitted Strayer to advance the idea that in a de facto sense the schools were a custodial institution with the task of warehousing the young away from the labor market.[16]

Turning to pedagogy, an Albany, New York, teacher objected to the dry education courses which were "destitute of spontaneity and life." Given this dull preparation, in his view, "the run-of-the-mill teacher does his work acceptably, avoids trouble and finally is pensioned to make way for others equally fitted to become cogs in the splendid machine. But the finer spirits, the innovators, those who comprehend the infinite possibilities of untrammeled teaching escape from this thralldom at the earliest opportunity. The tragic consequence is the steady compression of the teaching personnel toward mediocrity." While there were echoes of Matthew Arnold in the teacher's lament, the question remained unanswered how a "fine spirit" such as he had remained in the classroom.[17]

Seemingly in agreement with the foregoing teacher, an irate citizen charged that "youth is led by teachers many of whom are wholly unworthy of the profession. When education is administered by teachers who, though they may know their subjects, are nevertheless primarily interested in their monthly checks, it is certain that youth cannot receive a proper education." Was this once again a call for a colony of saints in the classroom?[18]

Yet, despite criticisms of curriculum or pedagogy, the larger world intruded into the schools. Echoing President Roosevelt's plea for neutrality following the invasion of Poland by Germany on September 1, 1939, James Marshall, president of the New York City Board of Education, also called upon teachers to guard against expressions of hatred and intolerance. Otherwise, in his view, tyranny would ensue. More generally, his colleague on the board, Johanna Lindlof, concluded: "It is with a sense of anxiety that I watch 1939 draw to a close" because of threats to progress in education. Chapter 10 will amplify some of Lindlof's anxieties.[19]

However, in 1939 U.S. Commissioner of Education John W. Studebaker took that year a more sanguine view of the state of education. He approvingly cited numerous experiments across the country including Dallas County's abolition of report cards and the opposition of Minnesota's teachers to saddling students with too much homework.[20]

Not so sanguine was another observer of the educational scene. In a year-end review, Frederick L. Redefer, executive secretary of the Progressive Education Association, pointed to some ominous portents. Redefer recalled that in 1916 impending wartime hysteria had wrought untoward effects in the schools and society. On the eve of another impending world war he was not sanguine that intolerance would not return. He sharply stated that "as a profession, educators are not prepared to defend freedom of speech or thought in times of peace, let alone in times of national mobilization." Summing up recent events, Redefer commented, "Schoolmen with ears to the ground hear the rumble of economy drives. . . . Reports and studies of national and state groups, such as the Regents Inquiry of New York State, all point to the need of drastic changes in education, yet schoolmen are slow to act." Also with congressional witch hunts such as the Congressional Dies Committee on the loose, teachers were likely to become more timid "in a profession already fearful." As a result, "Innovations and experiments face the double assault of the labels 'communistic' and 'fads and frills.'" Concluding on a dramatic note, Redefer stated, "There seems to be no clear clarion call in education as the curtain sinks in 1939."[21]

Aside from intramural criticisms of public education, throughout the decade, the Hearst newspapers had launched a crusade against "reds" in the classroom. While this quarter of criticism was familiar, the birth of the Dies Committee in the Congress to investigate "un-American" activities disturbed Redefer and many others in education from the lower grades through the university. Typical of the criticism of the schools that the Dies Committee encouraged was the testimony of Harper Knowles, chairman of the California American Legion, that California's schools from the lower grades to the college level were inculcating students with "radical and liberal thought." Knowles singled out Stanford University as a notoriously liberal institution with some of its professors under the presumably baneful influence of George S. Counts of Teachers College.[22]

Red-baiting aside, the more fundamental issue of equal educational opportunity rarely surfaced. Writing in 1934, Eunice F. Barnard, a *New York Times* education writer, raised the issue. She began by insisting that "our school system, of which we have boasted . . . is in fact no system at all" Barnard added, "The fact remains that some of our children are paupers and some are millionaires in educational opportunity. . . . An American public school at the moment may connote anything from an unheated, dilapidated one-room shack, closed until further notice, to a 200-room palace whose frescoed walls, swimming pools and air-conditioned interior a Roman Emperor might envy." Given the disparity of educational opportunities across the land, she advised parents "who would give their children the most and best education would better choose with care the town and state in which to live."[23]

Along with others who had questioned the persistence of rural schools, Barnard added that "service on the school committee is one of the popular and time-honored America amateur sports, enjoyed today by 423,000 of our fellow citizens." But this active participation came at a price. Summing up with a scalpel, she stated that "our twin philosophies of local *initiative in school matters and equality of opportunity* for all children have not in practice proved compatible. Local initiative has run away with the game, to the immense benefit of some children, and the equal disadvantage of others." Thus in Barnard's view, the deficiencies of public schooling were not so much attributable to teacher preparation, or curricula changes as to institutional cross-purposes. Was this cherished concept of local public education a contributing factor as well to the "blindness system" enumerated above? Having wielded her scalpel, Barnard recommended the consolidation of rural schools and the establishment of national standards and financing of the public schools.[24]

Five years later, U.S. Commissioner of Education John W. Studebaker stressed the need for the states to equalize educational opportunity within each state. "In this way, the States," he averred, "are more and more making it possible for good schools to be provided in all localities within their respective borders." Given the New Deal's retrenchment in domestic programs, it was a politic move by Studebaker to place the initiative upon the states. Of course, this recommendation ignored the realities of malapportioned and gerrymandered state legislatures, a future issue for the federal courts in the 1960s.[25]

Despite the foregoing disparate comments, there remained two opposed views in education both claiming lineage from John Dewey. The first group established as its guiding principle the child-centered curriculum. This viewpoint found expression in the activities and journals of the Progressive Education Association. The alternate view insisted that individualism was an anachronism in an age of rapid social change and large scale institutions. In the latter camp, George Counts was a leading advocate of the social reconstructionist view. The Great Depression seemed to lend credence to this view with the economy and society seemingly at breaking point.

To give expression to these views, Norman Woelfel and Mordecai Grossman held discussions with Professor William H. Kilpatrick of Teachers College. After further discussions, George Counts was persuaded to become editor of a new journal, the *Social Frontier,* with Woelfel and Grossman providing heavy editorial support. With Counts in the editor's chair, John Dewey was joined by fellow colleagues from Teachers College and other academics in writing articles. Beginning in the fall of 1934, contributors included among others Merle Curti, Ferdinand Lundberg, Lewis Mumford, Charles A. Beard, and Sidney Hook. The birth of the journal is an oft told tale.[26]

To whom was the journal addressed? In an end-page blurb, the journal insisted that it brought "to teachers: keen analysis of the various aspects of our civilization especially as they bear upon the work of the school. Forthright advocacy of social pioneering in education. Fearless support in the struggle of the school for the right to discharge its obligation in *building a new social order*." The utopian motif appeared at the outset.[27]

To John Dewey, a frequenter contributor, the journal "exists, as I understand it, to promote among teachers, and among parents and other who are responsible for the conduct of education just this intelligent understanding of the social forces and movements of our times, and the role that educational institutions have to play." It was a moderate statement given the polemics of the editors and other writers for the journal.[28]

The title and talisman of the *Social Frontier* became synonymous with other pet phrases such as class struggle, social reconstruction, collectivism, socialism, and the new social order. The patron saints of the journal were Thorstein Veblen, from whom they appropriated technocratic and social engineering motifs; John Dewey, from whom they borrowed freely ideas of social change and social reconstruction; and Condorcet and Jefferson, from whom they absorbed on faith the role of reason in human affairs that led if unhindered to the perfectibility of human kind and the good society.

While addressed to teachers, the *Social Frontier* felt no urgency in enlisting teachers to write for its pages. The basic format of the journal consisted of editorials, signed articles, a John Dewey page, book reviews, letters, and two potpourri columns extracted from the press under the rubrics of Notes for the Future Historian and Voices from Olympus, the later quoting educators and public figures ostensibly dedicated to the status quo.

A review of some key ideas and positions from the pages of the first year of the journal is in order. In a series of editorials, the writers recalled the many changes in science, technology, and the scale of society with the effect that "an age of individualism in economy is closing and an age of collectivism is opening." Of necessity, in their view, the American people had to make difficult choices of "social reconstruction" especially "whether the great tradition of democracy is to pass away with the individualistic economy to which it has been linked historically." Also "while recognizing the school as society's central educational agency, it refuses to limit itself to a consideration of the work of this institution." There was a hint that perhaps the larger politics of society might be under scrutiny. On the other hand, Goodwin Watson insisted that "education comprises all that makes a social order distinctive" and that education was the social frontier. Watson went on to note that "people able to see new questions or to experiment with new answers, must inevitably be products of a different education." Who were these seers? Presumably the writers of the journal.[29]

While cautioning his colleagues over the idea that the schools could literally "be builders of a new social order," Dewey was equally insistent that the "plea that teachers must passively accommodate themselves to existing conditions is but one way—and a cowardly way—of making a choice in favor of the old and the chaotic." Thus he hoped that there were enough teachers to make the "schools active and militant participants in the creation of a new social order."[30]

Echoing Matthew Arnold, W.H. Kilpatrick, a key founder of the journal, stated that "youth must learn to live richly. The school must then bring to growing youth 'the best that has been thought and said,' and all else that serves to make life rich and sweet." In his view, the obstacle preventing this condition was the profit motive nullifying all hopes of fulfillment. Hence, "efforts for private gain must give way to cooperative efforts for the common good. The educator must, with others, accept the task of effecting this reconstruction." But the conclusion did not follow from the premise. Even assuming a completely socialistic society, would individuals choose the liberal arts over a vocational or technical education?[31]

Considering that the journal was an organ produced by professional educators dedicated to reshaping the conventional wisdom in politics and economics, they remained deaf to the pejorative ring of their slogans. To those who objected to the label of "collectivism," the editors responded that the denotation of the word existed in the realities of technology, production, communication, and transportation—"a vast and complicated economic mechanism." Granted that a technological imperative might be on the loose, it did not follow that the "collective" label with its connotations of the Soviet Union was a wise choice by the editors unless polemical diatribes rather than persuasion were the ultimate ends. At times it appeared that the *Social Frontier* was but a junior sibling of the *Nation* and the *New Republic* in style and polemics rather than a platform for the teachers of America.

Taking a Veblenian tack, the journal wondered whether the economy would be managed for the few, or the "great masses of the people"? On this question, the editors noted "the American people must in the years ahead make one of the truly grand choices of history." On the side of angels, the journal announced that it would fight so that "no child will be starved and dwarfed, coddled and pampered, by reason of birth and circumstance." Having reviewed these thoughts and sentiments, the editors were "confident that it will have the support of at least ninety per cent of the teachers of this country."[32]

Perusing the first year of the journal, one is immediately struck by the love/hate relationship that its editors exhibited to its presumed audience— the nation's teachers. Again and again, the editors called upon the teachers to shake off their timidity, to organize, and to seize the banner of the new social order. As 1935 dawned, the journal reminded teachers that *class struggle* did not permit retreat into neutrality—they had to choose sides. Given the cultural lag in the dissemination of new ideas, so the editors averred, there remained "an enormous task of intellectual orientation" for the American people. They advised teachers to "positively and consistently . . . seek to develop in the population those values, attitudes, ideals, and loyalties consonant with the new way of life." Curiously, in a final paragraph, the editors offered their readers a caveat that the school was but one agency of education which "may still be *weaker than either the family or industry*." But it was a qualification and insight that the editors chose quickly to ignore in its pages.[33]

Similarly ignored was Charles Beard's advice in its pages when he remarked that "after the founding fathers and their immediate successors disappeared from the scene came the sciolists and daydreamers who thought that the perpetuity of American society was guaranteed if every boy was given an elementary education and then the ballot on reaching maturity." He added that "it was a pleasing illusion rudely shattered by events." In passing, Beard urged teachers to study their Federalist Papers rather than Marx for clues to class conflicts and their resolutions.[34]

Also taking issue with the *Social Frontier*'s editorial view that class struggle in America was sharp, clear, and inevitable, Ernest E. Bayles pointed out that "the business of arraying class against class in this country is not nearly so simple a matter as it may be in European nations, and we are far from justified in drawing dead parallels." He added, "Those who possess great wealth, and therefore wield large influence, are a shifting lot." He suggested that some would lose their wealth and fall while others would rise given opportunities. Pointedly, Bayles advised that "to array the workers against the wealthy in the hope of bringing about a revolution which will establish Utopia is foolish, because both groups *believe in the same set of ideals.*" If this were true, then the journal's attempts to recast the American mind were doomed. Or as the Lynds had observed that in times of strain, most people's set of cultural clichés tended to stiffen not to unwind.[35]

In an entire issue devoted to a discussion of indoctrination, the journal reiterated that it was much "more than an organ for the assembling of diverse ideas and opinions . . . it is an instrument for the positive fashioning of programs and philosophies." Hence it was less than patient with its polemical sister, the *Nation*, which objected to the use of teachers to espouse partisan causes. To such a view of neutrality, the *Social Frontier* objected. Why? Because an avowed disinterestedness "is a philosophy which is little concerned with the need for bringing American life as a whole into step with the accomplishments of modern engineers and technicians." Once again the shade of Veblen was invoked.[36]

Given their technocratic vision of planning from the top down rather than from the bottom up in a market economy, the editors found reforms of any kind repugnant. To the editors and other writers in its pages, the New Deal by definition was a failure. Harry Fairchild, for example, distinguished between President Roosevelt's political liberalism and his economic conservatism, which led, in his view, to the New Deal's pragmatic lurches without a clear philosophy. Lamenting Roosevelt's predisposition not to challenge the profit system, Fairchild judged that the New Deal could only remain a tragedy.[37]

In similar fashion, Broadus Mitchell, an economist, took issue with the New Deal's propensity for tinkering, especially with regard to the Tennessee Valley Authority experiment in producing power, reclamation, and irrigation of the land. He observed that "though business supporters of Roosevelt are disposed to scoff at it as an economic bastard, it is presented naked except for a snowy diaper, while its father delicately explains, as sufficient apology, that it is a love child, conceived in a random rapture that must be its own excuse for occurrence." Continuing his attack on TVA but shifting his metaphor, Mitchell cried out that "in the name of mercy, the Poor

Whites of five or six southern states are being gathered at the national bosom and nourished. The victims of ignorance and exploitation, their magnificent natural heritage, long abused and snatched from them, is to be returned to them under the fostering hand of government. The costs are not to be counted." But the political, economic, and social costs of poverty were counted by the New Deal.[38]

To rectify the ad hoc quality of the New Deal, Mitchell urged the teachers of the land to reorient the images in "the minds of the millions" and above all "to become propagandists. The truth is not something to be searched for and, when found, put in one's pocket. It should be handed about generously with a will. That is apparently the reason for the founding of this publication."[39]

In the following issue, the editors continued their attack on the president with an editorial entitled "The Roosevelt That Might Have Been." The editors took the president to task for tinkering since ad hoc responses had meant the loss of "economic socialization [that] would have been accepted without serious objection by the bewildered business leaders" in 1933. Having second thoughts a few lines below, the editors admitted "that Roosevelt held no mandate to inaugurate a revolution is true." Then turning the argument once more, the journal editors asserted that "the method of revolution acceptable in the American scheme of things at the present time is that of education." Next, echoing an earlier slogan of Counts, the editorial asked, "Dare a President harness the press, the radio, the cinema, the public educational system to the star of a new, economically secure and culturally free, social order?" Dictators abroad were "harnessing" the instruments of persuasion while in a democracy a president could only seek to lead by bully pulpit or by fireside chat.[40]

While daring the president and teacher to usher in the new social order, it, nevertheless, spoke highly of the National Education Association (NEA), an organization dominated by school superintendents. Rather than discuss salaries and working conditions of teachers, the *Social Frontier* chose to discuss academic freedom as the primary concern of teachers and professors. Ironically, the pages of the journal served as an unintended roll call of fired teachers across the land. What did the editors propose? "There is only one protection," the journal asserted, "for socially-minded teachers who are unwilling to be grovelling hypocrites. Only powerful national organizations, ready to fight at the drop of one name, can protect teaching integrity."[41]

On a related matter, the journal took issue with the imposition by the state of New York of a loyalty oath upon teachers. Having called upon teachers to man their classrooms in overturning the social order, the journal deplored the fact that the press and periodicals were tearing "down the traditional attitudes of tolerance that have been carefully nurtured by public schools." Such disingenuousness and lack of logic did not disturb the polemics of the journal.[42]

While repeatedly urging others to shed so much intellectual baggage as deadweight, the *Social Frontier* was loath to unburden itself of custom. Consider that in November of 1934 it hoped against hope that the new secretary of the NEA would have "social vision and courage" since "the post is, potentially, the *most strategic position in American education* in the present critical period." A large claim, indeed. Indeed, this supportive editorial of the NEA despite John Dewey's association with the smaller rival American Federation of Teachers (AFT) revealed how much the journal was enthralled with, and unable to detach itself from, the NEA. As an umbrellalike organization, the NEA membership consisted of superintendents, college professors, school principals, and classroom teachers. Ironically it was the AFT that began placing advertisements in the journal, not the NEA. Despite this the editors called for a unified profession of all teachers "from kindergarten through [the] university" in the NEA.[43]

In the main, the journal pinned its hopes on an ideal superintendent to lead the teachers in their respective school districts across the land. This ideal superintendent "knows that laissez-faire individualism is played out and that *a planned economy of some kind is inevitable*," and "he knows that the danger that threatens this country is the danger of fascism and not of revolution to the left." Lending some credence that national planning was on the way had been the passage of the National Industrial Recovery Act by the New Deal. Although shortly thereafter the U.S. Supreme Court declared the act unconstitutional, the editors ignored the decision's meaning.

Nor did many real-life school superintendents, as we shall see below, such as Harold Campbell of New York City and Worth McClure of Seattle, fit this heroic mold. Yet continuing its ambivalence toward the NEA, the editors chose to review the annual resolutions of the Department of Superintendence from 1907 to 1934 and found them wanting. "The Department has been neither consistent," the editors wrote, "nor persistent in the causes it has advocated. Never has it come to grips with the main issues of American life." True leadership to the editors meant the use of the schools "for the realization of . . . a social structure that has its basis in the rights of man and in creative effort rather than in property and profit." If the department espoused these thoughts, then "superintendents, principals, teachers, and laymen will follow [them]."[44]

Closer to the truth, Dewey indicated how restricted the typical school administrator was in reality for "by the nature of his calling he has a large amount of detail and routine to which he must attend. . . . Large systems work almost automatically toward isolation of the administrator." (There was a hint here by Dewey of the "trained incapacity" of administrators noted above.) Rather than becoming a chief clerk of the school, Dewey felt that the administrator must "have a definite idea of the place and function of the school in the ongoing processes of society, local and national." But if the principal's handicap was his "trained incapacity" how would this be circumvented by a course in sociology and economics? Of course, we can not be certain that with regard to this concept Dewey had read his Veblen.[45]

Others in the journal could only repeat the shibboleth of virtuous leadership. Given conflicting opinions and vested interests in society, Jesse Newlon concluded that the "educational or social leader has no alternative but to lead." It was an easy sleight of hand to replace Locke and Jefferson with the virtuous pedagogue. Newlon asserted that the educator "has no alternative to interpret as best he can what the needs of the people are and to act on the interpretation." As with the ideal superintendent, for Newlon the ideal educator had unlimited knowledge: "knowledge of society, insight into its processes and major trends, knowledge of its structure, of the various groups in it and of their respective prejudices and modes of operation" and more.[46]

But the adherents of the *Social Frontier* were to be disappointed. At the annual convention of the Department of Superintendence in 1935, the primary issue had not been a stout defense of academic freedom as the journal had wished but a "milk-and-water resolution." The love affair of virtuous superintendents had cooled quickly to the extent that "if teachers are ever to have freedom to do their work, they will not receive it from the hands of the administrators, but will have to achieve it themselves." But the editors chose not to consider the option of support for the AFT, or separately an alliance with John L. Lewis.[47]

After the annual convention of the NEA the following month, the journal found even less to cheer. With schools closed, children on the loose, and Hearst-led attacks on subversives in the schools, the journal intoned that "during times like these the teachers of the nation must have courageous and enlightened leadership." Having discounted the NEA, the AFT and any other options, what remained? The hectoring posture of the journal. The paramount issue was "freedom in the schools." To implement this posture meant "funds for investigators, legal counsel, tribunals, and publicity." Angrily, the journal warned, "If the NEA refuses to meet this challenge, it will be compelled to surrender its claim to leadership to some more virile organization. And that organization will not be the Department of Superintendence." Was this finally the attempt by the *Social Frontier* to break out of its own "patterns of mind" and to reach out for the likes of John L. Lewis?[48]

2 A Cause without Leaders

> *"Education" has been, during the New Deal years as in virtually all previous administrations, just one of those fine, clean words—like patriotism, manhood, character, etc. It certainly hasn't been recognized as a vital force in American life. You surely do not have your Norris, or your Wagner, or your [John L.] Lewis. . . . Your crisis has no identity.*
>
> —*Forrest Allen, 1937*[1]

Revisiting the *Social Frontier* in 1935, was it likely that the journal would propose an alliance as Forrest Allen hinted between classroom teachers and John. L. Lewis' CIO? It did not. Instead the journal chose to exhort teachers to assume their "new" roles as handmaidens of the impending social order. The call for the new had become shopworn. Only rarely did the journal choose to speak of the effects of the Depression upon the schools and the family. More typically, it deplored teacher loyalty oaths and in particular objected to the demand by a school board member in New York City to bar subversives from the classroom.

Reminding its readers that "an educational profession that is alive to its social responsibilities and free to function in the educational guidance of children and adults . . . can do much to shift social forces from reinforcement of our price and profit economy to an alignment backing a collectivistic [*sic*] economy of social utility." The editors added that "it is these considerations which make academic freedom an objective of paramount importance to the teachers of the nation."[2]

To the journal, for example, the importance of international affairs in the life of teachers seemed self-evident. As to the armaments race, "Will the teachers of America respond? How soon? How deeply are they concerned? How much danger are they willing to risk in order to play an unambiguous role?" No doubt, the journal would have approved of

Hemingway's Robert Jordan (in *For Whom the Bell Tolls*) forgoing his college classes in favor of joining the Loyalist forces in Spain.[3]

Aside from asking others to make sacrifices, the journal persisted in calling for disarmament. With *The Merchants of Death* as a Greek chorus, the editors insisted that "the race of armaments is on—America too, is engaged in building a bigger and better army, navy, and air force. Where will it all end if the individuals and groups who dread war . . . do not make a start somewhere?"[4]

To the dread of the armaments race was added the possible deleterious role of science in weapons making. Benjamin Ginsburg asserted that "voices were raised in many places accusing the scientist of being responsible, if not for the [First World W]ar, at least for the gigantic engines of destruction and for the lethal weapons of poison gas." (All this fingerpointing before World War II's Manhattan Project.)[5]

No doubt echoing Eugene V. Debs' principled opposition to the First World War, the journal noted that "sundry dissenters who take seriously their professional duties to society should find it difficult to refrain from correcting the untrue and socially harmful notion about freedom" or its lack thereof. Thus "such dissenters" could reshape the American mind.[6]

After calling teachers from their slumbers, the journal asserted that "education properly conducted in the modern world, is an enemy and not a benign supporter of inherited ways of doing things. Education in its profoundest meaning is revolution." Since the demise of free enterprise was at hand, "teachers must sow the seed and society must learn not to fear the whirlwind." Was the humble classroom teacher to venture forth as an agent of revolution? Goodwin Watson wrote, " A civilization which wished a high level of initiative must take pains to develop in children the habit of violating tradition in a constructive way. Teaching in the new America may not be so comfortable, but neither will it be so monotonous." Perhaps boredom drove the Robert Jordans from the classroom. But then again, Watson may have had Jefferson's aside of a little rebellion now and then in mind rather than thoughts of storming the White House on a winter night.[7]

As 1935 beckoned, three remarkable editorials were published. The first, in January, was entitled, "1,105,921." The journal made much of the increase in the ranks of classroom teachers since the Civil War and that teachers constituted a potential monolithic bloc. Of women teachers, the journal observed that "with the enfranchisement of women the teachers of the country have become a potential political force to be reckoned with." Moreover, the strength of teachers was "strategic and functional as well as numerical. They spread over the country in a fine network which embraces every hamlet and rural community." Still the editors insisted that teachers had to ally themselves "with the masses of the people and refuse longer to make obeisance to the badges of wealth and rank. All they lack is organization, vision, and courage. Perhaps these things will come."[8]

Aside from the journal's hot-and-cold romance with teachers, the editors had chosen to ignore some difficulties. For one, altar-bound teachers were not predisposed to take the long view. For another, they ignored too the aspirations of white-collar workers. These workers at the time took a view of upward mobility contrary to that of blue-collar workers, who chose to make their daily existence bearable within a collective bargaining agreement. These mass production workers were equally ignored. In short, the middle-class modus operandi had been to withdraw from unpleasant work, marriage, or residence. Moreover, the editors had chosen to ignore as well Ernest Bayles' observations in their pages that rich and poor alike in America "believed in the same set of ideals" of opportunity.[9]

Considering their presumed audience of teachers, the *Social Frontier* rarely chose to delineate in its pages the daily life of teachers. In the second editorial that touched reality at least in summary fashion, the journal itemized some educational realities: the shortened school year; construction curtailments; salary slashes; increased class loads; and in some cases school closures. "In the face of a widespread and organized assault upon public education," the *Social Frontier* reported that "the teaching profession, supported by democratic forces in the community, has struggled valiantly and with a large measure of success to keep the schools physically open." But keeping the schools open without a new conception of the school's role in society amounted to special pleading. Nor did the journal call for bread-and-butter leadership of the likes of John L. Lewis. Instead, it once again praised the NEA and hoped that teachers would organize since "potentially the teachers possess great power."[10]

Given their class struggle orientation, the editors rarely chose to discuss social class, political power, or the place of the public schools in society. They did report the truism that school board members were drawn from a "small segment of the population." Undoubtedly, this observation drew on Counts' earlier work, which had discovered the fact that society is not an apolitical Garden of Eden. Rather than Marxian motifs of "masses" and "class struggle," the editors chose to ignore Beard's advice to read the Federalist Papers. Reluctantly admitting to the realpolitik that governed communities, the journal suggested that the schools were powerless to remake society."[11]

And if the schools were powerless to transform society, then teachers were subjected to gratuitous barbs. "Unfortunately, most teachers are too busy," the editors wrote, "handing out cut-and-dried subject matter in class rooms and chewing the pedagogic cud in conferences . . . to discuss the present-day implications of basic national and human ideals." There was no discussion if the foregoing were true, why teachers should be berated for shop talk instead of reading the works of Marx and Lenin. Even Dewey, who was generous on most occasions, still could talk of the "lethargy and timidity of all too many teachers" without probing for the historical and institutional causes of the "condition." In the following chapters we cite some factors in the Depression that contributed to "lethargy and timidity." But these factors of fear and uncertainty affected not just teachers but most Americans who still held jobs.[12]

Rather than probe and discuss these mundane factors that affected all who worked, the journal persisted in its discussion of the issue of academic freedom despite Beard's admonition that the subject had elicited "a lot of nonsense." Was Beard in fact more perceptive on a tangential issue when he noted that the early New Deal NRA codes, especially section 7A, which permitted the institutional machinery to establish *due process* for teachers. Aside from John L. Lewis, who sensed the significance of the NRA codes to labor's ability to organize the unorganized, the NRA codes were a lost opportunity for the teachers of the land. Doubly ironic was the fact that the NRA codes were the closest thing to the repeated call by the *Social Frontier* for national planning. Having seen the reality, the editors blinked. But even Beard may have been overly optimistic that school officials "would welcome the adoption of some such program [of *due process*] by teachers and would cooperate with them in the process of realization." The following chapters reveal how far from reality this was likely to be.[13]

On occasion the editors could paint a picture that bordered on half truth and hatred of the classroom teacher. But all would be forgiven if teachers could only be what they were not. The third editorial itemized the deficiencies of teachers both as to character and professional competence. The teachers were accused again of being "timid and docile." Their professional skills were limited in dispensing "hackneyed facts and fix[ing] a few simple skills." With the result that "socially they present a *bad case of clinical isolation.*" They were also accused of being "politically and socially illiterate." More bitingly, the editors insisted that teachers were "strangers to literature, to music, and to the plastic arts." Teachers were enthralled by "newspaper stereotypes, movie sentimentality and popular 'wisdom.'" Although of middle-class origin, teachers had no conception of their own self-interest.

Their salaries were no higher than those of manual workers, yet "teachers do not recognize that they are workers." While these points were straightforward, the editors then added that teachers "have no property to depend on for an income and nothing they can sell at a profit." But having made these judgments, the editors still felt that the teachers of the land were "capable of participating significantly in *directing the course of history*."[14]

Were there many college professors who had separate incomes or could sell their services for profit? Yet within this diatribe there was the perception of the teacher's isolation within the classroom and within the Balkanized school systems of the land. How odd that they could couple the teachers' middle-class origin and then wonder why they were not quick to don the mantle of workers. But even the journal continued to turn to the NEA, which gave the patina of respectability to teachers rather than embrace John L. Lewis.

What images of the future did the journal espy? Of the good society, once the means of production had been "socialized and democratized, opportunities would be equalized . . . insecurity would be eliminated . . . and broader outlets for human creativity would be brought into being." Presumably once the labels of capitalism and socialism had been swapped, creativity and social usefulness would replace self-interest. The editors added that it was "also reasonable to expect that such a change in the social order would bring a greater kinship of the masses of the people with the social group and a greater identification with the group culture." How did the "masses of the people" differ from the "social group" and the "group culture"? Once again here was a reminder of Dewey's caveat on empty word-mongering.[15]

But to the true believers, the good society could not issue piecemeal through reform. In an issue devoted to a review of the press, Lawrence Martin concluded by observing that William R. Hearst was surely a product of his society but hence no more venal or corrupt than other businessmen who catered to the consumers' wishes. "The dope of Hearst is no worse," Martin wrote, "than the dope of the moving picture industry and the radio industry and the commercialized sport and theater industries." Since the public hastened to the products of these aforementioned "industries," this was proof in his view that society "stands convicted of a fundamental maladjustment." Rather than pragmatic attacks on particular evils, the moral was clear: the system was beyond the pale and had to be purged.[16]

Forrest Allen, a former newspaper reporter, took exception to the journal's view that public ownership of the press would usher in the new social order. For one, he questioned whether mere transfer of title from private to public ownership would alter automatically the press' performance.

Touching on sacred grounds, Allen observed that "are not most of the evils of the profit-motivated press extant in public-owned schools and school systems?" He added that a candid appraisal of the schools would question the "belief that social, group, or governmental control and regulation of the press would make the press free, socially-minded, intelligently fearless, intellectually honest?" Continuing his parallel, Allen asked if the schools had been "as willing a tool of special interests, or selfish 'rights' as has the yellower portion of the press?" Also he chided the *Social Frontier* for its concern with shadow rather than substance in writing of the press. In particular the journal had failed to note the oligopolistic nature of news gathering restricted to the three news agencies of the Associated Press, United Press, and Hearst International. As to content and editorial policy of a socialized press, Allen asked which yardstick would be used: one similar to the *New York Times* or the *New York Daily News*? Allen concluded that the press could be improved but only incrementally in response to higher levels of education of the public.[17]

Another advocate of apocalyptic change, Bruce Bliven, contended that "the sickness of the press is only a symptom of the sickness of society; it cannot be cured alone, and it will be cured, or greatly ameliorated, almost automatically when and if society is healed." How? By replacing the present corrupt society. But Harry D. Gideonese took sharp issue with these views. He suggested that "much of the generalizing about the breakdown of laissez-faire or capitalism is just depression katzenjammer." Warming to his task, he added, "We have antiquated banking institutions for the simple and satisfactory reason that we do not care enough about the problem to go out and get ourselves better ones. We have corrupt local politics and a yellow press for the same reason." Pointedly Gideonese concluded, "If we wanted change, it wouldn't be necessary to change the nature of the 'social order.' . . . Dreaming about the future utopia is as fruitless as a defeatist withdrawal into the supreme glories of the past."[18]

But Selden Rodman questioned the role of reason in human affairs, for "liberals make the mistake of thinking that man will always see the light," he wrote, "and act rationally if you only reason with him." Did these critiques within its own pages have any effect on the editors and its stalwarts?[19]

As the journal began its second year of publication with slightly over 6,000 in circulation, the editors announced with remarkable clarity that "to believe that the beautiful theories of the professor when expounded to other professors and to students will cause a shift of power in society is the *worst form of utopianism.*" A few paragraphs below, however, it shifted to the familiar once again by lapsing into the Jeffersonian crusade against ignorance by asserting that once the "masses of people" recognize the virtues of a socialized society, the recognition would be "enough to effect the necessary change." Still a few pages further in the same issue of October 1935, the editors announced a new section entitled "On the Battle Line." It would report events "wherever the struggle rages between the forces of reaction and forces of educational advancement." Clarity and common sense gave way to the "worst forms of utopianism" within the same issue.[20]

Eager to give advice, the journal chose to ignore not only Allen, Gideonese, and Rodman's comments but as well a future editor of the journal itself, George Hartman. As a professor, Hartman had run for a congressional seat in 1934 on the Socialist Party ticket. Defeated, he drew a few conclusions. For one, his "campaign has given evidence that a clear majority of the voters actually approve of 'Socialist' measures." But how could this be? Hartman presented a primer on semantics and the efficacy of labels. But heavily laden slogans could be approved by an electorate if presented as "simple propositions removed from a 'Socialist' context." And even more people were uncomfortable "in the presence of the term 'Socialist.'" He repeated that the voters wanted socialism but "not under that label." Norman Thomas would reach a similar conclusion when he referred to the New Deal's co-optation of socialist planks by the adoption of social security, a fair labor standards act, and more. Hence the Socialist Party joined the ranks of countless third parties in American history who having announced a grievance then passed on.[21]

"If this new social order has any basis in fact," Norman Boardman, a staff writer, opined "the constant reference to it might be all to the good, but the *mere talking about it* without doing anything to bring it about only conveys a false optimism." Despite this welcome admission, Boardman proceeded to indulge in the wish fulfillment of a closet revolutionary (unlike Hartman, who had actually run for political office) by asking what were "the characteristics of the new social order that make radical changes necessary?" As Boardman offered six propositions not prescriptions, the answers were tautological. The circular six propositions were as follows: a "socialized collectivism," the principle of cooperation; a classless society, a planned economy, an economy of abundance, and finally the wish "to make a peaceful world possible."[22]

Some days after the U.S. Supreme Court had declared the National Industrial Recovery Act unconstitutional in late May 1935, Norman Boardman concluded his call for the new social order by writing that "our present policy is pretty definitely committed to trying to save capitalism rather than to building a new social order. The human animal seems to be a great bear for punishment, and perhaps we may choose to go on groaning under capitalism."[23]

Stepping out of editorial anonymity, Norman Woelfel, an associate editor of the journal, noted in a review of Lewis Mumford's *Technics and Civilization* that Mumford had developed a "complete rationale for technological invention which frees this phenomenon once and for all from dependence upon the profit motive and a capitalist economic system." Did this imply that technology was a disembodied entity much like Venus sprung from the brow of Zeus? Or in turn did technology become the new determinism even under socialism? The questions were not broached.[24]

So transfixed on the new social order were the journal editors and its contributors, such as Henry Fairchild, for example, who took sharp exception to the New Deal's proposal to establish unemployment compensation as a "red herring" since "every insurance scheme is a confession of failure: the failure to eradicate the evil for which the insurance is provided." Presumably in Fairchild's utopia, insurance companies would wither away as accident, fire, death, illness, tornado, flood, and unemployment would be banished. Specifically, Fairchild urged a federal guarantee of a job to every breadwinner in the land. Otherwise, the "agitation for unemployment insurance serves mainly as a red herring across the trail of genuine social advance."[25]

Perhaps while waiting for utopia, the editors might have paid attention to their so-called basement. Innocently, the *New Republic* asked, "Should a college run a sweat-shop?" The reference was to a labor dispute involving low pay for cafeteria employees at Teachers College, the intellectual home of the *Social Frontier*. No doubt with tongue in cheek, the *New Republic* advised that in settling the dispute, Teachers College "can and should set an example to the whole country, especially in view of the liberal philosophy that underlies much of its classroom instruction"—and we would add the radical talk of the *Social Frontier*.[26]

While humor was at a heavy discount in the pages of the journal, during its second year occasional light verse appeared. In the manner of Ogden Nash, Florence Becker's sarcastic "No Matter" appeared:

> Professor So-and-So is sitting in his last year's bathrobe Nibbling his lifetime fountain pen, Musing on the Golden Age of Greece (When "pedagogue" meant "slave who takes care of children"). His fingers are fiddling with a letter from the Dean, Asking him to talk on the N.R.A. Surely it is the aluminum age of America, And what has a professor to do with politics?

Professor So-and-So has proved there is no such thing as matter and the business of a philosopher is to live the good life, Not to mix in ephemeral affairs.

Mrs. So-and-So in the next room, Is putting an invisible patch in her good man's trousers. Or he might be standing at the blackboard, Making a diagram of the nothingness of matter, And some dumb Pennsylvania Dutch sophomore, Might see a square inch of B.V.D. And think it was really there.[27]

As 1936 opened, the journal took note of the NEA's establishment of an Educational Policies Commission (EPC) with its concerns about long-term goals. But the journal wondered "if the masses of teachers are not carried along and converted into an intelligent and effective agency for translating policy into practice," the EPC in the editors' view would be of little value. More so, since the EPC members were "for the most part . . . the elder statesmen of American education, persons whose creative period lies behind them, educators who might be expected to formulate excellent educational policies for the nineteenth century." Whereas to the Young Turks at the *Social Frontier*, the future was in their pens.[28]

In October 1936, the S*ocial Frontier* began its third year of publication with declining subscribers. It replaced the format of "On the Battle Line" with "On the Educational Front" to appear less strident. The main editorial functions fell upon Normal Woelfel. It was a presidential election year, too. Earlier in the year the John Dewey Society had been founded, draining away some of the time and energy of the journal's founding contributors. The financial health of the journal had always been precarious, but it became even more so now.

A month before the presidential election, the journal called upon teachers to press for repeal of loyalty oaths and to push for the passage of federal aid to education since "there is no time to lose if teachers' organizations are not to be hopelessly handicapped in this struggle." Despite its misgivings, the journal insisted that "*upon the NEA . . . rests the chief responsibility for leadership* in all these matters." Yet the journal's patronizing tone toward teachers remained as it asked: "Are the teachers of the country prepared for these responsibilities? They are not . . . the great body of teachers is uninformed and indifferent."[29]

While the journal and its contributors generally ignored the New Deal until it favored federal aid to education, the editors took notice of the Works Progress Administration (WPA). Admitting that the WPA was "no model of efficiency," the journal announced that the WPA "has established a precedent for future public works that may be expected to develop, not suddenly out of emergencies, but rather as the result of long and carefully considered plans for realizing on a universal scale the boons of our potential economy of plenty." What is noteworthy is that the word "efficiency" should enter the thoughts of the editors at any time given its lock-stepped socialist views. Second, not unlike Keynes' call for a counter fiscal policy which entailed a shelf of public works project, the journal seemingly grasped the larger significance as well as the human need. To those hired on WPA projects, attitudes of "defeated pride" had been replaced by ones of "alertness." Yet it cautioned that if with economic recovery, the WPA and the Public Works Administration (PWA) were dismantled then "we may be sure that the New Deal is only the Old Deal in disguise." But if both agencies thrived, then "the New Deal may prove to have been a vital transitional agency in socializing America."[30]

Again the *Social Frontier* was at the time out of step with public perceptions of the WPA that it might be necessary as pump-priming but that it was a costly agency at best and at worst a boondoggle. Forrest Allen, earlier unheeded in its pages, asked why the most important educational accomplishments of the New Deal had nothing to do with professional educators. To Allen, it was "an educational experience for hundreds of thousands when a national government debates and finally writes into law enormously significant legislation." Why? Because education had become a platitude devoid of meaning. More importantly they lacked leaders equivalent to Senators Norris or Wagner or the likes of John L. Lewis. "Your *crisis has no identity*," he added. He did admit there were John Dewey and Nicholas Murray Butler among educators, but he felt that the average American did not understand the pedagogical chasm that separated the two. Finally Allen turned to the proponents of the journal. To those invested with the mantle of educators and presumed explicators of language and ideas, Allen declared that "the *American people simply don't know what you're talking about*." Brutal as this judgment might be, he went on to rake their political naivete for "my hunch is that most of you don't know how to get to work at the problem."[31]

A few weeks after the General Motors sit-down strike of January and February 1937 that resulted in the recognition of the United Automobile Workers by the company, the journal stated that the most needed development in American life was a powerful labor movement. As we recalled above, the journal had only a year earlier observed that labor was headed toward a "prolonged and bitter conflict" that might lead to its destruction. Once again, as with the New Deal, the editors had misjudged events. Instead of dissolution, John L. Lewis had organized the unorganized of the mass production industries under the mantle of the Congress of Industrial Organizations (CIO). Despite the CIO's success, the ambivalent mood of the journal continued into 1937 when the editors doubted whether the new union leaders would display insight and wisdom. Reversing gears, the editors were pleased that "labor is lifting its eyes from preoccupation with immediate and local concerns" in favor of surveying "the larger social scene."[32]

Ten months after the CIO's victory at General Motors, the journal called to its readers' attention to the schism between the industrial unionism of the CIO and the craft orientation of the AFL. While announcing its sympathies for the CIO, the editors backhandedly, if not begrudgingly admitted to the talents and successes of John L. Lewis, but they took no heed of Forrest Allen's comment that education had no equivalent organizing genius akin to Lewis. Curiously, the journal observed that "in some respects, labor progressivism found a strange leader in John L. Lewis, whose earlier Republican affiliations, ruthless crushing of opposition in his own miners' group, and late emergence as a 'liberal' have occasioned surprise to those familiar with his career." Condescendingly, the editors concluded their vignette of Lewis with the observation that "God sometimes employs strange tools to accomplish His ends, and even the possibility of genuine growth in intellectual stature is not to be eliminated." So spoke the voice from Olympus.[33]

As this review of the *Social Frontier* has revealed, the journal was a master at Janus faced reversals. In January of 1936, the editors, not the Chamber of Commerce, wrote that "compared with most types of productive labor in private industry and commerce, teachers' salaries are high, their hours short, and their vacations long." With Teachers College and New York City as their fulcrum, one can only speculate whether the editors and contributors chose to read the tabloid *New York Daily News* or the *New York Times*.[34]

Among the founders of the *Social Frontier*, Harold Rugg presented a position paper in which he called for federal aid to education, the extension of child services in the schools to include free lunches and medical care, the launching of adult education programs, the defense of academic freedom, and the remaking of the curriculum to bring it abreast of social change. Aside from federal aid to education, the planks were familiar ones. Interestingly enough, alone among his colleagues on the journal, Rugg used the war motif, but four years after Roosevelt's inaugural. Rugg declared, "Just as truly as in April, 1917, we are at war! . . . This war situation must be met with a warlike psychological program." But here the similarity with the consummate FDR ceased while the academician went on to demand that socialism could be achieved predicated upon a nationwide adult education program. "Every agency of communication," he added, "must be coordinated into a great organism of education."[35]

Rugg illustrated only too well the intellectual's impatience, then and now, with the messiness of ordinary politics. Rather than dealing with political conflicts, the preferred mode was to let the "experts" loose on problem solving. Rugg insisted that "a critical period like ours is no time for palliatives and placating of politicians. Rather it is a time for swift information-getting, for intensive study, for prompt decision-making, and for immediate writing of decisions into law and executive action." In 1936 the personification of the leader above politics able to act decisively and expeditiously could be found in the likes of Hitler, Mussolini, and Stalin.[36]

To be sure, the *Social Frontier* had its detractors. Close to home: Dean William Russell of Teachers College labeled Counts' dare to build a new social order on the steeple of the schoolhouse a "period of Utopia construction, and I think this period has run its course." Counts replied, "I gladly admit this charge. A map of the world that does not contain the land of utopia is not worthy of mankind." How any map could be "worthy" much less useful if it contained *imaginary* continents begged the analogy. More prosaically, the superintendent of schools of Allentown, Pennsylvania, responded in 1939 that "those of us who have not taken leave of our senses know the school and schoolmasters are not generally going to be permitted to take the lead in changing the social order."[37]

Isaac Kandel, a colleague of Counts at Teachers College but not on the journal, criticized the social reconstructionists for their focus on the schools as a denial of historical evidence and common sense. More tellingly, Kandel observed, "Schools are a part of the environment which they serve; they are not autonomous or insulated against the social forces and influences around them; nor can teachers on the basis of a guess . . . help to build a new social order. *Society changes first and schools follow.*"[38]

Another critic was John L. Tildsley, associate superintendent of schools in New York City, who while taking issue with the socialist objective of the journal and questioning the use of the schools for political conversion, suggested instead the "cheaper, quicker, and really more effective medium of the organ, the tambourine and the other techniques of the Salvation Army."[39]

Not so strangely, the sharpest critique of the failure of the *Social Frontier* to usher in the revolution came indirectly in the writings of both Dewey and Counts. In his magnum opus, *Democracy and Education*, Dewey had warned in 1916, "Words, the counter for ideals, are however, easily taken for ideas. . . . Because of our education, we use words, thinking they are ideas, to dispose of questions, the disposal being in reality simply such an obscuring of perception as prevents us from seeing any longer the difficulty." Critically, Counts had observed in 1929 that the founding of a new party or movement unless "rooted in some profound social movement or trend . . . can be but an instrument of deception." He added the caveat that "in spite of all the well-intentioned efforts of intellectuals, society stubbornly chooses its own roads to salvation." A fit epitaph for the *Social Frontier*.[40]

With subscriptions falling below 4,000 and the departure of Woelfel, Grossman, and Counts in the spring of 1937, the days of the journal were numbered. While the John Dewey Society had absorbed the publication and George Hartman had been named interim editor, two years later the journal in turn was absorbed by the Progressive Educational Association and renamed the *Frontiers of Democracy*. After his departure George Counts went on to take part in the internecine warfare over the communist-dominated Teachers Union in New York City. Just as the *Literary Digest* had misread the electoral pulse of the nation in 1936 so had the *Social Frontier* and its offshoot. Both the *Literary Digest* and *Frontiers of Democracy* expired without fanfare during the Second World War.[41]

To recapitulate, the *Social Frontier* remained semantically deaf to the pejorative connotation of words like "collectivistic," "socialist," "class struggle," "masses," "new social order," "social reconstruction," and other phrases even when advised to heed them by Hartman and Allen in their own pages. Mentally, the minds of the men at the journal were closed. Furthermore, they misunderstood a basic psychological principle. To a man hemorrhaging, for example, the immediate need is to stop the bloodletting, not to act as a pallbearer. Still other examples come to mind of the victims of earthquakes, and floods, who often return and attempt to restore where possible their former lives. For most Americans the cataclysm of the Depression induced the same human need for *restoration*, not excursions into utopia.

Thus radicals of the left in the 1930s located for the most part east of the Hudson River remained strikingly out of step with the politics of most Americans. Fifty years later, in a mea culpa, Sidney Hook could write that "serving [in 1934] on the political committee of the American Workers' Party was a rewarding and humbling experience for me. I got to realize how little I knew about the nature of the country whose system I was trying to revolutionize."[42]

On international affairs the journal was no less obtuse. With their aversion to rearmament but under the spell of the *The Merchants of Death* prose and peace marches, the editors perceived the looming menace of fascism, but not the unlovely purges by Stalin. Further, they were unable to use the war motif to harness the wills of its readers. Yet when the metaphor was used by Rugg, it had the unlovely overtones of neo-fascism.

More pointedly, as students of society neither Counts nor Dewey and others on the journal were able to articulate a new social policy that placed the restoration of the *family and school* at the center of political action. Such a policy never entered their consciousness. As to the war metaphor, they did not use the analogy of a "conscientious objector" to the "war" of the Depression. Could one argue that the noncombatants of school and family be given ample resources to recover, heal, and return the "wounded" into the daily fray of life? Or a call for the CCC to serve as a civilian medical corps? But then as Allen noted above, there were few grudging words of praise for the New Deal in general and for the WPA in particular. In short, the editors remained enthralled by old "patterns of mind" despite the incantatory call for the "new." Truly new ideas were not evident in the pages of the journal.

In terms of economics, the editors and most of the contributors were blissfully ignorant of the subject. They ignored Keynes, much less Hitler's economics minister, who pumped up the economy with military expenditures. Instead, the journal fastened its gaze upon the labels or titles of politics. As such, they mistook metaphorically the ribbons for the contents of the box. Various writers, in its pages, never tired of calling attention to the rapid pace of life, the rapid social change, and the changes in the scale of corporations without distinguishing, for a moment, the rate, scale, level, nature, and morphology of social change. At times the phrase "social change" became a mantra. If social change had become the new determinism, did it matter how much energy was expended understanding it, if one could? If so, could one only watch the trajectory of this receding process?

Obsessed with the new social order, and assuming as self-evident the institutional legitimacy of the public schools, the men of the *Social Frontier* were reductionists of words "easily taken for ideas." Close as Counts and his associates at Teachers College on the doorstep of New York City were to the evidence of the plight of schools in the pages of the *New York Times*, to the vivid presence and experiences of teachers taking summer classes at their institution, the social reconstructionists remained unreconstructed in their self-sealing dogmas. The writings of Keynes, Burke, and Mannheim passed them by. Close as they were to the realities of the schools, they were remote from the citadel of power and drama at the White House. The frontiersmen were awash in summer stock in a play without author or lines before empty seats, waiting for a Pirandellian rescue.[43]

Pointedly—an attempt to unravel the bureaucratic blindness of the schools and an attempt to unlock the classroom teachers from their trained incapacities—were never breached. The editors had hinted at the last mentioned factor when they spoke of the clinical isolation of the teacher and Dewey had hinted at the administrative roles that precluded dealing with nonroutine events. But they were wisps of the will.

But were the men of the *Social Frontier* more wanting than the Butlers, Russells, et al.? To a degree the answer must be in the affirmative. As frontiersmen, they viewed themselves in the vanguard of history on a mission of deliverance. One is reminded of that haunting advice of John Peter Altgeld from an earlier generation: "The fact that you met with an accident or got your legs broken, your neck twisted and your head smashed is not equal to a delivery of the goods." Counts and company promised much, but intellectually *their slogans did not touch reality*, they did not deliver the goods.[44]

All over Alabama, the lamps are out.
—*James Agee*[1]

Despite the inauguration of Franklin Delano Roosevelt, despite the promises of spring, and the repeal of prohibition in the offing, the winter fastness in 1933 clung to the land. Despite Roosevelt's denial of a "plague of locusts" sweeping the land, in Alabama in the spring of 1933, 85 percent of the public schools were closed as revenues evaporated. Dr. A.F. Harmon, the state superintendent of education, stated that "despite all the sacrifices by teachers, the schools of 50 counties [out of Alabama's 67] were closed." As of the first of April he noted that "7,000 teachers were out of work, and the doors of 2,400 school buildings were closed in the faces of 265,000 white children."[2]

Dr. Harmon added that higher education in the state was equally threatened by the collapse of the "boasted free school [which] is no more." "Merchants are notifying college professors," he continued, "that they must pay something on account or stop buying food." More pointedly, "Few teachers of elementary, high school, or college rank have been paid their entire salaries to date," he revealed, indicating that the payments were in arrears from three to eight months and in some cases over a year. As to what they were paid, Dr. Harmon stated, "The white teachers received in cash salaries $44 per month for the 12 months, and even a part of this was from wages due the previous year."[3]

Etching a chilling portrait, Dr. Harmon remarked that average annual salaries of $140 had been paid partly in cash and partly in scrip for two years, but merchants had increasingly balked at accepting the latter. Evoking echoes of the district schools of the 1830s a century earlier, some teachers in Alabama were working simply for room and board in a community-round robin. And of others not so fortunate, Dr. Harmon related that "rare instances are known of teachers 'camping out' in schoolhouses and living on gift vegetables cooked on the schoolhouse stove."[4]

Westward in Texas, school officials watched helplessly as tax revenues shriveled sharply. Dealing out of desperation, the Texas electorate voted a constitutional amendment exempting homesteads from state taxation up to $3,000, but the action in turn precipitated a further drop in state revenue, most of it earmarked for the schools in the amount of $7 million. To offset such a loss, a state sales tax was placed on the ballot but defeated. In turn discussion centered on the option of resubmitting a similar measure or a state income tax. In such a crisis atmosphere, urban schools in Texas fared no better than rural ones. With a conservative superintendent of schools and school board, the Dallas public schools had "for years practiced care and economy," so that teachers until 1933 "have suffered only a 14 percent reduction in pay and have been paid regularly and not with warrants. Now they face a 50 percent cut if the schools are to be run for the full nine months." For the rest of Texas, the reporter concluded that unless new tax revenues were forthcoming "a five-month term and pay cut seem inevitable."[5]

In North Carolina, the scenario was slightly different as the state assumed the funding of the pubic schools after the passage of a 3 percent state sales tax. Two months earlier, in March 1933, federal funds from the Reconstruction Finance Agency in the waning days of Hoover's administration had been granted to the state in order to hire unemployed teachers to instruct unemployed adults.[6]

Northward in the coal fields, however, in Scranton, Pennsylvania, the home of anthracite mining, 32 teachers went on strike over nonpayment of salaries for seven months. For the students the strike meant an extended Christmas vacation. In neighboring New Jersey, the secretary of the Camden school board with apparent pride noted that "yearly costs for sending children through Camden's schools have been reduced from $109.51 to $96.77 in the school year past," but with "no false economy." In Newark, the city council slashed the school budget by $6 million for the coming school year.[7]

North of New York City in the city of Yonkers, the teachers had seen their pay cut in September 1933 by 15 percent. Six months later the teachers had not been paid, at which time the school board announced the grim news that 60 school employees would be laid off and that as of December 1934 a "payless furlough" would bring the total teacher salary cut to 25 percent. Retrenchment and survival, much less restoration, were the order of the day.[8]

And what of the nation's largest school system? When Albert Einstein paid a social call to New York City's Board of Education, he was impressed by "the largest university in the world" of 1,250,000 students, and 36,000 teachers. Impressive as these numbers were, school attendance dipped in January 1933, but by the fall of the year they had risen above the June figures. Nevertheless, salary cuts, increased class loads, and curtailment of school construction as well as deferred maintenance illustrated a common national experience. As with other large cities, the school budget was part of the city's budget and under the control of the mayor, who appointed the board members. But these aspects of urban schools were unlike the countless independent school districts across the land. When schools were constructed in New York City by the middle of the decade, they were invariably built with funds from the federal Public Works Administration[9]

In New York City, teachers were no more effective in stemming slashes in school budgets, but they were rarely silent. When a delegation from 74 teacher organizations within the city schools personally protested further salary cuts to Mayor O'Brien, he assured them that "I am opposed to, and shall be opposed to, any reduction of teachers' salaries." But a lame-duck as well as an interim mayor, O'Brien had little more than two months in office to implement his promise. In a rare display of unity, a joint committee of teachers organizations urged the incoming mayor, Fiorello H. La Guardia, not to impose salary cuts in one guise or another especially the device of "payless furloughs."[10]

New York City schools differed in another regard from elsewhere. In the best of times, in order to obtain a teaching position, a candidate had to pass a battery of medical, written, and speech examinations. Once past this formidable hurdle, the candidate secured a substitute's license to teach full time pending the future issuance and subsequent passage of the permanent teacher examination. In practical terms, the substitute's license simply had a lower salary ceiling for full-time work. Thus in the worst of times, the Board of Examiners by not issuing permanent license examinations denied otherwise qualified teachers the opportunity of a higher salary. For the school system, it was a bureaucratic cost-saving device.

Yet if there were countless teacher organizations in New York for working teachers, even the unemployed but licensed teachers joined by recent college graduates formed their respective organizations. The latter groups were largely under communist influence. An appeal by the unemployed teachers to the state commissioner of education requesting class size reductions in order to create new teacher vacancies was turned down by the acting commissioner, E.E. Cole. Dr. Cole upheld the New York City school

45

board in its refusal to reduce class size. Dr. Cole noted that while a number of classes in the city had 40 or more students, the number 40 had "no magical significance." More important, he went on to note that "questions of cost and finance cannot be entirely disregarded, and the city . . . is at present in serious financial difficulties."[11]

Why was New York City in such financial difficulties? During the previous mayoral administrations of "Red" Mike Hylan and "Beau" James Walker from 1918 to 1932, the city's population had risen by 15 percent while the city budget had risen by 250 percent. How was this possible? During this period, the city payroll doubled with "salaries paid as political rewards at levels far above those paid for similar work in private industry." In fact, the public salaries were almost three times those of private enterprise. Not the least of Tammany Hall's misrule of the city was the letting of contracts to political cronies. The result was costly and shoddy public works. As a result of this fiscal malpractice, one-third of the city's budget in 1932 was devoted to servicing New York city's indebtedness of principal and interest. While school construction contracts were also plundered, New York City's teachers were rewarded in 1930 and 1931 for their honesty and political innocence with layoffs of 11,000 colleagues and salary cuts for those who remained. Appointed by the governor of New York, Franklin D. Roosevelt, Judge Samuel Seabury investigated the corruption of New York City's courts, government, and politicians. Into this morass as mayor strode Fiorello La Guardia in 1933.[12]

Vociferous but limited in numbers, the radical Teachers Union of New York City made its presence felt. A union official reminded Mayor La Guardia of his campaign pledge to restore salaries "to the 1932 level" at the earliest time. Two weeks later, a mass meeting of about 1,000 teachers led by Teachers Union officials marched on city hall to vent opposition to the mayor's announced "payless furloughs." Emerging from a meeting with the mayor, one union aide remarked that "payless furloughs" of one or two weeks instead of a month might be necessary as a result of financial stringency. But the Teachers Union had other interests to pursue. A year later in 1935, as Sol Cohen has written, "after years of internecine warfare, the Communist Party gained ascendancy in the . . . Teachers Union over the Linville-Lefkowitz (Right-Wing Socialist) administration." It was to join this fray that George Counts had left the editorship of the *Social Frontier*.[13]

Freelancing, a few teachers took pen in hand to offer their solutions and to recount their plights. One teacher felt that if the public was informed of the "problems" affecting the schools, corrective action would ensue. Along with other Americans, this teacher believed that social frictions flowed from ignorance and not deep-seated clashes over matters of substance, wealth and power. And surely not from circumstances such as plague and depressions. But another teacher, Fannie B. Biggs, a high school in New York City, wondered aloud at the low status of teachers in America. Plaintively she remarkedly "Neither does the press, nor do the people like teachers, and we wish we knew why." To underscore her point, she related a personal vignette. Attending a dinner party, an adjacent male guest, impeccably attired, exploded when Fannie Biggs informed him that she was a teacher: "I never in my life knew anybody who did so little and got paid so much for doing it as teachers." Perhaps this gentlemen was a closet chauvinist and a secret reader of the *Social Frontier*. In any event, Fannie Biggs went on to mention the so-called "ease" of her position in a high school of 7,000 female students with a daily class load of 200 students. She mentioned as well some of the daily tragedies that affected her students. Finally, she took exception to the proposed salary cuts with some rhetorical flourish: "You think we're crazy not to object to it?"[14]

Another aspect of our petit-drama involved the dunning of teachers for charitable contributions. Again and again, the superintendent of schools in New York City called upon teachers to divest themselves of contributions from their shrunken pay checks. Month by month, Superintendent William O'Shea appealed for contributions to continue relief work in the city. Even though salary cuts ranging from 6 to 33 percent had been instituted by January 1, 1933, Superintendent O'Shea exhorted supervisory personnel to persist in their solicitations of donations. Dr. O'Shea described the school relief work as the "holiest of causes" and expressed his confidence in the willingness of teachers to give. He went on to add that if relief work depended on government, the cemeteries of the city would be crowded with children who had died of starvation. "But thank God," he stated that "the situation is not as bad as that": 62,000 children were daily fed by relief funds.[15]

"Hunger is not debatable," Harry Hopkins had insisted as he took the reins of the initial efforts by the New Deal to institute direct relief to the public. What was debatable was the role of involuntary teacher philanthropy in fighting hunger. In 1932, the *New York Sun* editorially had noted that Judge Samuel Seabury, who had cleansed the corrupt Walker administration in New York City of men with "tin-boxes" full of graft, now called for an investigation into the New York City Relief Fund. Why? A Seabury staff inquiry had revealed that teachers had been coerced to contribute 5 percent of their salaries. Seabury also wanted to find out if a dollar limit had been placed on the relief fund as a whole. In October 1931, teachers, including daily substitutes earning $6 per week, had been asked to contribute 1 percent of their salaries "voluntarily." Despite protests from the Teachers Union and other teacher groups, the *New York Sun* noted that "nevertheless, the work of collecting the 5 percent went busily ahead." Unwilling teachers were harassed, dunned, and threatened that their names would be made public if contributions were not forthcoming.[16]

Undismayed by public criticism, Dr. O'Shea in March 1933 again called upon teachers to donate to the relief of children in distress. Noting that February contributions had fallen off from the preceding year, and while acknowledging pay cuts, he still urged everyone to contribute. Nor was he disturbed by "the lower rate of contributions from other city employees [which] has little to do with us." Proposing a new role of philanthropy for teachers during hard times, Dr. O'Shea observed that in normal times the pecuniary rewards of teaching "are small as compared with the rewards of industry and trade, but in these times there is no gainsaying the fact that as a whole they are in a more favorable position from the standpoint of salary and security than any other." The daily facts belied the "favorable position" of teachers. But what was clear was the magisterial calm in dispensing the dollars of teachers and their families.[17]

Again in April, Dr. O'Shea called upon teachers to loosen their purse strings to the tune of $100,000. In Olympian fashion, he stated, "Do not imagine that you or any other group can retire to the shelter of a safe statutory security and watch unmoved the efforts of the multitude to cope with the storm." Safely ensconced at school headquarters, administrators could "retire to the shelter of a safe statutory security" and watch the Fannie Biggs grappling with daily tragedies in their classrooms.[18]

School administrators were not alone in dunning teachers. Editorially, the *New York Times* could ask after citing the pay cuts of 6 to 33 percent that "few of us believed for a moment that the men and women whose work lies with the school children of the city would let possible resentment of their own somewhat narrowed circumstances [to] interfere with their splendid relief work among the little ones." Two months later on the eve of Franklin D. Roosevelt's inauguration, the *Times* posed a Hobson's choice for teachers. Given salary reductions, larger class loads, and other economies, "*we* would prefer to make personal sacrifices rather than the children denied their educational birthright." Then adding psychic insult to pecuniary injury, the editorial contemptuously stated that "the service of teachers is, after all, one of meekness."[19]

Superintendent Willard Givens of the Oakland (California) public schools, and secretary of the National Education Association, observed sadly in 1933 that teachers were "criticized, brow-beaten, sued, and vilified" if they like other citizens turned to politics for remedies. Givens asked, "Is there any reason why 1 million of our best educated people should be barred from real citizenship?" Rare was it indeed for a school administrator to mention the unmentionable—the declassed status of teachers in America.[20]

If Franklin D. Roosevelt could speak of the "forgotten American," W.H. McKeever of Oklahoma City could similarly speak of the "forgotten classroom teacher." McKeever itemized the factors that reduced teachers to the status of hired hands. Initially, he observed that the myriad of bureaucratic rules, regulations, and routines barely permitted the teacher each day to stay afloat and to teach. Second, the thinly veiled extortion of money from teachers in "rackets" such as the "voluntary" membership in state and national professional organizations as well as contributions to community funds did little to establish the autonomy of teachers. Third, he called insulting behavior the denial of the right to vote by teachers in PTA elections, who instead were asked to leave the room when elections took place. Last, he viewed the dismissal of women teachers who married as a symptom of the impotence and injustice surrounding teaching. In passing, he was critical of teachers who attended the NEA conventions, but rarely as speakers only to be told by various administrators and college professors about their "great responsibilities" and their "splendid devotion." In McKeever's conclusion teachers were permitted at these conventions "to assist with the applause."[21]

Along with two other schoolmen, Superintendent O'Shea responded to McKeever's criticisms by insisting that the points were overgeneralized. He averred that in New York City syllabi were necessary and that student intelligence tests were to be used at the discretion of teachers. Also competitive teacher-licensing examinations were equally essential in attracting the best talent to teaching. On the question of "rackets," he stated flatly, "I have expressly forbidden coercion of any kind as far as [teacher] contributions are concerned." As to professional organizations, he added, "most teachers rather want to belong to one or more associations." To be sure, 74 teacher organizations posed no threat to the prerogatives of the superintendent and school board.[22]

Dean William Russell of Teachers College weighed in with the statement that "fundamentally we've got to come to national financing of education," an idea that warranted discussion. But Russell went on in the manner of O'Shea, the *Times*, and the *Social Frontier* to state that "it seems obvious. . . . *We are not worried about salaries now.*" In addition, "one of the best things that will come out of this depression will be a soft pedal on the *materialistic trend in the teaching profession. We have got to fight for the children of this country.*" Presumably the same children would enter a materialistic world taught by teachers taking vows of poverty.[23]

Taking a similar view, John S. Brubacher of Yale University speaking before the National Council on Education asserted that education's status at the height of the previous decade's prosperity had been a "fool's paradise." Moreover, he added that education had suffered relatively little in the Depression. "We may *congratulate ourselves*," Brubacher declared, "that while our national income is nearly halved, school expenditures have suffered so much less." In the aggregate sense, Brubacher was correct as a glance at Table 3 of the Appendix will confirm. Turning to particulars, the Fannie Biggs of the country knew the meaning of the Depression but knew not a "fool's paradise." Less in the spirit of Russell and Brubacher, Dean Charles H. Judd of the University of Chicago's School of Education contended that "teachers whose salaries averaged $1,400 a year could hardly be accused of robbing the people." Or could Alabama teachers earning $140 be so accused or Kansas teachers earning $280—when they were paid.[24]

Upon his retirement, Dr. O'Shea called for the removal of teachers who "sow seeds of disloyalty to our country." What was the definition of loyalty? He provided a clue when he deplored the entrance of new teachers "of like temperament, who find in the destruction of established customs and principles keen satisfaction." He urged, accordingly, that entry into teaching be "rigidly controlled" or face shortly "a larger number of teachers with little sympathy for present school organization, social proprieties, professional traditions and American outlook." As evidence, Dr. O'Shea cited the case of two teachers who had interrupted a school board meeting in the summer of 1933—but who were dismissed for their pains.[25]

Warming to his task, Dr. O'Shea instructed that "no teacher who ardently holds an extreme view can avoid injecting it into his teaching. . . . A sneer, an intonation of voice, an imperceptible gesture, a one-sided presentation will carry their meaning to the impressionable and observant children in the class." Flattering as this view of teacher effectiveness and student perception was, most teachers trimmed their sails. With the Hearst and McCormick newspapers calling for teacher loyalty oaths, it was not long before school administrators picked up the cues. In the summer of 1934, Governor Herbert Lehman signed a teacher loyalty oath bill into law in New York.[26]

In his farewell address Superintendent O'Shea, while espousing evolutionary growth for teachers, took issue with radicalism that had little patience or knowledge of "existing structures and institutions." He called upon supervisors to uncover subversive teachers. Yet he admitted that a "patriotic" teacher need not turn a deaf ear to various injustices and "to denial of civil rights." Yet an alleged "spectacular exhibition of bad manners" by two teachers had warranted instant dismissal. Was this unwitting self-parody?[27]

In the wake of Dr. O'Shea's parting comments, one letter writer praised him completely and asked: "Does the public wish to retain the old-type American teacher, forward looking and progressive, imbued with fine personal, professional and national traditions of the past, or does it prefer a type enamored of all that is untried and bizarre?" Still another correspondent took Dr. O'Shea's definition of a radical to task by subjecting it to historical analysis. He noted, for example, that "emancipation was a radical notion prior to 1863, but afterwards a status quo concept." Therefore the writer announced as a first principle that institutions and social relationships are "wrong functionally when they fail to promote desirable ends." Moreover, "institutions are not ends in themselves. Loyalty to them, as such, is not a measure of a teacher's fitness."[28]

In February 1934 the American Civil Liberties Union (ACLU) provided another clue as to a "teacher's fitness." In a pamphlet entitled "What Freedom in New York Schools?" the ACLU charged that "during the past few years cases of violation of academic freedom, of victimization of teachers and of suppression of student activities" had been on the rise. The report indicated that the Depression had fostered a greater solidarity and outspokenness among teachers. This at first had been welcomed by school officials, but in short order, the officials grew alarmed at the potential strength and unity of teacher groups. Then, according to the ACLU report, other tactics were used to curb "outspoken" teachers, including the labeling of teachers and the use of the police when deemed appropriate. To all the infirmities plaguing teachers, the ability to be branded a modern-day heretic by school officials came to the fore.[29]

Before moving westward once again in our odyssey, we must consider a report issued by New York State Commissioner of Education Dr. Frank Graves. Above we noted that consolidation and centralization of public schools were legacies from the progressive era that were predicated on grounds of efficiency, economy, and disfranchisement of ethnic groups by holding elections at large rather than by ward or neighborhood. Concerned as we are with the responsiveness of institutions to its clients, it bears reviewing the efficacy of centralization, per se, as an organizational principle that would make schools respond more attentively to students and parents.

In response to charges leveled by the National Republican Club in 1931 that the New York City Board of Education was "top heavy with politics and mediocrity," a state investigation had been initiated. When the

Graves Report was released, seven reforms of the school bureaucracy were proposed: (1) that the school board delegate authority and concentrate on policy not administrative matters; (2) that the superintendent's power be enlarged; (3) that all future administrative appointments be made on the recommendation of the superintendent; (4) that the executive functions of the Board of Supervisors be transferred to the superintendent with the former board reduced to an advisory role; (5) that each associate superintendent be given a major citywide function; (6) that district superintendents (of nominal districts within the city) should be appointed on a functional rather than on a geographical (ward basis?) basis; and (7) that the schools "capitalize the best thinking of teachers." Clearly, the superintendent emerged from this report with greater power. But this thrust for tinkering with administrative machinery had begun in the 1890s when Nicholas Murray Butler had launched a crusade to centralize the ward schools of the city and continued during what Diane Ravitch has called the third "school war" on the eve of the First World War.[30]

To return to Dr. Graves' report, he found the professional behavior of principals wanting. "There is a tendency for New York City principals," he wrote, "to look upon the school system as sufficient unto itself, to be thoroughly satisfied with things as they are, to be provincial in their outlook on education, to be the willing or unconscious victims of the system." Principals, of course, were less the "victims" than what came to be called the organization man, and even Dewey had hinted above of the "trained incapacity" of the principal's task. Nonetheless, the Graves Report is significant in serving as a touchstone of the degree of the bureaucratization of the schools. Suffice it to say that, in the main, the report viewed the dilemmas of the schools as tractable—a consolidation here, a letting out there, a pep talk to shed provincialism, and all would be well. But to what pedagogical end? Conspicuous for its absence, the Graves Report had nothing to say about the classroom mode of instruction. While praising the Graves Report, one correspondent claimed that a perusal of the superintendent's annual reports from 1911 to 1932 revealed no "comprehensive educational plan that has taken the schools forward." In short, the "blindness system" had been in place and in practice since the 1890s when consolidation took place and its corollary of "trained incapacities" of administrators and teachers took root.[31]

Perhaps the greatest accolade bestowed upon the Graves Report was that the implementation of its recommendations would take "politics out of education," a phrase whose efficacy was dubious in the extreme. By definition, public schools supported by taxes are always subject to political purposes, constraints, and criticisms. As we noted, the Teachers Union after the mayoralty campaign urged that politics be removed from the schools. Since the 1880s, if not earlier, "removing politics from education" had meant two disparate but overlapping concerns. One element as old as the age of Jackson centered around removing the spoils system in hiring teachers in favor of merit, certification, and tenure beyond the reach of changing political parties. The related strand involved removing the power of the political bosses from controlling jobs, construction, and other contracts in the schools and checking as well their power in city government. The progressives' call for reform at the turn of the century under the banner of civil service examinations, consolidation and centralization of the schools, and the need for experts, which led to efficient government, became the new watchwords. And if in the wake of "honest" government certain ethnic groups lost their patronage and power, such was the price of democracy. Putting aside Boss Tweed's distinction between "honest" and "dishonest graft," progressives took one perspective while ethnic groups took another on the subject.[32]

If teachers dabbled at protest, even parents, high school and college students were driven on occasion to demonstrate and picket. In the spring of 1933 in New York City, 300 parents marched to city hall demanding free lunches and clothing for the children of the unemployed, more playgrounds and parks, and, finally, abolition of double and triple sessions in the schools. They were politely ignored. Of course, there was real suffering, as Fannie Biggs noted of her students, some of whom were "out six, eight, even ten weeks, sick. . . . There are others whose attendance is fairly perforated with absences.[33]

When Columbia University fired an instructor for being an avowed communist, an all-day rally in May 1933 was staged by 1,500 students. For their pains, "many students received bloody noses, blackened eyes, and torn clothes," reported the *Times* man on the scene. Among the speakers at the rally had been Diego Rivera, who had been dismissed shortly before as resident artist for the new Rockefeller Center, for his political affiliations. Rivera exhorted the students to "wrest control of the university from Dr. Nicholas Murray Butler."[34]

Across the Hudson River, in Riverside, New Jersey, 700 students went on strike in April 1933 against the reinstatement of an allegedly unpopular woman principal. Northward in Brockton, Massachusetts, 1,000 high school students in September 1934 stoned their school and jeered at the superintendent in a wild demonstration that was finally curtailed by the police. Curiously, the ostensible cause of the student strike had been the lengthening of the school day by 30 minutes. In the students' concern, the longer school day interfered with after-school jobs. Once again school officials while well intentioned ignored the primary need for family income.[35]

A month later in October in Chicago, students struck over a very different matter. At Morgan Park High School, 1,700 students struck to protest the attendance of black students. A delegation of 100 parents informed the superintendent that unless black and white students were separated, the parents would keep their children at home. However, speaking for the school, the principal of Morgan Park stated that the school would remain open, and that teachers were on duty to conduct classes.[36]

As elsewhere in the country, Chicago's teachers were subject to the litany of pay cuts, payless furloughs, increased work loads, and fear of unemployment. Like their colleagues in New York, teachers were aroused by moments of desperation. In fact, 5,000 teachers stormed five city banks in April 1933. Wearing arm bands signifying that they had not been paid for ten months, militant teachers stormed the banks to negotiate their warrants. While these teachers were engaged in direct confrontation, their colleagues called on the mayor, Edward J. Kelly. Upon learning that the governor was present with the mayor, the teachers chanted, "We want Horner," whereupon Governor Horner emerged to address the crowd.

"I can give you pretty nothings or the truth," the governor announced, "which do you want?"

"The truth!" echoed the teachers.

"Well, then, the truth is that every one who knows the situation is extremely concerned. Not only concerned, but alarmed. The only way that we can get money is through taxes—and payments are far overdue."

In another part of Chicago, still another contingent of teachers 500 strong shouted, "We want Dawes." Down to the lobby came General Charles G. Dawes, chairman of the board of the bank, to meet with the teachers.

"Well, here I am," retorted General Dawes flanked by bank guards but soon encircled by teachers. Sympathizing with their plight, Dawes suggested the mayor be given a chance to work things out. When hecklers ruffled his composure, he snapped back, "To hell with troublemakers."[37]

What was to be done? Mayor Kelly responded by filling seven vacancies on the school board and naming a close friend and coal merchant, James B. McCahey, as chairman. By midsummer of 1933, the school board announced a draconian program of retrenchment added to the already critical issue of unpaid salaries. The board proposed to *close* all junior high schools, junior college branches in the city, and the parental school for delinquents. Kindergarten classes were to be reduced in number; classes in art, music, and physical education were to be curtailed as were pupil welfare services. As to personnel, central office positions were to be eliminated and one-half of the elementary principals eliminated as well. Teachers and community groups were shocked by the severity of the retrenchments in order to save $9 million. Despite protests, petitions, and legal challenges, the board's unilateral actions were upheld, and reluctantly Superintendent of Schools William Bogan announced that the schools would open in the fall ready to render instruction.[38]

And so the lot of teachers worsened. Not until the summer of 1934 was a federal loan secured in order to pay some of the arrears to Chicago teachers. All told, 14,000 teachers were to receive fourteen checks, two for each of the then seven months in arrears. At this juncture, the *New York Times* editorially did not speak of the life of teachers as "one of meekness" and of "narrowed circumstances"; rather it simply stated that "Chicago teachers, if memory serves, were among the first to get the unpleasant taste of payless paydays. . . . They have been carried by landlords, tradesmen and friends who will now be in a position to start paying their own bills." Then adding a coda of possible pump-priming via teacher spending, the *Times* asked if this might "signalize a nation-wide upswing?"[39]

Superintendent William Bogan remarked in a rare moment of candor for school officials that "our teachers have suffered immeasurably during these years . . . some lost insurance, homes, and investments." Bogan's untimely death on March 24, 1936, shocked his supporters and deepened the fissure between school board and teacher/citizen groups.[40]

As in New York, Chicago with federal assistance continued the construction of five high schools. In the fall of 1934, three high schools were opened. Despite the joys of paydays and school construction, stringent economies were the order of the day with the new school board. In addition to the above measures of principals administering two schools, high school teachers taught six classes, instead of five, along with increased class enrollments. In brief, with teachers serving more students, their productivity rose.[41]

Into the parched fields of Kansas the blight of the Depression moved. As the price of wheat plunged, farm income declined with the result that tax revenues fell. In turn, school budgets shrank. "Kansas, true to her genius," so wrote a Kansan in the summer of 1933, "for engaging in reforms on a heroic scale, had an economy legislature that really did things." The taxpayers's association was jubilant while school boards were bewildered. In a quiet tone, the writer, Avis Carlson, observed, "Two years of twenty-five cent wheat followed by a year of drouth make a sad combination for Kansas." She added that "taxes dribble into the courthouse in slow, thin streams. As a result, some rural school boards had decided not to open schools." Much as in Alabama, the lamps of learning were dimming. Dean William Russell had advised teachers to soft pedal the materialistic appetite. For Kansas, Avis Carlson delineated the contours of materialistic teachers:

> More than one rural teacher has contracted for $35 a month, which in an eight month's school year means an annual income of $280. How many books and magazines these teachers, who are supposed to form the cultural leadership of rural Kansas, can afford to buy during the next year is open to any one's estimate. Their teaching will consist of a *plodding sort of routine drill*—when they are not worrying about the problem of how to replace the shoes which have just sprung leaks.[42]

The *Social Frontier* when not bellowing at teachers to initiate the new social order had mentioned but once the "clinical isolation" of teachers. Carlson noted the absence of income and the lack of a material base. In such straits, teaching was often a plodding chore.

Yet even in rural Kansas there were oases of stability, particularly among the Amish and German farmers, who displayed a good deal of neighborliness. For the teacher in a one-room schoolhouse, the day began at seven in the coal pile with a sledge hammer. Reduced to chunks, the coal served as heat in the pot-bellied stove upon which a donated daily bucket of soup simmered until lunch time for the students. For the youngsters of all eight grades, the school day ran from nine to four. Invariably, the teacher driving home deposited youngsters along the way. To the teacher in this community, there appeared no visible sign of want. For an eight-month school year, the remuneration came to $600. While salaries were not cut in this community, warrants had to be held by teachers for a short time in 1933, or face a discount when cashed. Moving to an adjacent county sitting on newly discovered oil, our peripatetic teacher received a boost in salary to $900 for a nine-month school year. Quite typically he taught in a new one-room-schoolhouse with certain modern conveniences, such as central heating, a basement library, and in the main classroom such apparatus as a moving stage platform, mounted wall screen, and a projector. Clearly, this was a far cry from Carlson's portrait of straitened teachers elsewhere in the state.[43]

For the most part, rural schools though celebrated in folklore were in terms of physical plant vestigial hangovers from the nineteenth century. As noted, since the turn of the century the conventional wisdom had called for consolidation of rural schools. As to rural schools within New York State,

Dr. Orrin E. Powell of Teachers College, a leading authority on the subject, observed as a result of a study that economy and pupil achievement were inversely related. He suggested not only higher expenditures immediately, but also consolidation over time. Within the state, Powell had discovered 21 schools each with one pupil.[44]

Aside from the reality of retrenchment in the schools, what pieties from high and low quarters issued forth on education? President Hoover could say in 1932 that "however, the national economy may vary or whatever fiscal adjustments may need to be made, the very first obligation upon the national resources is the undiminished support of the public schools. We cannot afford to lose ground in education. That is neither economy nor good government." Was this the obligatory nod to the shade of Horace Mann? What was the "very first obligation upon national resources" if not federal aid, which was not forthcoming?[45]

Months later as a lame-duck president, Hoover addressed a conference of educators and urged "the day-to-day care and instruction of our children" not be delayed. Again he insisted, "There is no safety for our Republic without the education of our youth. That is the first charge upon all citizens and local governments." So the charge was returned to local governments who were at the mercy of falling tax revenues. Quite cooly, Hoover went on to say that "I have confidence that with adequate reduction of expenditures there can be ample amounts obtained from reasonable taxation to keep our school system intact." How this three-hat trick of *adequate, ample, and reasonable* would come about was unclear. He concluded in January 1933 that "if we are to continue to educate our children, we must keep and sustain our teachers and our schools." That summer the Chicago school board would make quite ample reductions that were not construed as reasonable by teachers and citizen groups.[46]

Most revealingly, and unexpectedly, Hoover's commissioner of education, Dr. William J. Cooper, called for a national sales tax earmarked for education—a daring proposal. In the remaining time in office, Dr. Cooper took every opportunity to preach his fiscal solution, but the proposal fell on deaf ears. Commenting on another occasion, he noted, as had others, the "heavy incubus of small rural school districts, which are a useless legacy from pioneer times."[47]

With jobs scarce for adults, the time seemed propitious for raising the school leaving age in order to keep youngsters off the labor market. But a New York State bill to raise the attendance age to 15 was defeated as a result of largely Catholic pressure. On religious grounds? No, as one clergyman remarked that the "measure unduly infringed on parental control." Here was still another reminder that extending the school day or raising the leaving age were not simply pedagogical issues but social issues as well that affected the family and community.[48]

In a far-ranging attack on the alleged dictation by bankers of school finances, John Dewey cited the experience of a New York teacher delegation that had sought restoration of schools cuts at the state level. Before Governor Franklin D. Roosevelt would see the delegation of teachers, he conferred with two Wall Street bankers and then issued a negative response to the delegation. Of the presumed bankers' dictation, this factor reflected in Dewey's view "a pathetic and tragic commentary on the lack of social power possessed by the teaching profession." Accordingly, Dewey called upon teachers to seek solidarity with other workers and also to recognize the large forces loose in society, themes, as we have seen, that flourished in the *Social Frontier*. Once again it was easy to condemn the bearer of bad news as the bankers' role manifested itself; or alternately it displayed economic ignorance with a view of banking as a charitable enterprise.[49]

Harold Rugg of Teachers College decided in May 1933 that "if a choice must be made between liquidating the banks and liquidating creative youth, it will be wiser to cast the banks into the discard rather than youth." Besides a false analogy, Rugg had chosen to forget the distress of countless Americans who had seen their life savings disappear as thousands of banks had gone into "discard." Three months earlier in February, Rugg had also urged that the RFC, the agency created by Hoover, advance $2 to $3 billion a year for cultural reconstruction of the creative unemployed. While the fiduciary restraint of bankers had been seen as villainy, the dispensing of tax dollars to artists was seen as necessary. Indeed, by 1935 the New Deal had mounted WPA projects for unemployed artists and writers.[50]

Taking issue with Dewey and Rugg, John Brubacher of Yale University thought it "unfortunate that they should think those calling for economy in public school outlays are actively hostile to the schools as such." Rising to his principal point, he remarked that "if there is usurpation of political functions by banking groups, let us blame the political machinery or the man holding public trust rather than the hen that lays the golden egg." As noted, the persistent misrule by Tammany Hall in New York City created vast indebtedness, which the banks serviced. Brubacher was correct as Harry Gideonese, too, had observed, particular evils had to be challenged and corrected rather than "systems" vilified.[51]

With the coming of the New Deal, Harry Hopkins, relief administrator, in the summer of 1933 released funds to assist rural unemployed teachers. Of the scope of the need, Hopkins stated that the need "for relief to teachers is clearly apparent. Thirty-three states through educational officials have reported approximately 80,000 teachers are unemployed." By the following summer additional funds were released by the federal government to permit the hiring of 40,000 teachers to counter illiteracy among unemployed adults.[52]

To a women's conference on current problems, President Roosevelt admitted that "the economic depression has left its serious mark on education." But echoing Hoover as he had done during the campaign of 1932, Roosevelt went on to state, "Nevertheless, with good business management, and the doing away with *extravagance and frills* and the unnecessary elements of our educational practices, we must [restore] . . . the useful functions at least to their pre-Depression level." Going further, the president deplored the oversupply of teachers, for "even today we are turning out too many teachers each year." As to the quality of teaching, Roosevelt insisted that "we need to make infinitely better the average education which the average child now receives." Roosevelt thus joined professional educators in broadcasting bromides and bombast. Finally, while the rhetoric of Hoover and Roosevelt was similar, the New Deal practice in assisting teachers and building schools was dissimilar.[53]

Those within the schools were aware that close to three-fourths of operating school budgets went for salaries of teachers, administrators, janitors, and clerical workers. Were these salaries examples of "extravagance and frills"? At its annual convention in May 1933, the National Congress of Parents and Teachers deplored the wholesale cuts in school budgets. Similarly, the National Council of Education denounced further retrenchments in school budgets and called on President Roosevelt to create a national council on social and economic planning. At the same conference, William H. Kilpatrick of Teachers College took special issue with the slogan of "fads and frills." Before cutting school budgets, Kilpatrick asked school boards to carefully examine the slogan since "Americans are prone to fads." Without irony, he asked, "May budget cutting become a fad?" Such droll humor was lost on business groups and school board members.[54]

Given the birth since the turn of the century of the high school and of booming enrollments and construction in the wake of compulsory attendance laws, the Depression brought a respite to this growth. Initially, the Depression served as a moratorium on escalating school costs. With teacher turnover reduced to zero, the typical practice of replacing experienced with inexperienced but cheaper teachers was unavailable. Also students stayed longer in school since opportunities in the labor market were few. Various strategies to urge or coerce teachers to retire or face dismissal were broached, as we shall see below.

Nevertheless some businessmen were impatient to slash school budgets. In fact one businessman in Minneapolis was quite confident of the inevitability of cuts. On another front, *Nation's Business* editorially criticized the notion that public education had an unlimited claim on the public purse or that the schools were sacrosanct. The editors then asserted that "the growth of education costs in this country is startling." After citing the rise in costs, the periodical indulged in the dichotomies dear to businessmen, namely, that while businesses *invest*, governments by their nature *spend*. Moving to its own non sequitur, the editorial chided government officials that "our states and cities have still to learn that they cannot always justify spending by the desirability of the thing to be bought; and *waste* in education is as evil as *waste* in *garbage* removal." Whatever the difficulties that schools faced in remaining wedded to the status quo, they hardly deserved this unfortunate triple metaphor of waste.[55]

Another businessman and traditional critic of education, Robert R. McCormick, publisher of the *Chicago Tribune*, delivered himself of bromides. In a free-wheeling attack before the Advertising Club of New York he called upon fellow businessmen to enter politics in order to fight the "subvertists [*sic*], those who wish to destroy the economic system of the country in which we have grown to prosperity." In his mind, he singled out excessive taxation as the primary cause of the Depression. McCormick then launched into a broad-gauged assault upon education. "The fact of the matter is that the seat of radicalism, socialism and communism is in the city," McCormick averred, "in which we all are today." He added that the "pink doctrines" which had been disseminated throughout the country had their source in institutions of higher learning along the Atlantic coast, particularly Harvard and Yale. McCormick would have been closer to the mark if he had singled out Manhattan from 14th Street in Union Square to Morningside Heights as the likely redoubt of radicals. Flattering indeed was the attention given by the Hearst newspapers and McCormick to the cranks and crackpots across the land and to the intellectual ideologues of the left who made Union Square their forum.[56]

To many in education, John Dewey remained the voice of forward thinking. In April 1933 Dewey delivered a lecture at Teachers College entitled "Education in Utopia." He called for schools with special rooms for studios and workshops under the tutelage of married teachers as in a well-furnished home. In addition, textbooks would be abolished since they were "instruments of torture of a departed age." What is significant is that Dewey proposed nothing new. As one reads the lecture, the familiar Dewey canon unfolds of the stress on individual experience, the need for growth and a suitable garden-like setting for learning enveloped with "what the best and wisest parent wants for his own child, that must the community want for all its children"—ideas that appeared in *School and Society* in 1899. The challenges of the Depression both politically and educationally elicited from the 74-years-old Dewey not the vaunted reconstruction of thought, but the reprise of the familiar in a utopian label.[57]

And the responses from the AFT and NEA? The New Deal's NRA offered a truly innovative fulcrum for the teachers of the land. But only the AFT initiated a response. The American Federation of Teachers (AFT) executive board drew up a code for submission to the National Industrial Recovery Administration (NRA). As noted, the NRA was the initial attempt by the New Deal to stabilize business output and prices. In addition, the NRA welcomed codes from labor and management. The AFT code sought the end of school budget cuts; equal pay for women; indexing of teachers' salaries pegged to that for federal employees and certain professions; a federal commitment to education to assure a national minimal standard; security of teacher tenure; decent working conditions; the right of teachers to organize; and, finally, adequate pensions. Gingerly, the NRA refused to accept the code even for consideration. Parenthetically, the unemployed teachers association of New York City regretted that the AFT "had submitted a code for the public school teacher without making the code public." But this response was a continuation of fractional politics among teacher groups in the city. Public or not, two other educators denied the need for such a code by insisting that teaching was a profession and a public service, not a business. As noted above, the *Social Frontier* also missed this opportunity to pursue the NRA codes as an avenue of political leverage for teachers.[58]

Aside from the miniscule AFT, the NEA, laden as it was with superintendents and administrators, remained the principal teacher organizations whether by choice or coercion. Given its ties with state and local affiliates the NEA gave a gloss of professionalism to teachers; at the lowest rung, the local NEA affiliates resembled company unions under the dictation of superintendents. Aside from a clearinghouse function, the NEA collected and published educational statistics. For the most part, the NEA's efforts rarely touched, if ever, the lives of the Fannie Biggs of the nation. Most revealingly, the NEA was but another illustration of the "blindness system" in which the organization provided those services that it was capable of producing regardless of the wishes of its putative clients: in terms of numbers, the teachers.

In 1933 the NEA established a Joint Commission on the Emergency in Education, which, typically, issued reports and denounced school cuts. As an example of the conventional wisdom, consider the particulars of the NEA's publication, "Meeting the Emergency in Education." It was a potpourri of platitudes, polemics, and selective data along with a wringing of hands with a genteel horror at the prospect of social conflict. "The American ideal of education," the report stated, "has grown up along with the American idea of democracy." Then the report took note of a particular fact, to wit, that between 1930 and 1933 with the same number of teachers, there were a million more students in school. (See the Appendix, Tables 1 and 2.) But side-stepping the economics of this increase in productivity of teachers, it did not raise the question of remuneration. Instead, the NEA sought to secure "the advice of consultants who can inform the Commission as to the facts about the crisis in education." Would they call upon the likes of Dean William Russell or Fannie Biggs? Not surprisingly, the consultants included presidents and directors of educational organizations, editors and school board officials, but *not a single teacher*.[59]

Reading the publication, one comes away with the conclusion that education was misunderstood by the public or so the report would have us believe. The commission's "important activities" included an exhibit "to present the case for education to the people." Another activity sought to identify influential policymakers in education; still another objective was to formulate basic issues. Also articles were commissioned for public dissemination, and, finally, a series of radio programs were planned to recount the schools' needs.

As to why school costs had risen over time, the NEA report advised principals to "give reasons for increased costs since 1914." The reasons included inflation, a longer school year, lower drop-out rates, and improvements in educational services. The remainder of the report served as a first-aid kit to coddle critics of the public schools, including this piece of piety in dealing with the public:

> Be temperate in your statements. The case is strong; it need not be over-told. Above all refrain from attacks on other groups or workers directly or by innuendo. The public school is strong enough to stand on its own feet. Sell it on its own merits.[60]

Warming to its prissy tone, the report advised, "Be moderate. Respect the attitude of those who differ. Most of them are honest American citizens, but misinformed." Like so many other school men since Horace Mann, the

NEA report asserted: "Assume a natural good will towards the school on the part of your hearers. Almost every American is at heart an ardent believer in the public school system." For the true believers at the NEA the wish was self-fulfilling.[61]

Dedicated to the status quo, the NEA disseminated reports and indexes of lagging teacher salaries as if the larger society and school boards were moved by dry numbers rather than by the shape of power. The NEA made the world safe for school administrators, professors of education, and bureaucratic compilers of dusty tables. Rather than a spur to action, the NEA's reports, conferences, annual meetings, and emergency calls simply ratified the "hired hands" status of teachers by those above. In sum, the publications of the NEA were the scarlet letters, the indexes of infamy that teachers had to wear.

And how had teachers fared in Middletown? After the pioneering study of Muncie, Indiana, in the 1920s, Robert and Helen Lynd returned in the 1930s to assess the impact of the Depression upon the life of the community. Perhaps rebutting the article of faith displayed above by the NEA report above, an attempt in Middletown in 1935 to restore teacher salaries to pre-Depression levels over a four-year period was sharply rebuffed by the local chamber of commerce and by a local circuit judge who ordered the new teacher salary schedule into the hands of the board of tax adjustments for review. The Lynds observed sharply that "here one sees the familiar situation of a business culture slashing the social services in which it may believe, but in which it does not believe as much as in the goodness to business and to the city, in its competition for new industries, of a low tax rate." Finally, the Lynds astutely reminded the innocent that "in a culture organized around competitive private business, all interpretations of the 'public interest' that do not relate to this *central pursuit* occupy a vulnerable position and are the *first to suffer in time of strain*." Isaac Kandel had said as much on the schools' place in society as a peripheral institution.[62]

Like embattled teachers elsewhere, Middletown's "teacher class loads rose in 1936 to an average of 35–6 from an average of 30 in 1923." And excellent teachers were penalized further since "administrative thrift prompts . . . [the] use [of] better teachers as a device for increasing pupil load." Teachers "regarded it as characteristic of the trend toward administrative dominance that in one recent year eight administrators and *no teachers* had their expenses paid to the National Education Association convention."[63]

Neatly summing up a recurrent dilemma since the arrival of the child-centered schools, the Lynds noted that "the announced new emphasis in Middletown's schools on the 'individual student' and 'education for individual differences' however attenuated in actual practice, introduces sharp conflicts at this time when the local culture is putting renewed stress on elements that make for solidarity and unanimity."[64]

As 1933 came to a close, many Americans hoped that the trough of the Depression had mercifully passed. In a gesture of national reconciliation, President Roosevelt in a yuletide radio address offered greetings to the American people and exemplified the spirit of the season by restoring civil rights to 1,500 Americans who had served sentences opposing our entry into the First World War.[65]

THE LITTLE LIST OF DR. ALTMAN

Attrition among the insane teachers in the city schools has operated ever so much faster than among the little Injuns who sat on the fence. The unbalanced teachers started out to be 1,500. The next day they were down to 700. The next day there were none.

—*Editorial,* New York Times, 1934[1]

Divided by ten, the New York City public schools would still yield ten very large school systems. But as a single entity—simply from the scale of operations—New York was atypical. Atypical as it was in many respects, it was quite typical in facing the retrenchment that the Depression bestowed. Aside from institutional survival, school systems in general were loath to make basic changes in organization and in the mode of teaching—unless compelled to do so. Nor were school boards and administrators eager to reexamine the premises and promises of the public schools, for they were self-evident. Self-evident, the collateral axiom called for more dollars in public education that would lead to better schooling of students.

In this chapter, the three matters under review are the reorganization of schools in New York City, student academic standards and assessment, and the competencies of teachers including their mental health.

During the interregnum of the superintendency in New York City while Dr. O'Shea departed, the state Graves Report on administrative reorganization hung like a cloud over the city's schools. Moving to implement the Graves Report, discussed above, the new superintendent of schools, Harold G. Campbell, a veteran of 32 years in the system, suffered an initial rebuff when a legislative measure to increase the statutory authority of the superintendent was defeated by the state Senate. Nevertheless, a *Times* reporter waxed optimistically a few weeks later over the intended reorganization. "A reorganized education system," he wrote, "which is expected to function *more efficiently* and provide the best instruction possible for New York's 1,200,000 public school children was set in motion . . . with the opening of the spring term" in February 1935. If efficiency meant greater classloads for teacher, he was correct.[2]

In an historical study, Sol Cohen has observed that Harold Campbell and the Board of Superintendents "wooed the elementary school principals and other supervisory heads of instruction through conferences, meetings, special committees, and appeals to *amour-propre*." Cohen added that "the rank and file were given orientation via study groups composed of principals and teachers formed for the purpose of exegesis of the Graves Report."[3]

Two years later, the New York City Board of Education consolidated the powers of the superintendent by a vote of 6 to 0 with one abstention while reducing the powers of the board of superintendents. Under the consolidation, the superintendent would (1) grant or deny leaves of absences, (2) alter the educational ladder of the schools, (3) select school sites and determine school boundaries, (4) recommend the acquisition of library books, and (5) recommend the appointment of attendance officers. Surprisingly, the consolidation was justified on grounds that the board of superintendents would not "be bothered by the small administrative matters" that now cluttered their calendars. But why cluttering the superintendent's calendar was an improvement defied comprehension. Relieved of petty duties, would the board of superintendents exert leadership, examine institutional premises or would they practice bureaucratic mischief? In short simply designating the superintendent the chief executive officer of the system did little to assure that institutional effectiveness and efficiency, much less economy, would follow.[4]

By 1937, in a two-year study of New York City's schools sponsored by the Carnegie Foundation, Professor Isaac L. Kandel of Teachers College found, as had the earlier Graves Report, evidence of administrative inbreeding. To Kandel, this factor denied school administrators a "notable part" in local and national policymaking. Further, he charged that administrators had become "educational enclaves unto themselves" leading to "professional provincialism." To remedy such inbreeding, Kandel recommended the use of competitive examinations that would sift the most talented candidates from throughout the land for both teaching and administrative posts. As to the existing set of examinations, he suggested that a modified speech test be utilized to stress practical rather than literary speech and that teachers demonstrate classroom competency before they received tenure.[5]

As to administrative searches for talent, Kandel saw little purpose in a perfunctory "combing of the country for talent" only to fall back on home-grown people. As to the locus of change, he averred that inbreeding could "be met more successfully by introducing 'vigorous vitality' at the top than in the ranks." To be sure, Kandel added, he was not opposed to securing the talented for the classroom, but if a choice had to be made, he would prefer men of talent at the top rungs. It was all so reminiscent of William James' dictum that the "renovation of nations" commenced at the top. Yet would a superintendent, chosen from outside the system, unless accompanied by a staff of his choice, be more effective in shaping and kneading the school bureaucracy? Of the Graves and Kandel reports, only the latter hinted at the existence of a bureaucratic blindness system. Thus a new superintendent with his own staff would be a necessary, but not necessarily a sufficient, condition in revitalizing the schools.[6]

One of the assistant superintendents in the New York City schools, John L. Tildsley, suggested a further clue as to why the bureaucratic blindness system persisted. "You must understand," he wrote in a letter to Howard K. Beale, "that there is really no public opinion in New York; that our school system is so large that no one at the top knows all that goes on thruout [sic] the system; that the average supervisor is not looking for trouble, that he is rather inclined to avoid it than seek it." If this were so and the school system was too large by ten, then the Graves Report's recommendations aggravated the administering of a gargantuan system. Second, what the Graves and Kandel reports perceived as "inbreeding" Tildsley as an "insider" recognized implicitly as the behavior of organization men. Could such institutional behaviors be more responsive to heroic superintendents or to external forces?[7]

More often than not superintendents were likely to fall back on traditional roles. With the growth of urban school systems at the turn of the century, the traditional role of a superintendent as master teacher and reigning father-figure became an anachronism. Given a bureaucratic institution, the need emerged for a chief executive not a patristic figure. Reverting to type, Superintendent Campbell, fearful that the new generation of students might find the public dole attractive, called on teachers to stress the principles of hard work, thrift, and self-reliance without permitting the "idea that come what may—the government will support [them]." Finally, he urged teachers to familiarize themselves anew with Franklin's autobiography. Fundamentally was this gratuitous advice to the unemployed on the dole? In normal times the virtues Franklin lauded might be applauded. But consider as an example individual thrift. Ironically, Keynes had demonstrated in his *General Theory* that individual *attempts* by those still employed to save a few dollars, if numerous in a Depression, had the unwanted effect no less of creating unemployment among the would-be savers. Thus individual prudence practiced collectively could lead to economic and social folly. Clearly, the world was upside down, requiring new conceptions.[8]

Reinforcing the Lynds' observation on the central role of business in American life, Campbell in reviewing 40 years of schooling in the city praised the business community for its contributions to education. "I think," Campbell stated,"that from time to time the public schools should be given an opportunity to understand the close relations existing between business advancement and the development of educational facilities. The two go hand in hand." Was this "understanding" directed at administrators or teachers, or both? But Campbell went on to note that between 1898 and 1937 the schools had earlier operated on a "survival of the fittest basis" whereas in the 1930s the schools provided a democratic education with a wide curriculum. "The aim today," in 1937, he added is "to *adjust* the regular schools to the needs of the individual child so that he will not be tempted to truancy." Was this an announcement that the "system" would meet the needs of its clients? In chapter 6, we examine the truth of this assertion.[9]

Although an article of faith that a close relationship existed between years of schooling and the securing of a job, the Depression snapped that fragile tie. Many youth harkened to the lure of the open road. At other times, in the cold of winter, youth gravitated into the schools seeking shelter, a hot lunch, and possibly a shower. In Middletown, the Lynds had sensed that the high school no longer served "as a screen sifting" out the vocationally oriented from the college-bound students. The academic subjects appeared as "a luxury to these hard-working folk" seeking employment. Amid severe economic downturn, the school solution was to erect another layer of bureaucracy. "As a partial answer to this problem," the Lynds wrote," a 'guidance program'" had been inaugurated to *adjust* Middletown students to the life of the school.[10]

What did adjustment entail? In New York, Superintendent Campbell banished scholastic failure by substituting what Sol Cohen has called "New York's program of progressive education." In the language of the time, schooling and the three Rs gave way to the "activity program." The program was begun as an experimental program in 1922. Space was provided in a school, PS 61, for a demonstration of the tenets of progressive education. Central to the principles of the experimenters was the conceit that pedagogical and emotional engineering was necessary and sufficient for the good of students, schools, and society. The beneficent activities would include numerous field trips, robust student behavior while singing, hammering away, dancing, playing to the end of "constantly creating and solving problems." In Benjamin Bloom's lexicon, cognitive learning assumed a subordinate role to pursuits of the affective and motor domains. In the hands of enthusiasts, the danger of Gresham's Law operating in driving out the cognitive domain was very real.[11]

Given the scale of New York City's school system, educational experiments could wax or wane with no one the wiser. Again, John Tildsley sheds additional light on this point. He noted "that in this great city, no one is constantly observing the teacher's conduct and utterances. Possibly the freedom of the teacher is *accidental* rather than planned." No doubt 36,000 teachers could not be scrutinized daily but then salary cuts, dunning for contributions, payless furloughs, increased work loads, fear of layoffs all worked their message of social control—unless some teacher chose to call attention to his teaching or behavior.[12]

Granted that here and there in the classrooms of the city teachers enjoyed a measure of supervisory benign neglect. But not always. One senior high principal removed a number of literary works from the school library and placed them under lock and key. He was concerned that the students of his schools not be subjected to "perverted pictures." What books had merited censorship? He had removed Sinclair Lewis' *Arrowsmith* and Victor Hugo's *Les Misérables*. The principal assured parents that the students at John Adams High School would have "an abundance of sound, healthful reading matter." To his divided faculty, the principal cautioned, "If there is any criticism of any action of mine, it should be directed to the superintendent of high schools. When a group claiming to be teachers takes any other course such as anonymous sniping in newspapers, it is evidence of bad taste on their part." But teachers understood that more than "bad taste" was involved.[13]

Aside from what some students might not be able to read in school, there was the continuing problem of unwilling students and others classified as retarded. The substitution of affective for cognitive approaches did little to reach this audience of students. The mismatch between a group of students and the schools became one of "maladjustment." Some of these labeled children were youngsters not predisposed to traffic in the world of writing, reading, and arithmetic. Their bent, perhaps, lay elsewhere. Rather than call them nonstudents they were labeled "overage," "maladjusted," "backward," and "retarded." Rather than reexamine institutional premises, a panel of educators called for a flexible curriculum, smaller classes, and greater authority by school officials "to decide the course of study for backward children." But their mild recommendations were likely to benefit the other students rather than the presumed nonstudents. In turn, the New York

City school board sought a study of the extent of backward children in the schools. A few months later, the problem of backward students appeared less tractable in favor of a suggestion that public and private agencies coordinate their efforts.[14]

A year earlier, Superintendent Campbell had noted with pride that over the decade 1924–1934 the percentage of children "overage" had dropped. In 1924, 28.6 percent of all elementary pupils had been overaged whereas by 1935 the figure had dropped to 15.4 percent. A year later in his annual report, Campbell again noted that fewer students had been "held back." Had the schools improved significantly in dealing with this difficult group? Rufus Vance, an assistant superintendent, provided the answer. He revealed that 6,000 students in 70 elementary schools had been *automatically promoted*. The goal of such administrative sleight-of-hand would be to eliminate by fiat student failure and to dress up handsomely school statistics.[15]

At a conference of civic groups in New York City in 1937, William E. Grady, an associate superintendent of schools, observed that "school failure at any level gives rise to emotional maladjustment, frustration and inferiority complexes that are often the bases of much juvenile delinquency." What was to be done? Grady assured his audience that the schools would *adjust* the curriculum to the child. With "more active occupational experience and subordination of the textbook to realistic experience at all levels," the result would be to preclude student failure. There was no mention by Grady that the youngsters presumably could be best served elsewhere than in school.[16]

If there was any doubt as to the administrative "solution" to unwilling students, the new line was clearly enunciated by Superintendent Campbell. He noted that formerly a teacher who had failed as many as 50 percent of her students was thought to be doing excellent teaching. But in 1937, a "good" teacher was one who advanced as many students as possible with few "left-back." Thus administrative fiat could redress embarrassing school statistics and overnight declare excellent teaching by the expediency of automatic promotions. Were the schools as a result more effective or more efficient?[17]

Nor was this administrative tinkering restricted to New York City. In the fall semester of 1936, the failure rate in Chicago's public schools stood at 4.9 percent, while plane geometry had the highest rate of failure at 8.7 percent. As Edward Krug has noted, William Johnson, Chicago's new superintendent at the time, "launched a comprehensive campaign against failure, including subject selection, revised student loads, and homework policies, plus one feature that might be judged almost surefire in its effect, that of requiring teachers to anticipate failure." From Chicago's school headquarters came the directive that "if between regular marking periods, the teacher feels that the work of a student is likely to be graded unsatisfactorily . . . the teacher is required to report this fact to the office, *in writing*, giving what seems to him the reasons for the unadjusted situation." As in New York, so in Chicago the failure rate the following year declined to an all-time low of 2.3 percent.[18]

Superficially, the use of activity programs and automatic promotions was not an indication that the school bureaucracy was responsive to its clients. On the contrary, these were but stratagems that maintained the status quo. They gave the appearance of institutional adaptability when in fact they locked in the routines of the schools upon unwilling students. In the key phrase of the time, *students were adjusted* to the life of the school. The real question, as a *New York Times* reporter put it, was how to meet the needs of "emotionally sick children . . . who do not like school"? Programs could be relabeled as "opportunity classes" and restricted to 20 boys ranging in age from 9 to 12. The *Times* writer went on to note that "special equipment, consisting of movable furniture, tables and work benches" were provided. Guided by the student's interest, everything was done to make school life interesting and enjoyable. One way to do so was the use of field trips for the initial batch of 600 boys chosen for this program.[19]

Still another response in New York City to the school/student mismatch was the use of empty storefronts. Lacking space for extracurricular activities, Leonard Covello, principal of Benjamin Franklin High School, persuaded neighborhood landlords to permit the use of vacant, run-down stores, rent free for a year. It was done on the condition that the students in turn would clean and renovate the properties. In all, five stores were remodeled serving different school and community needs. Covello remarked that "the renovated stores supplement the work of the school. Our students come to the store, sit around and feel at ease. They [the stores] are much more cheerful than the ordinary classroom." Were the classrooms of the high school so run down and dreary from lack of maintenance? If so, then the students might have repainted their school's classrooms. Or were certain behaviors permitted in the stores but prohibited in the school, such as smoking? Finally, Covello asserted that "we are reducing juvenile delinquency by taking the children from the streets."[20]

Aside from the storefronts attached to Benjamin Franklin High School, another option was possible—apprenticeship programs. But there was no initiative from Covello to establish such programs in the community or in storefronts. Second, taking the children from the streets was an old theme from the days and fears of Jacob Riis, Robert Hunter, and Jane Addams that the streets were in fact the true mentors for many of the young.[21]

In due course, the diagnoses of the reluctant students took a sociological cast. In a survey of New York City schools in 1937, Nehemiah Wallenstein of Teachers College disclosed that 17 percent of the school population came from broken homes as a result of divorce, separation, or death of parents. In turn, Wallenstein found that these students performed "less competent school work than pupils from normal homes." For these beleaguered youngsters, remedial programs were planned. Aside from surrogate mothering, what could be done? Fannie Biggs delineated the effects of broken homes on her students. "There are always a number of orphans, half-orphans, and step-daughters whose anxious eyes land on the teacher for dear life. These girls are very sensitive and usually nervous; many of them have hesitancy in their speech." Of one particular student, she observed that "a thin little youngster stops at the desk to have her 'admit slip' signed after an absence. 'Feeling better?' you ask. 'Oh, I wasn't sick,' she answers in a thread of a voice. 'It was my mother. She fainted on the street and they brought her home. We didn't know she was so tired.' Your heart rushes out of you like running water waste in a gutter." Of another student who was not working, she asked: "'Something the matter, Olga?' She doesn't move; she doesn't speak for a minute—'Yesterday morning,' she says breathlessly, 'I saw my mother jump out the window—she's dead. My father thought I'd best be in school.'"[22]

Anticipating the Coleman Report of the 1960s, New York City schools' Bureau of Reference, Research and Statistics reported in 1937 the truism that success of students in school was directly related to their parents' socioeconomic status. The report discovered that "the smallest number of behavior problems and the greatest degree of satisfactory adjustment in school," as the *Times* reported the story, "existed among the pupils with highest intelligence quotients." A year later Superintendent Campbell suggested that separate academic high schools be established in the future for the college-bound students. For those students not so inclined, he suggested a "general education with vocational values." In the interim, "honors" classes were planned for the high schools although selected high schools had had such classes for over six years.[23]

If separate schools and classes were feasible administrative responses to a heterogeneous clientele aside from automatic promotions and watered-down curricula, then the adoption of the junior high school appeared as an exercise in institutional cartwheels. In 1938 the first of a number of school committees was established to ascertain the need for a 6-3-3 or an 8-4 school ladder. A year later, the New York City school board urged the conversion of the remaining 50 percent of the high schools that remained on the 8-4 ladder in favor of the alternate one. The pedagogical or social justifications for this quarantine by age had not changed in 20 years, to wit, that better "articulation" from the kindergarten through the twelfth grade would ensue. In this perspective the sharp transition from elementary to high school would be eliminated. Why *two* transitions would be better than one was never explained, nor the assumption that 14-year-olds were fragile beings in need of administrative shoehorns. If logically this were true, then one school would eliminate all the transitions. Yet, the junior high gave the illusion of administrative, not pedagogical, change.[24]

If the junior high reorganization seemed remote from the daily concerns of teachers and students, the question of teacher performance and school effectiveness was never far from public concern. Like European nations, New York State appeared unique in the nation by utilizing annual statewide student examinations in academic subjects. It was one method of assessing student, and implicitly teacher, performance. However, a committee of New York City educators discovered that the main outcome of the state regents examinations had been that teachers spent an inordinate amount of their time preparing their students for the tests. Once again, means could slide into ends. Was the purpose of public schooling the passing of examinations by students?[25]

Upon retiring after teaching for 35 years in the city schools, Johanna M. Lindlof had been appointed by Mayor Fiorello H. La Guardia in 1936 to the school board. Would she bring a fresh perspective to the board's deliberation as well as a teacher's view? To begin with, in a report submitted in 1938 to the Board of Superintendents, Mrs. Lindlof urged the elimination of the teacher rating system by principals and department heads as deleterious to teacher morale and efficiency. Her report was based on a survey of 28,000 teachers, of whom 20,000 were convinced of the rating method's inadequacy. Further, the teachers held that the rating was equivalent to a photograph that failed to capture the flow of the ongoing classroom teaching nor did the rating method improve rapport between teacher and supervisor. As a result, Mrs. Lindlof hoped that the abolition of the rating system would be an "intellectual emancipation" of teachers. However, the bureaucracy's response was to revise the semiannual rating by dropping the categories of loyalty, character building, cheerfulness, courtesy, tact, sympathy, and other intangibles from the rating list. Thus supervisors were left with a two-step instrument of either satisfactory or unsatisfactory teaching. If the latter was chosen, amplification by the supervisor was necessary. In all, Mrs. Lindlof had gained a token victory: the bureaucracy retained the rating system, and the quality of teaching remained a mystery. On another issue, Mrs. Lindlof admonished teachers to take to the outdoors for their health. On the board she pleaded for recreational facilities within the schools for teachers. In grandmotherly fashion, she advised teachers that "a little less bridge and good deal more play in the open would work wonders in vitalizing the teachers and making them able to do better classroom work."[26]

On the crucial issue of licensing examinations for prospective and substitute teachers, Mrs. Lindlof remained silent. In 1938, the Board of Examiners of the city's schools issued a speech manual in an effort to stem what the board considered slovenly speech by candidates. Dr. Joseph K. Van Denburg, the board chairman, in issuing the report asserted that the slipshod speech had reached the "menace" stage in the city. Others like Leonard Covello took a different view of the difficult speech test: it was a means of screening out ethnic candidates who spoke the *patois* of New York.[27]

On another occasion, Mrs. Lindlof called upon the schools to enlarge their functions to include many of the former tasks assigned to home and community. "Teachers will have to clarify and accept," she asserted, "many of the *former responsibilities of the home* and the agencies for moral training"—*not* an alliance with the home but an announcement of its demise. Thus Lindlof, like Campbell, called for greater stress on vocational courses for students and an expansion of tasks for the schools. By doing so, her lifetime in the classroom offered no new perspective. It suggested that her "trained incapacity" as a teacher could not be breached and that she accepted her position on the school board safely ensconced within the blindness system of the schools.[28]

Whatever difficulties those seeking teaching positions had in passing the battery of tests, those within teaching had their own fears. The fact that 2,648 candidates had applied for 240 high school positions "the greatest number of applicants . . . since the depression began" played its part in keeping classroom teachers prudent in behavior and utterance. The financial lot of the teacher was a familiar refrain. Speaking of payless furloughs, a *Times* reporter noted that "as no employee will leave his post on actual furlough, the plan virtually is a pay cut, ranging from 2 per cent to 8 1/3 per cent" from June 30 to November 30, 1934.[29]

Nor had the *Times* changed its attitude toward the "voluntary" contributions of teachers except to bestow a small bouquet. "No one group in the city has given more generously during all the years of the depression than have the teachers . . . . Their obligation to give help in these emergencies is no greater than that of other citizens, but they have out of their first-hand acquaintance and sympathy doubtless *given far beyond their proportionate part.*" Yet such an admission by the august *Times* did not cause a cessation to such dunning except to lament a decline in giving. "The substantial reduction of their salaries," the editors of the *Times* opined, "during 1934 under the 'furlough' plan has prevented their giving on the scale as in former years."[30]

Once again the players of our drama moved to well-worn cues. Threatened with a reduction in state aid to education, a joint committee of teacher organizations in New York City, before mounting a statewide campaign to arouse public opinion, sent a letter to Governor Herbert Lehman objecting to the omission of educators on the state commission to study the effects of the state cuts in education. The teachers' group charged that the state commission "represents but one group in the community, the banker group." Apparently, if bankers did not exist, they would have been created out of whole money. Instructive in this regard was Mayor La Guardia's attempt to nullify a 1933 agreement between the city and a consortium of banks over a $200 million revolving fund for city use with interest rates adjusted every six months. Honoring the contract, the city's Board of Estimate refused to terminate the financial arrangement that ran through 1937. Again and again, the joint committee of teacher groups was driven to reflex postures of pressing for restoration of pay cuts and the denunciation of payless furloughs. At times, the political efforts of teachers appeared amateurish, at other times an exercise in civic futility.[31]

Sometimes a teacher, defying prudence, protested too vehemently in public. A near melee transpired at a New York City school board meeting over the dismissal of a teacher, I. Blumberg. Various spokesmen for the New York ACLU, the Unemployed Teachers Association, and the Unappointed Teachers Association charged that Blumberg had been fired for his public duties as a chairman of a teacher group against cuts in teachers' salaries. However, Dr. George Ryan, president of the Board of Education, took exception to the charge by insisting that Blumberg had been dismissed for his inability to maintain classroom discipline and for falsification in 1929 of his service record. After the uproar at the board meeting, Isidore Begun and other teachers were arrested. However aside from police charges, Isidore Begun and Mrs. W.J. Burroughs, a black teacher, were both suspended from their teaching posts without pay for "conduct unbecoming a teacher" at the board meeting. About a month later, before an orderly audience of 500, the Board of Education announced the dismissal of Begun and Burroughs. (The two were also active communist members of the Teachers Union.) Osmund K. Fraenkel, the attorney for the two teachers, asked the board whether teachers and citizens had the right to address the board. Failing a response from the board, Fraenkel sought to mitigate the outbursts of Begun and Burroughs as spontaneous over a colleague's dismissal. The board remained unmoved.[32]

Two years later, Isidore Begun as a spokesman for the Unemployed Teachers Association (a communist faction within the Teachers Union) disrupted another board meeting to demand the reduction of teacher class loads, thereby possibly creating new teaching positions. Once again, his nemesis, Dr. Ryan, remarked that such demands were out of order. In short order Begun was evicted from the meeting. Later, Dr. Ryan remarked that class reductions would have cost the city if implemented an additional $9 to $13 million.[33]

In due course, federal funds from the Works Progress Administration (WPA) began to flow into the schools. In the summer of 1935, Superintendent Campbell dismissed 59 WPA novice teachers for staging a three-hour strike. Taking issue with Campbell, WPA administrator Hugh S. Johnson held that "no WPA employee should be discharged for participation" in a brief strike. Johnson admitted that while federal funds paid for the salaries of the 59 in question, the Board of Education was the final judge as to the qualifications of the appointees. The 59 were employed as playground and park instructors. The following day, Dr. A.C. Bonaschi, the mayor's most recent appointee to the Board of Education, objected to the dismissals since "this indiscretion did not warrant such inhuman treatment, particularly, in view of General Johnson's lenient and judicial attitude" in the matter. A week later the New York City Council president also objected to the firings and asked whether "employees . . . cannot protest against hardships and seeming injustice without facing the danger of immediate dismissal."[34]

But Superintendent Campbell remained intransigent. Harking back to echoes of Calvin Coolidge in breaking the Boston police strike in 1919, he remarked that "walking out is always forbidden where a teacher is concerned, or a policeman, or a member of the army or navy." Pending a compromise with the Board of Education, Johnson reassigned the dismissed teachers to other projects not under school control. A week later the Board of Superintendents ratified Campbell's prerogative in the dismissals. A month later, General Johnson announced that most of the dismissed teachers would be reinstated if they signed a pledge that stipulated that they would not leave their posts and duties without express supervisory permission.[35]

Aside from protesting or staging brief strikes, other grounds for dismissal of teachers included smoking in the recesses of school buildings. A junior high teacher, J.F. McCarthy, for example, had been dismissed for smoking twice in the building. When a diligent reporter pursued the matter, a member of the Board of Examiners "expressed certainty" the denial of a promotion license had not been based solely on the charge of smoking. "The chances are that there was a whole series of matters which led to the decision. In all probability there were criticisms that entered into the heart of Mr. McCarthy's teaching ability." The anonymous administrator "expressed certainty" over "chances" and "probability" over McCarthy's "teaching ability." Were these circumlocutions by the system an attempt to be compassionate toward the dismissed teacher? Or was this the flexing of bureaucratic muscle to rid itself of a troublesome teacher? Was minimal *due process* at work? In any event an appeal by McCarthy to the state commissioner of education was to no avail.[36]

As the dismissals of obstreperous and novice teachers continued, the Fannie Biggs in the classrooms knew only too well that the bureaucracy in its countless permutations was not benign. One actor illustrated this drama with a vengeance. The low point in the drama of New York City teachers involved its chief medical officer since 1924, Dr. Emil Altman. After receiving his medical degree from Columbia University, he joined the city schools' medical board in 1919 and five years later became the city's chief medical examiner. In April of 1928, H.R. Linville, president of the Teachers Union, accused Dr. Altman of intimidation and mistreatment of teachers and asked for a full-scale inquiry. A year later an investigation dismissed the allegations as baseless.[37]

Five years later in March 1934, Dr. Altman charged that the incidence of mental disorder among teachers was about the same, of about 3 percent, as the general population. Accordingly, he asserted that 1,500 teachers currently employed were emotionally unstable or insane. After Altman dropped this time bomb, Mayor La Guardia felt compelled the following day to call for the removal of unbalanced teachers and of any unfit city employees. But the next day the "numbers" game took another turn when Dr. Altman reduced the number in question to 700 teachers. Disingenuously, he declared that "there was no reason for a rumpus being stirred up." Despite having created a rumpus from a statistical average, he went on to insist it was "not unnatural that such cases exist, but they should not exist in the schools." But a day later, Dr. Altman insisted that there were emotionally unstable teachers but he repudiated "the impression that these people are insane." Immediately the high school teachers association called upon Dr. Altman to "present a bill of particulars couched in the language of science rather than in that of prejudice." More sharply, the Kindergarten–6B Teachers Association called for the dismissal of Dr. Altman. A day later, Dr. Altman virtually retracted his sensational charges.[38]

While Dr. Altman was withdrawing his allegations, the *Times* chose to pick up La Guardia's call that 700 unfit teachers had to go for "even this rate is too high if only we can find a satisfactory test." The editors concluded with this oblique comment, "Countless generations of blackboards have been decorated after school hours with pictorial comment on Teacher's peculiarities." The *Times* did not explain how student graffiti confirmed the mental health of teachers. Pained more than ever that teachers were not available for wholesale dismissals, the *Times* the following day noted that "attrition among the insane teachers in the city schools has operated ever so much faster than the little Injuns who sat on the fence" from one figure to another to none.[39]

Once alive, the issue of the sanity of teachers would not die despite retraction. Nor did the bureaucracy have a satisfactory way of dealing with the issue. Two years later, John L. Tildsley, assistant superintendent, called for a jury of teachers to weed out incompetents since the attempt by administrators to do the same had been met by the charges of persecution, prejudice, and invasion of tenure rights. Tildsley estimated that there were several hundred incompetent teachers whose lack of abilities were detrimental to their students and to staff morale. Tildsley's call for a jury of teachers only confirmed that the bureaucratic system was not only incapable of ascertaining the quality of teaching, but even less so in removing ill teachers.[40]

Nevertheless, the bureaucratic stirrings continued. Two weeks after Tildsley's invitation to teachers, Dr. A.C. Bonaschi, school board member and chairman of the Teacher Retirement Board, proposed that the school board broaden its definition of teacher capacity to include emotional and pedagogical fitness as well as physical and mental states. Otherwise failing this new standard, the retirement board in Dr. Bonaschi's view would remain an insurance agency rather than an administrative arm of the Board of Education. Aside from the call for redefinition, Dr. Bonaschi did not present criteria for pedagogical competency. Yet under the existing guidelines 17 teachers had been examined for incompetency, of which 13 had been retired and 4 cleared in the period from January 1935 to May 1936.[41]

On a related matter of school board discretion, Governor Herbert Lehman signed into law the Feld bill, which empowered a committee of the school board rather than the full board to hear and try teacher cases. Two years later, the shadow of Dr. Altman surfaced when a committee of the United Parents Association in January 1938 agreed to study teacher tenure since the UPA asserted that there were hundreds of emotionally and physically incompetent teachers who were unduly protected by tenure laws.[42]

Five years after Dr. Altman had dropped his bombshell, the Teacher Retirement Board in February of 1939 asked Superintendent Campbell to investigate the "sensational" magazine article which had charged that among the teaching corps of New York City there were 1,500 insane teachers. Upon the revival of these grim numbers, Mayor La Guardia sought to bend with the wind by calling for the earlier proposal by Dr. Bonaschi to strengthen the discretion of the school board. A month later, Dr. Bonaschi proposed a new and different solution. He called for a Board of Education resolution requiring all school officials from assistant superintendents to principals mandatorily to report all unfit teachers. Failure to do so by principals would result in disciplinary action. However, Dr. Bonaschi cautioned that the purpose of his proposal was not to "make sleuths or spies of principals and superintendents but to require them to report the conclusions that any layman in their position could reach." But school officials were not laymen. Yet Dr. Bonaschi was satisfied that he had proposed a system that is "kind but efficient." The alternative was the mayor's proposal for a medical board with "inquisitorial power."[43]

Slowly the school bureaucracy asserted itself rather than leave external agents to usurp its putative prerogatives in the broad issue of teacher competency. As the school year came to a close in June 1939, Superintendent Campbell announced that after three years of probation a novice teacher would be subjected to a second medical examination prior to receiving tenure. Echoing Dr. Bonaschi, Campbell ordered principals to report those teachers over 65 who appeared physically or mentally unfit. In short order, medical and academic standards were raised for entry into teaching, to wit, a chest x-ray became mandatory for new teachers.[44]

But in August of 1939 came an unhappy augury through the mail for 250 teachers—a command to each to report for a medical examination in the office of Dr. Altman. According to the Times reporter, the 250 teachers were "listed technically as mentally or physically unfit to continue active classroom service." Of the group, a number were over 65 while another large number had served the minimum 35 years for a pension. Closer to the mark, the Times reporter observed wryly that the retirements "will result in an economy move for the school system" with older teachers replaced by novice teachers on the bottom rung of the salary schedule. So the Altman campaign was revealed for what it was ostensibly—ignoble means in pursuit of economy.[45]

Continuing its cleansing of teacher ranks, the Board of Education in

September 1939 recommended the retirement of an additional 15 teachers. Dr. Bonaschi, again cautioned teachers, not be to be "unduly excited" by the campaign to weed out the unfit. While women dominated the teaching ranks, interestingly enough all of the 15 were women, with most over 55 years of age and with 20 years of service in the classroom. Of the 15 women, the ages ranged from 35 to 69. At this time teachers could retire at the age of 70 with full pension rights, but those with less service received proportionately lower benefits.[46]

One teacher when dismissed did not go quietly into the night. For example, when Ellen S. Matthews, a substitute teacher, was denied reappointment, she proceeded to turn the office of Dr. Jacob Greenberg, an assistant superintendent, into a shambles. Matthews was taken to Bellevue Hospital for observation.[47]

Faced with recurring budgetary deficits in the city schools, Benjamin Fine, the *Times* education reporter, observed that "everything has been done with an eye toward economy." He went on to note that "never before have principals suddenly discovered so many 'unfit' teachers." He added that retirement had become "prominent in the lives" of teachers. He concluded his review by stating that the taxpayer had the right to hire teachers who are "physically and mentally sound, vigorous and wide-awake."[48]

Very much in the bureaucratic saddle, Dr. Bonaschi denied in ousting the unfit of any intent to inaugurate a "witch hunt." But in a rebuff to Dr. Bonaschi and Dr. Altman, the Teacher Retirement Board (TRB) asserted its prerogatives and quotient of fair play by insisting that it would not retire professionally incompetent teachers who were otherwise medically or mentally fit. Pedagogical competence, the TRB stated, would be left with the principals. The TRB went on to note that the law was never intended to remove teachers "who although not robust were still capable of rendering efficient, satisfactory service." In essence, the TRB enunciated an implicit sense of institutional obligation for those who had remained through thick and thin of service. But the key question of teacher performance remained unanswered. Finally, with the passage of a new state law, the retirement age for teachers was lowered to 65 over a five-year period.[49]

In time, another government official generated a new list of unfit Americans. In Wheeling, West Virginia, Senator Joseph McCarthy in February 1950 held aloft a clutch of papers and asserted: "I hold here in my hands a list of. . . ." The junior senator from Wisconsin would embark on a numbers game of latter-day heretics and lend his inquisitorial techniques to a new name: *McCarthyite tactics*. With his list, was Dr. Altman, a precursor of McCarthy or a comic figure like Ko-Ko from the Gilbert and

Sullivan operetta *The Mikado* with his "I got a little list . . . They'd none of 'em be missed?" Upon his retirement in 1941, Dr. Altman remained convinced that the Board of Education "if it really wanted to, could get the unfit teachers out soon enough."[50]

Seattle's school buildings are not overrun with rats. But there are enough of them, particularly around the portable buildings. . . . Last week, Robert Propst, eight years old, was bitten on the finger by a rat. . . . The rodent . . . darted from one of three portable wooden structures.
—*Editorial*, Seattle Times, *1939[1]*

Nestled between the Olympic and Cascade mountain ranges on Puget Sound lay Seattle. But the Depression ignored topography and rolled into the Pacific Northwest. In comparison to New York City, Seattle's public schools were approximately one-twentieth the size with 60,000 students and 1,700 teachers. Of course, smaller size was no bulwark against the familiar scenario of retrenchment. Looking backward briefly will set the stage in order to assess fully the impact of the Depression upon Seattle's schools. From the turn of the century onward, Seattle like other urban areas had witnessed booming enrollments with the resultant need for classrooms and teachers.

Given these twin factors, Raymond Callahan has suggested that public school officials across the land during the first two decades of this century were obsessively concerned with financial "efficiency" and with repeated attempts to economize on school expenditures. The experiences of New York, Middletown, and Seattle would appear in part to confirm Callahan's thesis. Yet Callahan uses efficiency and economy repeatedly as synonymous terms, whereas the former is a concept involving how well one does something per unit of time. It is a measure of productivity of labor, or of capital, or of land. Nor does Callahan take cognizance of the ability to reach institutional goals, which is what effectiveness connotes. Nor does he address the systemic blindness of the bureaucracy or the *trained incapacity* of the teacher's persistent use of the recitation method.[2]

In the 1920s public employees' salaries for the most part lagged behind those of the private sector. Despite this, a Seattle school board member, Ebenezer Shorrock, asserted that living costs in 1921 were the same as in 1914. He simply ignored the wartime inflation of 74 per cent. Thus Shorrock allowed nothing to interfere with his proposed austerity plan. Since "eighty per cent of the budget is for salaries," he noted," we must cut there if we are not to harm the education of children." As a result, teacher salaries were cut by $150 for the school year of 1922–1923. The following year a portion, $60, of the pay cut was "restored." By 1925 the pay cuts had been restored. Yet enterprising, if not desperate, male teachers were also denied moonlighting work by school regulations. Nor did this regulation permit moonlighting on Saturday. Why? Because the board insisted that it was "paying liberal salaries and would be denying employment to others" if moonlighting were allowed.[3]

While it was not typical of teacher behavior across the land, a group of Seattle teachers launched in 1927 a teachers union affiliated with the American Federation of Labor. On the whole, the membership consisted primarily of high school teachers who also retained their membership in the High School Teachers' League. As in New York City, a number of teachers belonged to one or more teacher organizations; however, the number in Seattle did not approach the 74 of the former. In a bulletin to its members in the spring of 1927, the Teachers' League observed that "it is impossible for those with dependents to live on our maximum salary of $2,400. The typical high school teacher is not a young woman, living at home and partly supported by her parents as seems to be the popular notion." As a result, the group petitioned the board for a 25 percent increase.[4]

As was its wont, the *Seattle Times* damned the requested pay raise by the Teachers' League with faint praise by noting that if granted it would cost the taxpayer an additional $1 million. Going further, the editors stated as if to confirm the prevalent "popular notion" that "any advance would automatically be paid to women teachers; these salaries are for nine months." In a history of Seattle's teachers union, Francis Morris wrote that "several cities were paying teachers over $4,000 as against the League's request for $3,000." But the relative salaries of teachers could be ignored by the school board and press even though the income of other gainfully employed people had risen 25 percent since 1919. Reinforcing Callahan's claim of the stress on economy by school boards, the Teachers' League discovered in its research that while per pupil costs had declined from 1919 to 1927 from $149 to $119 per pupil, teacher class loads had increased in the same period. Thus the school system received a double dividend of increased economy and increased efficiency at the teachers' expense—with the assumption that institutional effectiveness had kept pace.[5]

This substantial 30 percent reduction in school costs was achieved at the teachers' expense in three ways: (1) in direct pay cuts, (2) in pay raises forgone, and (3) in increases in class loads as teachers became more productive. Expressed differently, it was a substantial subsidy from the teachers (and their families) to the community. In the Roaring Twenties, schooling was a sterling steal in Seattle.

While the Teachers' League presented their demands, the Teachers Union remained its alter ego. Unable to advance their own self-interests, the teachers' organizations were helpless to forestall on May 4, 1928, the adoption of a "yellow-dog" contract by the school board. Such contracts by employers were common during the 1920s to prevent employees from joining trade unions. Eventually the federal Norris–La Guardia Act outlawed the contracts. But it must be recalled that Seattle, while ostensibly a strong trade union town since the First World War, had also witnessed in 1919 a general strike.[6]

As Robert L. Friedheim has written, "The Seattle general strike was a revolt against everything and therefore a revolt against nothing." Nevertheless, the failure of the strike left a legacy of internecine union conflicts; "the destruction of labor's economic hold" on the city, and a green light to business to push its open-shop plan. Thus by adopting the "yellow-dog" contract, the Seattle school board simply echoed the dominant business and press sentiment toward unions and radicals. In this view, teachers were hired hands. Given this setting, the board held unilateral and unrestricted authority and power in the community. An apt illustration of the board's undiluted control of the schools came to light when the superintendent of schools, Thomas R. Cole, retired in 1930 to assume an academic post at the University of Washington. In a statement praising Cole, the board noted that the schools had attained their current "enviable position" because Cole had kept control in the "hands of elected representatives, undisturbed by any faction." On the eve of the Great Depression, control of the schools by the board and superintendent remained unilateral, undiluted, and undisturbed.[7]

Reading the *Seattle Educational Bulletin*, the monthly house organ of the schools, from 1929 onward, one finds little inkling of events beyond the schoolhouse. Not until September 1930, in one of his monthly messages to the teaching corps, did Worth McClure, the new superintendent, admit to outside events. Raised and educated in Iowa, McClure had come to Seattle in 1915 as an elementary school principal. Rising rapidly in the administrative ranks, he became an assistant superintendent in 1923 and in 1930 superintendent. In his initial message, McClure wrote, "During the year that has been so well begun, it may be that we shall have some pupils in whose out-of-school environment there will be much of discouragement and even of want." Was it quaintness or a typical blind spot of administrators in casting the home and family as an *"out-of-school environment"*? Or to admit "even of want" in pupils.[8]

If Superintendent Harold Campbell of New York City reverted on occasion to the traditional role of school superintendent as orator/chief-of-state, Worth McClure knew apparently no other role. Thus McClure's messages throughout the Depression with few exceptions provide a fund of homilies more at home in the world of the 1880s. Greeting the teaching corps in the fall of 1931, McClure wrote that "I think the message of our opening institute was unmistakable in its emphasis upon permanent values which are of the time and some which are of all time." Descending from this bromide, McClure suggested that "I believe education will come to realize this year, as never before, its duty to distinguish clearly between the means and the end . . . [and] to see that not only must it impart knowledge and skills, but that it must provide new disciplines of responsibility and build new attitudes of service." To this use of platitudes was added the confusion of personifying "education," which would "realize" what only a person could do. Finally, there was a bare hint by McClure in this turgid prose that affective activities might well displace cognitive studies in the schools.[9]

By the fall of the following year as the nation plunged deeper into the Depression, McClure once more greeted teachers in an optimistic vein by insisting that "the new year has been well begun. . . . Boys and girls and parents were never more interested in school than now." McClure added that "increased flexibility" by the high schools had resulted in "increased service" to students. By greater class loads for teachers? As to the electorate, McClure noted that "the public's two and one-half to one vote of approval of the $750,000 bond issue to fund tax cancellations has expressed confidence" in the schools so that "Education moves ahead in Seattle." While the rhetoric of "education moving ahead" was jaunty, the suspension of the *Bulletin* from September 1932 to March 1934 indicated one bite of the Depression.[10]

An earlier item in the *Bulletin* reported on the modified adaptation of the "platoon system" that had been inaugurated by Superintendent William A. Wirt in Gary, Indiana, before the First World War. It was a complex organizational device. Wirt sought to use school facilities more fully and intensively than other school systems and thus offer a more diversified school program. Challenging the received wisdom of the time, Wirt's plan signally departed from the prevalent school bureaucracies. But in the hands of school administrators far removed from Wirt's guiding hand, little remained of the "platoon system" except the slogan. In Seattle the idea meant that the overworked elementary school teacher would have someone else to teach music, fine arts, and physical education to the students on occasion. In Seattle the "platoon system" amounted to a limited specialization in the lower grades.[11]

Another *Bulletin* article took to task the fledgling radio—remarking in 1929 "that a mechanical device like the radio lacks the vital personal touch of the teachers *explains* the present lack of extensive use" of the radio in the schools. The writer went on to say that the "children as passive recipients of radio instructions can never be stimulated" as they are by a classroom teacher. Clearly, the verdict was premature before the halcyon days of radio in live broadcasts of sports, entertainment, and news such as Edward R. Murrow reporting on CBS radio from London during the Second World War.[12]

Still another clue to the mental horizons of educators manifested itself in the juggling of labels. A writer in the *Bulletin*, for example, stated, "'Physical Education' has definitely displaced 'Gymnasium Work'" in the high schools. Here again was the shuffling of labels. On a related matter, the schools had mounted a "Posture Contest to Outlaw the Slouch." The *Bulletin* informed its readers that the "debutante slouch has been virtually outlawed." Aside from the humor of the matter, what is interesting is that the public schools displayed any interest in so-called debutante behavior.[13]

Not to be denied, reality slowly intruded itself into the *Bulletin*'s columns. By early 1932 under a headline, "Child Welfare Board Assists Needy Children," the article delineated the scope of assistance in the form of lunch tickets, milk, car tokens, and clothing to over a thousand needy children. The Depression had reached the pages of the *Bulletin*.[14]

As in New York City, teachers in Seattle were asked to "donate" a part of their pay, their time, and their good-will. The *Bulletin* headlined: Seattle Teachers Proffer Services for the Unemployed. Surprisingly, Superintendent Worth McClure, in the bulletin, spoke of unemployment as a *theoretical* state. McClure wrote in September of 1932, "On the *theory* that conditions of unemployment, such as exist and may continue to exist through part or all of the coming winter . . . [presented] a challenge for unemployed citizens, to be taught by public school teachers who *volunteer their services* for this work." In dunning teachers, McClure joined his colleagues O'Shea and Campbell as well as the *New York Times*.[15]

Across the land and in Seattle the winter of 1933 was bitterly cold. In the heart of the city Green Lake froze over. What did the Depression mean to students? As elsewhere, on a winter day, the schools when open with their routines and rituals afforded an oasis of stability amid social upheaval—a place to come in out of the cold, to be fed, and sometimes to receive medical treatment. Teachers grappling with the effects of the Depression upon their students also encountered the first round of pay cuts in the spring of 1932 amounting to 11 percent.[16]

Along with pay cuts, teachers regularly received pay warrants that were often discounted by merchants and at other times nonnegotiable. As local tax collections diminished, the warrants drawn on the county treasury became essentially promissory notes. Monthly warrants consisted for a time of a $50 warrant and the remainder in $10 denominations to facilitate payment of bills without receiving change in cash. In addition, a clause was inserted into the 1933 teachers' contract that they would not be paid for three weeks during the school year as an economy measure. The "payless furlough" had arrived in Seattle too. In passing, it is worth noting that a prominent banker served on the school board throughout the Depression.[17]

Thus the bond issue alluded to earlier and passed by the electorate in 1932 served less to bail out teachers than to redeem warrants in the hands of local bankers and business people. As in New York and Chicago, Seattle bankers cautioned the school board that warrants would be accepted solely on a month-to-month basis provided further economies were forthcoming. McClure instituted one small economy in May 1933 when he announced that hitherto *free* school supplies to students above the fourth grade would be sold to them at a *savings*. In addition, the school board announced that a 5 percent interest rate on warrants would go into immediate effect to forestall further discounting of such warrants. At the height of the Depression, the *Seattle Post-Intelligencer* in May 1933 headlined School Cost to be Lowest in Many Years and went on to quote the state superintendent of public instruction to the effect that the state's schools would be operated at $2 million less than for the preceding school year.[18]

By January 1934 the school board recommended a 10 percent salary *increase*. To be sure, the board's announcement took no cognizance of its past actions from 1919 onward in keeping a tight lid on teachers' salaries except to note dryly that "the present increase is in accordance with the Board's desire . . . to relieve the severity of reductions in compensations as soon as revenues" permitted. But the "severity" was to become more severe.[19]

To implement the proposed salary increases that would barely restore the status quo, the school board decided to submit in the fall of 1934 a modest supplemental tax levy to the electorate. As in other states, the action of the board was necessitated by the passage of statewide initiatives, numbering 64 in 1932 and 114 in 1936. These measures granted property tax relief while still another initiative established a state income tax, which was declared unconstitutional. The two property initiatives established a 40-mill ceiling with 10 mills earmarked for the schools. However, supplemental or excess millages beyond the 10 mills required an affirmative supermajority of 60 percent and a devilish 40 percent turnout of voters based on the previous general election to *validate* the election. Thus, for example, a tax levy might receive 75 percent approval with a 35 percent turnout of the voters, thereby nullifying the vote. To those who wished to defeat any excess tax levy, this mechanism provided a premium by staying home. Despite these hurdles, the school board chose to submit an excess tax levy in the autumn of 1934.

As the school year started in the fall of 1934, a polio epidemic broke out in the city. Health officials immediately sought a delay in the opening of the schools. Undisturbed, countless volunteer workers canvassed neighborhoods to urge voters to support the upcoming school tax levy. However, property groups took exception to the tax measure. The Community Tax Bureau, for example, insisted that "the levy has nothing to do with either the minimum or maximum education to be received. It will provide pay for teachers and other employees and it will increase the reserve for warrants." Concluding, the group stated, "The schools can be run without an additional levy and this levy in effect breaks down the protection given by the forty mill tax limit."[20]

While a simple majority approved the tax levy, it went down to defeat as the approval was less than the supermajority of 60 percent needed for passage. The *Seattle Times* headlined: Crisis Looms in City's Schools. What was to be done? Echoing Ebenezer Shorrock's statement of 1921, John B. Shorett, president of the school board, stated, "Salaries are about 80 per cent of our costs. In making the reductions, I am satisfied we must make, the salary items will be the starting point. There must be a *squeeze* somewhere." The squeeze began as the school board ordered cuts across the board for the 1934–1935 budget by extending Christmas vacations, releasing 20 temporary teachers and 13 nurses, abolishing kindergartens, and closing the recently reopened Harrison Elementary School.[21]

As noted above, a state initiative for a state income tax had been approved but declared unconstitutional by the courts. (Ratified in 1889, the Washington State Constitution was basically a populist document with distrust of government written on each page. Its very length bespeaks its veto nature.) With a state income tax nullified, the only alternative revenue in the Depression was the passage of a state sales tax. By 1935, the state legislature did grant some relief to harassed local school districts by voting to restore free textbooks, by granting funds to hire additional teachers to reduce class loads, and by restoring 5 full days and 15 half days of sick leave for teachers.[22]

In the spring of 1934, the school board observed that "teaching and operating employees . . . are now serving under a 25 per cent reduction from scheduled salaries. . . . The Board directs attention to the fact that Federal employees have returned to full schedule." Meanwhile what advice did Worth McClure offer to the teaching corps? In the first issue of the *Bulletin*'s restoration, he bestowed a bouquet: "I am frequently told nowadays of the helpful influence of some teacher or principal upon a child. There is no finer tribute to teaching than this and no finer interpretation of the spirit of the schools in 1934." Despite the Depression, McClure insisted that each student "shall be learning through daily experiences a truly successful way of living."[23]

In June 1935 with a 25 percent salary cut, and substantial increases in work loads for school employees, McClure issued another bromide. Apparently innocent of economics and tone deaf to nuances of language, McClure chose to call his year-end message to the corps, "Capitalizing the Depression" in Seattle. While the message contained a pertinent thought or two, the message was replete with contradictions and bombast not unlike the NEA's advice, above, on "Meeting the Emergency in Education." Taking the high road, McClure averred that "the depression years have not been years of stagnation in the Seattle Schools." Correctly he added, "Pause in enrollment gains has provided opportunity to scrutinize all we have been doing and to look ahead." (See the Appendix, Table A6.) Aside from a "pause," McClure did not pursue this line of inquiry as to institutional purpose and premise. On the other hand, he stated, "*Improvement of service* rather than expansion has occupied our attention." A fair point that he immediately contradicted when he proudly boasted of the *expansion* of the schools as "the past two decades have made the common school in Seattle a thirteen year instead of an eight year institution." Was more better?[24]

"These are testing years for America," McClure wrote, in which the schools have met their "times of trial" and in the process "found new friends and quickened support." Despite this "quickened support," it was essential to look ahead and "to capitalize our present restricted status by considering new directions the schools should follow in order to meet the needs of changing conditions." Did McClure really mean that the best defense for a beleaguered institution was to take the offense by expansion? Or was it better to improve existing programs? Clearly, McClure played both sides of the street and also misused the infinitive "to capitalize."[25]

It remained for an assistant superintendent, Samuel Fleming, to broach the subject of those students the schools were serving poorly. He noted that in years gone by "employment was a safety valve" for high school students "who found the curriculum irksome." But in 1935 Fleming observed that given the Depression the "safety valve" was unavailable to a student "after his school fails him." Rare was it indeed for a school official to admit the limits of schooling as a beneficent agency or to note the role of business and industry as an alternate route for such youngsters. Rarer still when an educator took note of the "irksome curriculum" and the fact that the schools failed to benefit a segment of the student population.[26]

Less expansion-minded, Worth McClure three years later took note of the "custodial responsibility of the schools." Like Fleming, McClure admitted that a clutch of students remained in schools for nonpedagogical reasons of warmth, food, and care. Of these students, McClure disparagingly noted their "presence in purely academic classes has not been fortunate either for themselves or for the pupils with academic interests." Having diagnosed the mismatch between students and institution, McClure nevertheless eschewed the creation of separate schools. He looked askance at one avenue of training: the technical school. Why? He claimed that the experience in other cities was that such schools were costly and in his view denied such students a general education, "which is essential for good citizenship." It is a recurring question of whether individuals in a free society ought to have a liberal or a technical education.[27]

McClure chose to call his closing message in June 1936 "The Long View." The influence of the *Social Frontier* was clearly evident in this message. Safely ensconced within the bureaucratic system of the schools, he spoke glibly of the "new." As an example, "If it has been necessary to face *new* conditions educationally ... [, that] Seattle has not been laggard in educational *reconstruction* is evidenced by our studies in character education, guidance, and curriculum." Again, "we must expect *reconstruction* days to bring *new* and difficult problems. We need not be dismayed if we take the long view." Could dispossessed farmers and the jobless afford to take the long view? One is reminded of Keynes' acid remark that in the long run we are all dead. In fact, McClure's use of the reconstruction motif suggested that he was conversant with the *Social Frontier*'s writings, but more important, his examples of character education or guidance were as in Middletown merely *add-ons* that hardly constituted a change of kind as to what the schools were about.[28]

More prosaically, while enrollment dropped by approximately 10 percent, Seattle's population increased over the decade by 1 percent. Illustrating the time lags that affected governmental budgets vis-à-vis the decline in GNP, it was not until 1935 that the teachers received their most crushing body blow of salary cuts—or, conversely, that the community received such a sterling buy for its taxes.

Common as salary slashes were, cuts in spending for new textbooks were also quite common. In a poll of 832 teachers attending summer session at Teachers College at Columbia University in 1933, a majority objected to the numerous taxpayers' demands for substantial cuts in school budgets as unreasonable. More to the point, the *New York Times* reporter stated that "more than 75 per cent declared that the supply of books had suffered unduly in their districts since 1930 because of reduced budgets." In Seattle the expenditures for textbooks fell precipitously. (See the Appendix, Table A7.) Given the long lead time that school districts use in reviewing, selecting, adopting and securing textbooks in the best of times, one can only conclude that old textbooks were made to perform yeoman service in the 1930s.[29]

However, the occasional adoption of social studies textbooks aroused controversy. The principal texts in use fostered one of three viewpoints with regard to the Depression: to wit, (1) the need for government planning or (2) the status quo of laissez-faire, and (3) the need for moral regeneration of society. In a study carefully reviewing these texts, Michael Katz concluded that in the majority of the books the authors conveyed the view that the status quo was no longer tenable. Yet there were signs that a number of parents did not appreciate the slant of the new textbooks. During the spring of 1936 in Seattle, a group of parents led by John W. Sparling demanded that the school board withdraw a social studies textbook, *Current Problems in American History* by William Hamm and Oscar Dombrow, as a work that was "un-American and radical literature."[30]

While McClure had spoken that "improvement of service" "quickened support" for the schools and proclaimed that Seattle had "been no laggard in educational reconstruction," he was conspicuously silent as to the question of adequate classrooms in the city. Despite McClure's ebullient style, the reality of countless temporary or wooden portable classrooms plagued Seattle. In fact, a severe classroom shortage bedeviled the schools. To be sure, Seattle like other urban schools, as noted, had experienced since 1900 burgeoning growth rates in enrollment. If the community was in no mood to tax itself beyond a given point for the elevation of the young, then surely expedients had to be found. For Seattle this meant ringing existing school buildings with satellites of portable classrooms. In his annual report, the president of the school board had reported in 1925 that "although the average daily attendance is constantly increasing, we find the accommodations made available by this [1925 building] program have reduced the number of children in portables from 6,000 to less than 4,000."[31]

Four years later in 1929, the *Bulletin* proudly announced that "several hundred children will start to school in spick and span new schoolrooms instead of portables next September." With still more pride, another announcement a year later stated, "No longer will it be necessary for children to go out on damp days to get their lunch . . . children will now be able to partake of a hot lunch in their own building, every day." While this improvement was cause for joy, it still left 3,700 children out in the cold and damp of the inclement Pacific Northwest.[32]

What effect did the Depression have on the portable population? In the absence of federal aid, the school board noted in 1937 that a building program had been "held in abeyance." After a survey, the school board revealed that 14,000 children attended classes in portable classrooms. Compelled by necessity, the board submitted a modest capital program for the electorate's approval. Once again while a simple majority approved of the measure, it fell short of the supermajority.[33]

Two years later in 1939, the school board decided to submit again a capital levy to the voters. So modest was the amount of $750,000 that it was concerned less with building new structures than renovating rapidly deteriorating school buildings. Aware of this slippage, aside from the effect on teacher morale and effectiveness, a number of community groups stepped forward to support the measure. One such group, for example, was the conservative Municipal League. While the majority of the league's education committee supported the capital levy, a minority of the committee instead urged the school board to construct new schools out of the annual operating funds! To this scheme, the majority objected since to implement such a proposal would have meant severe slashes in teacher salaries, nor would this proposal have been a sound method for constructing capital items. The league also noted that no new buildings had been built for over ten years in the city and that the stock of schools was aging rapidly with 26 frame buildings that were over 50 years old. They also cited the inferior quality of the portable classrooms that were overcrowded "with poor heating and ventilation facilities." And one might add a fire hazard.[34]

Conspicuously silent when a similar capital levy had been submitted two years earlier, the *Seattle Times* joined the bandwagon, self-righteously. Editorially, the *Times* opined that it had "opposed at all times to unnecessary taxes and opposed most of the time to all new taxes," but the paper was in favor of this item. Why? In a front-page editorial, entitled Drive out the Rats! the *Times* endorsed the 3-mill capital levy. The editorial recounted that the school buildings were not overrun with rats, "but there are enough of them . . . so that to the disgrace of Seattle" a student had been bitten near a portable classroom. But the *Times* was also silent as to its share of the "disgrace" that had long tolerated the expediency of portables. So the levy passed not by appeals to reason but by touching a raw nerve in the community with its front-page story.[35]

Finally, there was no equivalent Altman affair in Seattle. But the impulse to utilize early retirement as an economy measure was similarly conceived. Worth McClure in his annual report for 1938 mentioned that "equitable policies for the retirement of persons long in the service should be developed this year" as to the "personal fitness of the school corps." A year later this statement became clearer. With salaries fully restored, McClure and the school board were confronted, despite economies, with rising costs. As elsewhere, female teachers who married were forced to resign. In normal times, as duly noted above, teacher turnover, however, served as a brake on rising expenditures. McClure was refreshingly candid on this point. "Due to the length of service," he wrote, "a relative [*sic*] large number of Seattle teachers are now in the upper brackets of the [salary] schedule." Thus "with practically no new teachers" costs had risen. Finally, whatever his shortcomings as a superintendent who harkened back to an earlier age, McClure did not invoke the psychological warfare of Dr. Altman upon the teachers of Seattle.[36]

Mayor La Guardia addressing the Virginia Press Association luncheon meeting at the Biltmore Hotel, New York, July 19, 1935. Associated Press photo.

John L. Lewis at desk with F.D.R. photograph behind him. 1934. Associated Press photo.

Lord Keynes (left), chairman of the United Kingdom delegation at the Monetary and Financial Conference, greets China's minister of finance, Dr. Hsiang-Hsi Kung, in the dining room of the Mt. Washington Hotel, Bretton Woods, NH, July 1, 1934. Associated Press photo.

John Dewey, this country's foremost philosopher and scholar, on his eighty-fifth birthday, October 20, 1944. Associated Press photo.

Fairview Elementary School. Courtesy of Seattle Public School Archives.

Seward Elementary School. Courtesy of Seattle Public School Archives.

Lincoln High School. Courtesy of Seattle Public School Archives.

Horace Mann Elementary School, 1934 graduating class. Courtesy of Seattle Public School Archives.

Worth McClure and Child Welfare Council. Courtesy of Seattle Public School Archives.

6 THE TUSHER CASE

We have the right to send our children to the school nearest our home.
—William Tusher, parent, 1939

Every parent strike that has ever been started has fizzled out.
—George H. Chatfield, New York City school official, 1939[1]

Were the schools responsive to parental wishes? Did the consolidation of the schools in the name of economy and efficiency overrule or contradict the institution's ability to be effective? What was the cardinal criterion of school effectiveness: student scholastic scores or the support of the home? To shed light on the foregoing queries, we turn to the evidence in New York City schools and elsewhere.

What was the view of school administrators to parental requests that countered administrative rule? One answer in part came from John Tildsley, an assistant superintendent in the New York City school system, when he observed that the sheer size of the system precluded active direction and supervision of the countless schools. Aside from numbers, Tildsley added that the typical school administrator was concerned with the avoidance of "trouble" and "that parents have a most profound and largely unwarranted faith in teachers and schools and so are not inclined to ask their children concerning their teachers' " performances.[2] But there were parents, acting singly and in unison, who did not display an "unwarranted faith" in the decisions of central office school officials. In fact, John Tildsley came under fire over an old issue. In 1935, the United Parents Association (UPA) of New York City objected to the continuance of a *student* loyalty oath as a prerequisite for high school graduation. Interestingly enough, during the big "Red Scare" that followed the First World War, Tildsley had written in 1919 the loyalty oath requirement. Yet by 1935, this legacy of intolerance had raised doubts even in Tildsley's mind as to its efficacy when he remarked: "I don't think the oath accomplishes any effective results . . . it doesn't make a boy loyal." Despite the protestations of the UPA and Tildsley's misgivings, Superintendent Campbell insisted that the loyalty oath would remain.[3]

The UPA objected also to the alleged indoctrination of students on the topic of military propaganda throughout the city. Composed of over 60,000 parents, the UPA also chided the school board for not permitting students to participate in a nationwide "strike for peace" on April 12, 1935. A year later the UPA again supported the right of students to march for peace. If the schools would not sanction the march for peace, the UPA supported the right of parents to absent their children for public demonstrations. Finally, the organization opposed demonstrations inside schools but approved of student assemblies on public issues if desired by the student body.[4]

Turning to enrollment matters, the UPA discovered in a survey of city schools that short, double, and triple sessions existed in some schools and that classes were held "in stock rooms, corridors, lunch rooms, backstage and in the indoor yards." While federal funds for school construction in the city had been allocated, the UPA concluded that "steps taken so far will supply but a fraction" of the city's needs. The UPA singled out one school, PS 89, which had one wing that was 40 years old, and another section that was 46 years old. While the school's capacity number stood at 41 classrooms, in fact 56 classes met daily. In addition, of the 41 nominal classrooms, 9 had been damaged by fire and were inoperative. Located in Harlem, the school enrolled predominantly black students.[5]

In a letter to the *New York Times*, a parent objected to classes of 50 or more students in elementary schools and the prospect for still higher class loads given the school board's intention to *consolidate* 287 additional classes throughout the city. Other parents sought direct contact with school officials rather than through the pages of the *Times*. But when representatives of a parents' association sought a hearing from the school board president, Dr. George Ryan, they were rebuffed. Dr. Ryan peremptorily stated that the parents had had their "day in court" at an earlier meeting with another board member. In Ryan's view, the matter was closed. But the persistent parents sought more than a token meeting for their complaints of dangerous conditions in their neighborhood school, PS 131 in Queens. The parents charged that the school annex was "nothing more than a cow shed" and that the annex roof leaked with the result that students and teachers had to keep their coats on at all times. Clearly, the Depression had exacerbated school building needs, but budget retrenchment had also curtailed expenditures for maintenance. William J. Carlin, a school board member and chairman of the finance committee, reported that after 1932 the maintenance budget had been cut each year. With these "skeleton amounts" allotted to maintenance, Carlin warned that "if we do not act soon to spend more for school repairs, we will soon be in a bad way."[6]

By the spring of 1937, Superintendent Campbell observed in his annual report that obsolete school buildings, triple sessions, and a high student/teacher ratio in the schools menaced the health and welfare of thousands of children. Furthermore, Campbell averred, overcrowding in schools offered limited opportunities for these children that led to student "retardation" and failure. Thus he called for an outlay of $100 million in school construction to remedy the deficiencies. A month later, the UPA again called for a reduction in class size and supported Campbell's call for new construction. Another protesting voice was that of Dr. Bella V. Dodd, legislative representative of the Teachers Union, who charged that large classes bred nervous children. As had others, she observed that "a surprisingly large number of elementary school buildings, including every single one in Negro Harlem, were built before 1900." Yet new schools were forthcoming. By the fall of 1938, 14 new schools were opened as well as 5 additions or annexes to existing schools. In turn, with federal aid largely through Public Works Administration funds, the city embarked on a six-year building program running through 1944. But the coming of the Second World War curtailed the flow of federal funds.[7]

Paradoxically, when school officials did move to reduce overcrowded schools and to replace obsolete facilities, the public reception was sometimes untoward. A minor incident, for example, occurred in October 1936 when the parents of 55 children out of 87 students transferred to new schools objected to the reassignment. Ostensibly the parents objected to the fact that the new schools were too far away. The idea of the neighborhood school whether out of habit or convenience was alive, but for school officials who had been badgered over the years to provide new facilities this opposition presented a quandary. Nevertheless, Superintendent Campbell warned the parents that if the children did not speedily attend the new designated schools, they would be prosecuted under the truancy laws. With this threat rather than accommodation, school officials unleashed a minor tempest.[8]

Secure as they were from isolated skirmishes from unorganized parents or even from the strictures of the UPA, the school bureaucracy and school officials were ill-disposed to grasp the tenacity of parents once aroused. Nor more fundamentally were school administrators predisposed to determine the benefits of institutional effectiveness versus family stability and neighborhood cohesion. Despite school overcrowding, school officials hiding behind administrative rules and implicit pedagogical ones were reluctant to persuade or accommodate. For school officials the temptation to "keep politics out of the school" could degenerate easily into "keep parents out of the school."

Thus despite schoolish paternalism, three years later, parents of children at two schools, PS 97 in the Bronx and PS 116 in Queens, objected to the student transfers although the moves were predicated on alleviating overcrowding. Representing the Bronx parents as president of the Eastchester Neighborhood Association, William Tusher called for Mayor La Guardia's intervention in the dispute and recommended that instead of busing the students that a new annex be built adjacent to PS 97. Unequivocally, he affirmed, "We have the right to send our children to the school nearest our home." In response, one school official, George H. Chatfield, an assistant superintendent, citing the provision of busing, obtusely stated, "I see no reason for the parents to object."[9]

School board members and administrators, while annoyed by the parents' pleas, nevertheless remained optimistic that the "strike" would pass within a week. Chatfield, in addition, unreeled a scenario that bespoke the usual conditions for teachers that by analogy applied to parents as well. Chatfield asserted, "Every strike that has ever been started has fizzled out. We always try to give the persons involved a little time to recover their balanced point of view." No doubt a "balanced point of view" implied one in harmony with administrative decisions. Chatfield concluded that "usually the strikes get down in the last analysis to the persons *who have started the trouble* and then we take action against them." Like unruly students? Or unruly teachers? Chatfield warned the parents that if compliance was not forthcoming, the police would be called into the matter.[10]

The following day it was discovered that four schools were involved with parent/student strikes in progress. Walter E. O'Leary, the city's school attendance officer, reported that 79 pupils from PS 97 in the Bronx, 18 from PS 40, and 20 from PS 123 in Queens were also on strike in addition to others from PS 116. Immediately six additional truant officers were dispatched to the homes of the truant students in order to seek compliance with the administrative decisions. At this point, the *Times* reporter stated that "the end of the three strikes was in sight." Nonetheless, parents and students continued to march in front of their neighborhood schools seeking readmission. But falling snow in February was instrumental in curtailing the demonstrations as shivering mothers and children retreated. Before doing so, William Tusher rallied parents with the cry, "We're coming back tomorrow

and every day until we are allowed to send our children to this school"—
PS 97.[11]

"We will be patient for another day or so," O'Leary stated, "we are hopeful that police action will not be needed." Another school administrator, Rufus Vance, an assistant superintendent, declared that the strikes "are practically over." However, the *Times* reporter could write after the close of the first week of the strike of a sense of neighborhood solidarity following a meeting that gave "the strike a new impetus." Instead of fizzling out, the strike entered its second week in chilling wintery weather. Despite freezing rain, 60 children and 30 parents picketed in front of PS 97 carrying placards for the first time with such messages as "This is not a strike, this is a lockout"; "We want our 3R's"; "We want to go to school"; "PS 97 is our school, let us in." With disaffected students only too quick to drop out, here was the spectacle by contrast of students and parents anxiously, gladly willing to go to school—"let us in." The irony was lost on school officials. Instead, the schools chose to preserve their prerogatives and to emulate the politics of Carnegie and Pullman in the days of the Homestead and Pullman strikes of the 1890s when lockouts, threat of force, and sanctions of the courts were used to break the wills of the workers.[12]

Continuing the resistance, William Tusher wired Mayor La Guardia that "close to 100 children are in driving rain in front of PS 97 waiting for admission to their classrooms. This inhumane situation must stop." Despite this militancy, a truant officer after visiting a number of parents concluded that there was no interest in the strike with no vital issues at stake. He predicted that since "*no clear cut issues are involved . . .* the strikes will peter out soon." Rufus Vance again predicted that the strike would soon be over: "The strikes have practically died out." The *Times* reporter added that the "Board of Education members were prone to take the whole affair rather lightly."[13]

Apparently losing their predictions and patience, school board officials summoned parents to appear at departmental hearings before the schools' Bureau of Attendance. The strike had entered its second week. To counter this demand, William Tusher planned a mass demonstration at school headquarters. In turn, when reporters informed George Chatfield that 15 children had come down with colds and grippe while marching, he commented that "because of the desire of the parents to demonstrate, the children are now sick. That is a silly thing to do." Chatfield repeated the administrative line that adequate schools existed, that no new schools would be built in the neighborhood, and that fewer than 250 children had been transferred from PS 97. "The clamor going on now," Chatfield added, "*has no meaning.* I think it is a good arrangement to send the children from PS 97, which is overcrowded, to PS 89, which has a new annex and plenty of room." Was this the same PS 89 that the UPA had denounced three years earlier as in a state of disarray? Yet at that time no busing had been initiated. If the "clamor had no meaning" for Chatfield and his colleagues, Tusher replied to the real and imagined threats, "We won't be intimidated. There is not a chance in the world that the parents will give in."[14]

With the line manned by 40 children and 30 parents, the picketing of school headquarters continued. Barring reporters, Stephen F. Bayne, associate superintendent, met with Tusher and a committee of parents. Bayne stated that he would not recognize the group but would speak individually with the parents. At this point, Tusher appeared crestfallen. The bureaucratic stonewalling had begun to take its toll. Meanwhile, with obvious relief, school officials announced that the two strikes in the borough of Queens had been "officially closed." The following day in a crackdown on the Bronx parents, the school board prepared to issue summonses to all parents who remained on strike. Again the threat fell on deaf ears. At a public meeting, Tusher and his group denounced Bayne, made plans to see the mayor, and vowed to go to jail rather than transfer their children. In response, school officials "indicated that they would not countenance the strike many more days."[15]

Again on the picket line, Tusher threatened not to appear at the departmental "trial" unless he and other parents could appear collectively. Taking a leaf from the pages of John L. Lewis and the CIO, Tusher chided school officials for not permitting collective bargaining with parents. Back on the picket line, February rain greeted the band of picketers. As the *Times* reported, "In the two weeks of picketing, the parents and children have experienced an undue amount of rain, snow, sleet and slush."[16]

As the strike entered its third week, the *Times* noted that "viewed lightly at first, [by school officials] the strike now has become serious." Shifting tactics, Tusher and his followers picketed city hall in an attempt to see the mayor. Unable to meet with him, the protestors met with an aide of La Guardia in a meeting termed "wholly unsatisfactory" by the parents. Tusher even extended feelers out to the ACLU for assistance. Meanwhile, the board acted: summonses were issued to the striking parents. When 20 parents arrived at PS 105 to attend departmental hearings for truancy, much to the group's anger only 5 parents were permitted individually to enter a converted classroom serving as a hearing chamber. On their part, in answer to the school officials accusations, parents hurled recriminations at the officials. Unable to maintain order at the hearings, the presiding school officer issued police summonses to 5 parents to appear in domestic relations court. Undeterred by the responses of bureaucratic processes and undeterred by temperatures of 17 degrees and a biting wind, other parents and their children continued their vigil at PS 97 as the strike closed its third week.[17]

Pending clarification of the board of education's authority to transfer students, Justice W. Bruce Cobb, the following day in domestic relations court, adjourned the case until March 3. Before Judge Cobb adjourned, the attorney for the parents, A.I. Goldstein, asked the judge to permit the children to attend PS 97 in the interim. Speaking for the schools, George Chatfield objected vehemently to the request, declaring that 150 children who had already transferred would feel "discriminated against" and that possibly the entire semester's work would be disrupted. He did not amplify the nature of the disruption to those already in school, nor did he address himself to the disruption in the education of those on the picket line. "Instead of diminishing as predicted by the Board of Education officials," the *Times* reporter stated that "the strike has won new adherents" and had entered its fourth week. As the picketing continued, Tusher announced that six more parents had withdrawn their children from PS 89, the receiving school from PS 97.[18]

Finally the day of judgment had arrived. Before Judge Cobb, school officials testified that the transfers were predicated on the best interests of the children. To the officials, the transfer orders had not been arbitrary but the work of many months of effort by the schools. Yet no mention was made of soliciting community and parental sentiments on the orders, nor did the bureaucracy even hint that they had considered voluntary rather than mandatory transfers. The received wisdom of the time perhaps did not permit these alternatives. Before delivering his verdict, Judge Cobb of the Bronx's Children Court complimented the school officials for their efforts on behalf of the children and parents of the city. He added: "I must confess that the evidence I have heard here today from the various witnesses [school officials] has been an eye-opener; I never realized the care and thought that the Board of Education provides for the children." He also opined that few students in foreign countries would have received the care as these children had received in the Bronx. Judge Cobb also felt the school board was concerned not only with the majority of students but was reaching out to "help the individual child." Hence, the decision by Judge Cobb confirmed the view that the courts and school officials' evaluations of students' needs superseded that of parents.[19]

Glancing at the four defendants before him, Judge Cobb pronounced that "each of the defendants is found guilty as charged." Under threats of fines and days in the workhouse, three of the defendants relented and sent their children to PS 89. But Benjamin Tusher, William's brother, remained adamant to the end. The former chose three days in jail rather than pay $10. As he was led away, Benjamin Tusher insisted that the decision was "unfair and unjust. Our kids are not footballs to be thrown around like rubber dolls." Despite the court decision the Bronx strike continued. The Eastchester Neighborhood Association immediately sent a telegram to Mayor La Guardia demanding Tusher's release. If not, they threatened to picket city hall again. Supporting her husband, Benjamin Tusher's wife observed that "I think my husband should be congratulated and the Board of Education should be ashamed of itself."[20]

And so the story moved from the front to the back pages of the *Times*, again. Upon leaving jail a few days later, Benjamin Tusher vowed to continue his fight and if necessary to seek arrest and a jury trial rather than send his son, Alvin, 9, to PS 89. In a similar spirit, his brother, William, announced that the strike would continue with 20 families committed to the cause. Two of the original four defendants complied with the court order, while two parents including Benjamin Tusher did not comply but daily called the schools to say that their children were "ill." Affirming what appeared to be his birthright, Benjamin Tusher stated that he would "stand on my constitutional rights. After all, if a father hasn't got the right to look after his own son, who has? When I went to school, I went to the school nearest my home." Thus principle, custom, and convenience were joined in his mind.[21]

The drama continued. A school official hinted that if arrested again, Benjamin Tusher would face a $50 fine or 30 days in jail. In turn, six new departmental summonses were issued by the central office of the schools. Despite this, the picketing continued into its sixth week. While two parents were summoned to appear for a departmental hearing, three other parents were summoned to court. When the latter appeared before Judge Jacob Panken, one defendant was released into the custody of his attorney while the other two parental cases were postponed for two weeks. At this stage of this saga, the law secretary to the Board of Education, Theodore F. Kuper, ordered the schools' truant officers to apprehend bodily the children on the picket line and take them into custody.[22]

Clearly, the strike had taken its toll of parents and children. At a meeting of the Eastchester Neighborhood Association, the group reluctantly voted to send the remaining eight children to the new school. Sounding the epitaph for the harsh lesson in democracy that you could *not* "fight city hall" *and* a school board as well, William Tusher sought to put the best light on this exercise of frustration. Tusher concluded: "We think even though our victory was not complete that we performed a service for the entire city." What service had this been? In his view, that the school board would "no longer decide on transfers without *first consulting the people involved*. We have taught the board the wisdom of thinking twice before acting." But had the parties involved learned the lesson? Closing the affair, Judge Panken, after delivering a lecture on the duties of citizenship and the privileges of a free education in a nation ruled by laws rather than in a totalitarian state, dismissed the charges against the three parents. This dismissal, the *Times* correspondent concluded, had "closed the longest school strike in the history of the Board of Education." As mentioned many times above, the bureaucratic blindness system would dispense what the system was *capable of delivering* not what the clients wished or needed.[23]

Did school officials elsewhere behave less imperiously to student and parent strikes? The record is replete with similar behaviors and significant exceptions. For the most part, student and parental strikes were precipitated by the dismissal of a popular teacher or principal. An exception to this rule was the strike by a 1,000 students in the coal fields of Walker County in northern Alabama. During September of 1936, while students struck, school officials were confronted by a teacher demand for union recognition. A union spokesman claimed that 110 of 375 teachers in the county were already members of the American Federation of Teachers' (AFT) local. As the strike continued, the Walker County school board, a few days later, refused recognition. In short order with students on strike numbering "between 7,000 and 10,000 of the county's 17,000 enrollment," nonstriking teachers were jeered at and called "scabs" as they walked into empty classrooms.[24]

As the strike entered its second week, the governor and a Walker County grand jury were drawn into the dispute. After conferring with school and labor leaders, the governor announced that "The school children shall not be crucified to attain any end whatsoever." At this juncture internal teacher politics unraveled the strike. Another group of teachers affiliated with the National Education Association (NEA) through its local voted behind closed doors not to join the AFT. The NEA local officials later claimed that the vote had been unanimous with only 15 of the 375 teachers absent. In addition the local group adopted a resolution *disapproving of the parent and pupil strike on their behalf*. In early October the strike collapsed when the governor agreed to act as an umpire in a "full and impartial" investigation of school conditions.[25]

More typically, the dismissal of a popular teacher in Hazelton, Pennsylvania, during Easter week of 1936, and the subsequent refusal by the school board to attend a joint meeting with parents to air the issue left a lingering pocket of resistance into the new school year.

In Ohio, 1,000 junior and senior high students struck in the town of Struthers over the dismissal of four teachers on charges ranging from "inefficiency" to "talking too much in class." Outside Youngstown, Ohio, the 900 students of Memorial High School struck in the town of Campbell over the transfer of a number of teachers, including a popular journalism instructor, Michael Grabon. In explaining the transfers, the superintendent of schools mentioned declining enrollments as the reason for teacher transfers. With all but 100 students still on strike, violence ensued as the police used tear gas to break up crowds of milling students around the high school. After a four-day strike, student strike leaders and school board president, William Glass, announced an agreement. Pending the return of students to class, the school board, and not the superintendent, would decide the fate of Michael Grabon's transfer to an elementary school.[26]

In Hazel Township, Pennsylvania, students picketed eight schools in protest over the dismissal of 12 teachers. While strike leaders sought to close all 21 schools in the township, school officials claimed that only 2 schools had actually been closed. Refusing to reconsider the dismissal, the school board stated that absent children would be classified as truants and that if absences exceeded three days, parents might be prosecuted under the state code. Similarly, a two-day strike by high school students in Nantucket, Massachusetts, ended pending a settlement of the dispute—a demand that two teachers be rehired. Belligerently, a student spokesman threatened to resume the strike "if we do not get what we want."[27]

In suburban White Plains north of New York City, 80 high school students struck over the dismissal of Esther Neubrand, a six-year teacher, for reasons of school economy. Accepting defeat, most of the students returned to their classes. Outside New York City, 500 students struck in Great Neck, Long Island, over the failure to rehire four teachers serving their last year of probation. Staging a morning sit-in at Great Neck High School, the youngsters set an example for their parents, who in the evening thronged, 1,500 of them, to the high school auditorium to protest the dismissals. The following day the school board simply agreed to notify each teacher in writing as to the cause of his or her dismissal.[28]

Occasionally popular administrators suffered dismissal. In Lenoir City, Tennessee, one-third of the high school student body struck over the failure by the school board in the spring of 1936 to rehire the superintendent of schools, Claude M. Mitchell. The strike then "settled down into an endurance contest between striking students and the school board." In

Cheotopa, Kansas, nearly 400 grade and high school students struck when the school board failed to appoint as the new superintendent the acting holder of the position. To the east in Leaf River, Illinois, the school board voted 3 to 2 to dismiss Stanley Finifrock, principal, because he was spending too much money. In protest, the entire student body of 100 went on strike and paraded through the main street of the village, and all the teachers and two board members announced their resignations. However, a few days later, the students returned to school pending the arbitration of the dispute by the county superintendent. Still farther east in New York State, 1,000 high school students marched through the streets of Poughkeepsie waving placards with slogans of "Keep politics out of the schools" and "We want Treharne back." School officials did agree to meet with student demonstrators to outline the reasons that Thomas O. Treharne, an assistant principal, had not been rehired.[29]

With a spate of student strikes across the country, the *New York Times* observed that "School children go on strike because" school boards would not rehire popular teachers with the result that "there are the usual demonstrations." Following this dismissive tone, the *Times* went on to cite two events of a mother ordered by a judge "to thrash her 16 year old son with a short wooden plank," and in another incident a father spanked his 34-year-old daughter for coming home after midnight. Where this dubious pair of examples were leading became clear later in the editorial. "Here is an obvious lag between the progressive school child who does pretty well what he pleases with his teachers' approval and parents' approval," the *Times* recounted, while other parents believed "in whaling the lights out of sons of 16 and daughters of 34." Did progressive education have such effects, much less producing the "usual student demonstrations"?[30]

To the *Times* in 1938 the student and parental discontents converged at the doorstep of the progressive schoolchild. Never mind that the so-called progressive or child-centered school was more likely to be found in private rather than public schools. With the decade of bonus army marches, peace demonstrations, and labor strife, student and teacher strikes seemed to the *Times* by comparison pinpricks and so dismissed.[31]

Our final high school strike took place not over the dismissal of a teacher or principal, but rather over the display of overt prejudice in the affluent township of Oyster Bay, New York, the one-time home of Theodore Roosevelt. These 300 high school students went on strike over the alleged scurrilous remarks about certain students uttered at a taxpayers' meeting in the community. After meeting with the school officials, a committee of 12 students issued a statement in which they resented "these insults." What had been these alleged insults? A school board member, Dr. Myron Jackson, had been present at the meeting, and he had taken exception to the utterance by a citizen that Oyster Bay High School "was too good for Negroes, Wops and Poles." However, Dr. Jackson refused to identify the author of the remarks to the students. The student committee concluded that "we the children of these different groups, feel that this school system is not too good for us and we as a group bitterly resent these insults."[32]

With the spanning of the continent by steel rails after the Civil War, the slow but steady movement of rural flight to the urban areas continued. Spurred by technology that increased output and productivity on the farm, the excess labor migrated to the factories of the cities. In turn the viability of rural America became an issue with the rise of the Populists in the 1890s. But if rural decline was inevitable as a result of market forces, then surely rural schools would suffer a similar fate. Thus by the 1930s the accepted remedy was the consolidation of one-room schoolhouses. Consolidation seemed self-evident given the antiquated buildings, lack of adequate textbooks, and ill-trained teachers. Also, as above noted, rural teachers received lower salaries that reflected their lesser training.

Giving vent to the popular views of the time, the *New York Times* editorially observed in April 1934 that one-third of the 7,059 one-room schoolhouses in New York State had enrollments of 10 or less. Hence the *Times* urged consolidation since the old schools worked to the "disadvantage of the children." Damning with faint praise, the *Times* went on to state that a "small school is not necessarily a poor school, but it is an incomplete school." But what of the wishes of the parents and students of these "inferior" schools? The point was not raised.[33]

One correspondent took exception to the consolidation movement and to the riddle of rural poverty without the consent of affected Americans. Without a rural renascence, the writer felt that the young would drift into the cities to "become hirelings with a disposition to swallow any political quackery that is provided them." It was an old theme and no doubt a half-truth that the "babes in the woods" would be shorn by city slickers. Nevertheless, in New York State, despite Governor Lehman's support of the measure, the state Senate defeated a bill to combine rural schools. Still another correspondent queried whether consolidating schools would be economical since an offsetting cost to closure of schools would be the cost of transportation.[34]

Echoing a similar point on rural schools, the New Jersey State Planning Board indicted the "little red school house" as uneconomical and inefficient. In a preliminary report, the board observed that there were 249 one-room and 153 two-room schools in the state crying out for consolidation. Taking a different perspective, Professor John K. Norton of Teachers College in a study entitled "Wealth, Children and Education" took note of the disparity in income levels among the states. Thus while intrastate consolidation might be useful in Norton's view, the true issue remained, as Eunice Barnard had noted above, the wide income disparities among the states. Hence the remedy involved some form of federal aid to education. By 1939 as the worst ravages of the Depression had receded, the New York State Board of Regents encountered considerable opposition in its attempts to "modernize" rural schools. At the very least, unlike the Tusher affair, the board wisely decided to hold numerous public hearings in the affected rural areas.[35]

Rare indeed was it for an educator to speak feelingly of the passing of rural America and its schools. At the annual convention of the American Association of School Administrators in 1939, Dr. John A. Sexson, superintendent of schools at Pasadena, California, spoke of the slow starvation for over two decades of village America. "Perhaps the most tragic result of the depression," he observed, "is the havoc it has wrought in the educational institutions of the smaller communities. *America has been and still is a nation of homes and neighborhoods* which have by kindness, cooperation and sacrifice built for themselves a rich, nourishing culture resting solidly upon local resources." Sexson as an educator was a rarity also for his implicit perception of the connection among school, home, and neighborhood.[36]

But the *New York Times* took quick exception to Dr. Sexson's address by missing his principal point—the revitalization of community. Instead the *Times* focused narrowly on the pedagogical delivery system, the one-room schoolhouse. Given that there was little cause for pride in New York's rural schools, it followed according to the editors that Sexson's comments "cannot be true except in rare instances." Supporting its contention, the editors reported that some schoolhouses traced their origins to 1812 while others had been scarcely altered since the Civil War. This meant that "boys and girls in 70 per cent" of the rural schools were not receiving "modern schooling." Typically, the *Times* confused or preferred the trees of the schools rather than the forest of the community. Nor had it absorbed the lesson of the Tusher case on its doorstep. But even the *Times* admitted a "rare instance."[37]

We turn to a revealing "rare instance." In the spring of 1937, Amish, Mennonite, and Dunkard residents of Lampeter Township school district of Lancaster, Pennsylvania, felt compelled to seek judicial relief. In federal court in the nation's capital, the three sects sought an injunction to *prevent con-*

solidation of their 11 one-room schoolhouses with its concomitant busing of their children to a new school, which would be built with Public Works Administration funds. Pending the review of the case by the courts, the three sects boycotted the new consolidated school. Approximately six months later, Federal District Judge George A. Welsh criticized "governmental benevolence" and "extravagance" on the part of Harold Ickes, the secretary of interior, for erecting the school. Judge Welsh argued that the school board in applying for PWA funds had "improperly represented the financial state of the school district." He then issued an injunction against the school board. But nine months later, Judge Joseph Buffington, of the Federal Circuit Court of Appeals, overturned the injunction and ruled that the federal courts had no jurisdiction over local education despite the fact that federal funds were used for the new school's construction. Nevertheless, the school had been built and completed.[38]

What avenues were left for the three sects? Francis Doyle, attorney for the Amish, spoke of appealing the appellate court decision to the U.S. Supreme Court on a *writ of certiorari*. Failing this appeal, the Amish had informed Federal Judge W.H. Kirkpatrick of their intention to secede from the school district and to once again set up separate schools. As the fall school year opened, anxious school officials of the East Lampeter Township awaited the decisions of the Amish parents. Taking their case to the state legislature, Amish and Mennonite parents testified before the legislative education committee. They spoke of their sincere wish to keep their children out of high school so they could work in the fields and avoid worldly contacts. The parents also urged the *lowering* of the compulsory school leaving age from 15 to 14. One Amish spokesman added, "Our children are our only source of building our faith. We want to educate them for farm and domestic work. We do not want them to work on public works or in cities." Another Amish father, Stephen Stoltfus, pointed out that "if we send our children to high school nine months out of twelve, it will lead them to worldly things and away from the church." It was all so reminiscent of the elder Pilgrims' similar fears and concerns for their children in Holland prior to their decision to embark for the New World to establish a city on the hill.[39]

Unlike the Tusher episode, the Amish and Mennonite case turned out differently. Early in November 1938, 10 red one-room schoolhouses were auctioned off for a total price of less than $10,000. These were the 10 of 11 replaced by the new consolidated school. Three weeks later, the legal turnaround came when the Pennsylvania State Legislature in a special session enacted a law permitting the establishment of independent school districts. Immediately one of the sold schools, Horseshoe Pike, was reopened by the

Amish. Ignoring its earlier and later editorials on student and parental rights, the *New York Times* waxed eloquent over the Amish victory.[40]

The *Times* reporter noted approvingly that "thirty children with Amish bowl-shaped haircuts rode in horse-drawn sleds" to their old school. Piling out from the wagon, they "went to work with a will carrying in coal from the shed . . . bringing drinking water" and doing other chores.[41]

Editorially, the *Times* found that when rustic virtues were contrasted with urban virtues, the latter were found wanting. Indeed, the editorial added that urban children in "chromium-plated and thermostated classrooms" will envy the Amish youngsters for their zest and hard work. Of the hard work, the *Times* asked: "What of it? Forty years later they will be the big industrialists and labor leaders and give orders to the graduates from our chromium-plated central schools."[42]

Once again the *Times'* editors chose not to read their own news columns very carefully, much as the *Social Frontier* editors had ignored writers of contrary viewpoints in their own pages. Aside from the *non sequitur* of supposing that other worldly Amish would wish to be "industrialists and labor leaders," what is noteworthy was the *Times'* ability to perceive virtues in rural schools if only through the exotic lens of religious sects. But of typical rural schools, and of parents seeking redress from school officials, the *Times* displayed the stance of the times in ignoring family preferences and cohesion and ignoring the community wish for involvement with and stability from its public offspring—the schools.

> *Teaching is not at present a profession for women; it is a job. . . . Their*
> *jobs are secured not by improving conditions but by remaining spinsters. . . .*
> *She is saved only by the consciousness that her humiliation is as temporary*
> *as her job.*
>
>   *—Raymond Fisher*[1]

For over a century, the specter of Horace Mann has hovered over public school teachers. In this chapter I review the historic "ceremony of professionalism" that issued from Mann and shrouded public school teachers. For one, Mann held a Ptolemaic vision of the public schools at the center of his universe with other institutions in a subordinate role. Given this spirit, Mann could intone that the common school was "the greatest discovery ever made by man: we repeat it, the common school is" and so on. At the center of society, the common school matter of factly countered countless social ills. "Education, beyond all other devices of human origin, is the greatest equalizer of the conditions of men—the *balance wheel of the social machinery.*"[2]

Was this a lofty vision or a quixotic exercise? More important, was it even remotely true? In retrospect, Mann's "balance wheel" was what Keynes later ascribed to fiscal policies of the national government—the ability to steer economies. To implement Keynes' ideas required political will and knowledge. What was necessary to implement Mann's conception? A clue may be gleaned from Mann's command that school board members were to stand as "sentinels stationed at the door of every school house in the State, to see that no teacher ever crosses its threshold who is not clothed, from the crown of *his* head to the sole of *his* foot, in garments of virtue . . . of pure tastes, of good manners, of exemplary morals." and more.[3]

In the real world such unworldly figures are always in short supply. And if male saints were unavailable, "is it not an unpardonable waste of means," Mann asked, "where it can be possibly avoided, to employ a a man, at $25 or $30 a month, to teach the alphabet, when it can be done much better, at *half price by a female teacher*?" Whatever the strategic role assigned by Mann to the public schools, the tactical means consisted of platoons of petticoated pedagogues at discounted prices. This legacy of Mann provides a clue to Fannie Biggs' plaintive plea noted earlier of why teachers hovered at the bottom of the social ladder.[4]

By the turn of the century as urban schools grew in numbers with an attendant bureaucracy, the training of school administrators was fostered, particularly by Ellwood P. Cubberley at Stanford University and George Strayer at Columbia University. By taking the appropriate courses and perusing the new textbooks, novice administrators received advanced degrees and the bestowal of legitimacy. Needless to say, as with any training, administrators were enmeshed in the trained incapacity of the new academic field.

Cubberley concluded his *Changing Conceptions of Education* in 1909 with a hortatory call so reminiscent of Mann that "the work of public education is with us, too, to a large degree, a piece of religious work. To engage in it is to enlist in the nation's service." He added that "Its call is for those who would dedicate themselves in a noble way. Those who would serve must be of the world, its needs, and its problems; they must have largeness of vision and the courage to do and dare; and they must train the young with whom they come in contact for useful and efficient action." If Olympian giants were not available, docile spinsters were.[5]

Until the latter part of the nineteenth century, the nation's economy dealt with sporadic labor shortages. As a result, Mann's use of women as teachers was a practical matter. Labor shortages normally induce rising wages, but social convention cordoned off teaching to women with its discriminatory wage. As with Irish and black workers at the time, the marketplace worked imperfectly in labor markets.

Women were restricted from acting as actors in their own right as equals since they lacked the franchise, were encumbered from inheriting property and suffered from social constraints on their movements. They faced a cruel choice of either discounted wages or acting as a burden upon their parents. Despite Mann's fostering of normal schools for would be teachers, teaching remained less a profession than a semi-skilled occupation. Also when teaching was cast in the light of "mothering," then a vast reserve army stood ready to supply the service.

Consequently, as a keen observer of education has written, "Prestige and glamor are not so likely to come if, like the typical mother . . . you spend your time in supervising a process which quietly and inconspicuously goes its own way." Another writer could ask in 1895 that "it must be a rather poor average man who would not find some opening which would pay him" more than in teaching. Thus with males drawn into the industrial operations of the nation, the writer believed that "a great army of faithful female teachers" were necessary in teaching. In fact, in Horace Mann's bailiwick of Massachusetts, 92 percent of the teaching posts were manned by women.[6]

By 1909, the president of a state normal school for teachers could astutely ask, "Is the employment of untrained teachers the cause or the result of low salaries?" To which he replied, "Surely when wages are low few will go to the expenses of professional training. It seems equally clear that when untrained teachers are acceptable the abundant supply will keep wages at the general level paid to *unskilled labor*." This was an astute analysis of labor markets. However by the 1920s, many urban school systems in an attempt to upgrade teaching standards began to insist on a bachelor's degree or its equivalent.[7]

Insist as they might about education requirements, school boards welcomed women into teaching for two reasons. First, women with lesser training could be hired for less, and women had to resign when they married. Replaced by novices, salary costs were kept in check. Despite this implicit policy by school boards, the percentage of women in teaching began a slow decline. By the close of the First World War, the percentage of women in teaching hovered at 86 percent; at the start of the Great Depression the figure had fallen slightly to 84 percent; and by the close of the decade, it had fallen further to 78 percent. In New York City's school system, where the education requirements for men and women were the same, the percentage of women teachers fell between 1933 and 1939 from 85 to 82 percent.[8]

As the preceding pages have made clear, the Depression brought a decline in income and host of restrictions for teachers. Pressed further by the persistence of the Depression, many school boards again retrenched. We already noted the attempt to "retire" teachers earlier than by choice. Of course, with mass unemployment stalking the land, even those spirits ill-disposed to teaching remained in the classroom. A pay check meant the difference between gentility and breadlines.

For school boards the dismissal of married women teachers seemed an inviting target in hard times. Yet, married women teachers had their supporters. Professor D. Peters of Teachers College, for example, in a 1934 survey declared that married women teachers were better than unmarried ones since the former, he found, spent more times in the classroom, were engaged in more extracurricular activities, and complained less about increases in school work. If this were so, then school boards were penny wise and pound foolish in removing these hard-working and experienced teachers. To return to Peters' survey, despite the enumerated advantages, he found that between 1928 and 1931, school districts had reduced the number of married women employed by 17 percent. Even city school systems in the same period became less tolerant in retaining married women teachers as witnessed by a 12 percent decline of married teachers in their schools. Thus hard work and experience were necessary but not sufficient causes for retention. The sufficient cause was the lowest rung on the salary schedule for novices.[9]

Will Durant, the historian, argued before the National Education Association convention in 1936 that "I would not permit unmarried women teacher in the schools. Teachers should be complete human beings and know the gamut of life." On the other hand, Leon C. Staples, superintendent of schools in Stamford, Connecticut, stated that "married teachers as a rule are at the center of every educational disturbance in every large school system. Replacing married women with men will be a blessing to the youth of the land. These men are available . . . elimination of married women will make the place." Still another view was expressed by an English educator, H. Gordon, who sought to protect English boys from "the infantilism of the American male," which he attributed to women teachers, married or not. To Gordon, beyond the early grades, men teachers should prevail since most boys were not "little dears" but "little devils" who preferred male teachers.[10]

Surprisingly, a number of Americans agreed with Gordon. Geneva V. Walcott, for example, noted that "it has always been a mystery to me why the system of employing female teachers for boys has been the general procedure in public schools." After an interview with the ghost of Horace Mann, the mystery would have dissipated. Responding to this dispute, the *New York Times* suggested that "if a community, for reasons of broad social policy, wants to keep men in the school, the way to do it is by *raising salaries*." It was good economic advice but poor timing. Competitive salaries were not forthcoming, nor more men.[11]

On the other hand, Professor J.R. McGaughy of Teachers College declared that across-the-board increases in salaries would not attract more men into teaching. Basing his conclusions on a survey, he contended that equal pay would attract inferior men into teaching and/or result in the overpaying of women. McGaughy added that salary increases would have to be justified on grounds other than "special privileges for their profession." Echoing Mann and Cubberley but in a deprecatory tone, he snorted that the "sentimental hysteria about the noble, self-sacrificing service which they render and the supposed fact that those in their profession are the chosen of God, somewhat as ministers are, should have no place in an earnest consideration of salaries which should be paid to members of a respectable . . . profession."[12]

Readers of the *Times* were quick to take exception to McGaughy's implicit salary differentials for men and women as contrary to the spirit of the times. Dismissing McGaughy's suggestions and conclusions, Isabel A. Ennis wrote that "we fought every inch of the way for years and in 1920 [Governor] Alfred E. Smith signed the first equal pay bill in this [New York] State." Professor John K. Norton, a colleague of McGaughy's at Teachers College, denounced his proposals as reactionary that would "wreck teaching service and set it back 100 years." Norton added that the "whole trend of thinking in recent years has been to take account of human rights as well as the operation of economic law in determining wages and salaries."[13]

In chapter 4 we met Dr. Emil Altman, chief medical officer of the New York City schools, with his little list. Having raised one fictitious list, Dr. Altman moved on to list-building of another kind. Unequivocally, Dr. Altman stated that his school system had too many married women teachers. In a study he found that of the 37,000 teachers in the corps, 30,000 were women and of the latter figure, half were married. As in so many other ways, New York City was atypical in having so many married women teachers employed. To Dr. Altman, married women hindered classroom efficiency, were absent more often than not, and did not display the same enthusiasm as, single women. He based his assertions on the office records of 50,000 teachers over a 14-year-period.[14]

Thus Dr. Altman's findings were diametrically opposed to Professor Peter's 1934 findings. When professors or doctors disagree, whom shall we follow? Dr. Altman added that a married woman teacher with a sick child or an ill husband at home became distraught in the classroom; while a natural reaction, he considered this an unfair situation for the students. "The point is," Altman went on, "these teachers can not give complete service to their own children or those in school. . . . Teaching is a big job and so is motherhood. I do not feel that one woman can carry both successfully."[15]

No doubt Horace Mann would have agreed to this necessary division of labor between mothering and teaching, with the latter filled by spinsters. Speaking of the role of woman in society, Mann intoned that "it is her glorious prerogative to lift our world from its degradation, to raise the soul of man. . . . I have no firmer belief than that a wise womanhood could take the race in its arms, as a mother takes her babes, and shield it from harm, and nurse it into immortal strength and beauty." To do so required heroic strength and undivided loyalties.[16]

Reaction to Dr. Altman's comments were immediate. James Marshall, a New York City school board member, took exception that "if there is anything that is debatable, it is whether we should have unmarried teachers, [but] the subject of employment of married teachers is no longer debatable." Similarly, Mrs. Jacob Schecter, of the United Parents Association held that married women were more, not less, sympathetic in dealing with children. Still another voice, Dr. Jacob Greenberg, an administrator within the schools, while admitting that there was no evidence to indicate that married teachers were inferior to single teachers, observed that pregnant teachers by leaving during the school year did disrupt student learning. But he did not elaborate whether this disruption was minor and how it differed from a prolonged illness of any teacher. Nor throughout this debate did anyone raise the corollary issue of unmarried versus married male teachers.[17]

Whatever the nature of the debate on this topic, the reality in New York City and elsewhere was clear. In the name of economy and efficiency, women were dismissed on the basis of age, marriage, health, weight or by some infraction of a bureaucratic rule. As an illustration, the New York Supreme Court upheld the authority of the New York City Board of Education in refusing a teacher's right to withdraw her resignation. Why? The school board, and the court concurred, had found that Mrs. D.L. Shapiro had *concealed* her marriage status. Apparently, Mrs. Shapiro could not "lift our world from its degradation" if she practiced little white lies.[18]

Similarly, Superintendent Campbell explained the dismissal of Mrs. Mary C. Williams, a black teacher, on the ground that she had falsified her personnel records by concealing the birth of her child in violation of maternity leave by-laws of the school board.[19]

Still another example of bureaucratic misstep involved the denial of a permanent teaching license to Rose Freistater because she was overweight. Cited for being overweight in 1931, Freistater had reduced her weight from 180 to 154 pounds. Despite this accomplishment, an attorney for the Board of Education averred that her normal weight should have been 122 pounds and thus he considered her a "sub-standard risk." While Freistater continued to work on a substitute's license from 1931 onward, she sought the advice of counsel and finally appealed to State Commissioner of Education Frank P. Graves. Taking a legalistic stand, Dr. Graves upheld the school board by implying an administrative statute of limitations had run its course. After noting that four years had elapsed between her rejection and her appeal, he wrote that "it may be that the *nature of the test* applied was *too severe or unreasonable*. But she did not, at the time of rejection, take any steps" to challenge the administrative decision. Nor was Dr. Graves sympathetic to Freistater's "ignorance of her right to appeal."[20]

And so the roll call of bureaucratic dictation continued. If Rose Freistater's denial of a permanent post appears debatable, the dismissal of Mrs. M.S. Cunningham on grounds of overweight would appear less so. Weighing in at 275 pounds, Mrs. Cunningham, 51, had taught from 1906 to 1940 in the New York City school system. In her 34 years of service, she had been absent 1,556 days and late to her school post 724 times. She walked with a cane and needed assistance in putting her coat on. During a special fire drill at PS 192 to test her mobility, she limped down the stairs while her students were a block away. Observing the test, Mrs. Johanna M. Lindlof, a school board member and former teacher, declared that Mrs. Cunningham was a "fire hazard" and ordered her case reopened. Left unanswered was how her absence and tardy record had been ignored over the years by principals and the bureaucracy.[21]

Speaking on behalf of teachers, Professor Roma Gans of Teachers College scathingly ridiculed the attempt to evaluate teachers on the basis of age, weight, sex, and loyalty. "Where are the facts to support the contention of superintendents," she demanded "that what the public wants in a teacher is that she be good-looking, unmarried if a woman, not too-fat nor too-thin, charming in manner, with powerful friends who have influence or pull and no ideas of her own?" Her lament was accurate unless she was being facetious in teachers having "pull."[22]

Nor was the situation much different in Great Britain, the mother of democracy, when in 1933 numerous teacher organizations protested the dismissal of married women teachers. Two years later, and after a dozen years of struggle, married women won the right to be employed as teachers and doctors in London by a vote of 76 to 37 in the county council. The *New York Times* editorially took note of the event and commented that "the action of the London county authorities is all the more significant because the trend of the times under the spur of unemployment, is against women."[23]

Across the Atlantic in New Jersey, the Wildwood school board announced in October 1933 that women teachers who married during the school year would be asked to resign. In addition, a Wildwood school board resolution demanded that all teachers reside in the community as a condition of employment. Three years later the New Jersey Supreme Court reversed the dismissal of two married women teachers by the Wildwood school board, holding that "the fact that a female public school teacher under tenure marries does not constitute a legally sufficient reason" for dismissal. Two years later, the same court ordered the reinstatement of two other married women teachers dismissed by the same Wildwood school board. The court also commented that the teachers had been dismissed not for economy reasons but to make room for unmarried teachers. But as we have noted, novice teachers began at the lowest rung of the salary schedule and thus the removal of senior teachers was in fact an economy measure.[24]

Elsewhere in New Jersey, the Elizabeth school board was upheld by the state Court of Errors and Appeals after six years of litigation. The court affirmed that the school board had not violated state statutes permitting salary discrimination based on gender. Yet the court while noting the 1925 statute prohibiting sex discrimination asserted that the law applied not to prior but to "new" salary schedules. Finally, the New Jersey Federation of Business and Professional Women's Club went on record as opposing the dismissal of married women teachers.[25]

True to the tradition of Horace Mann, 72 Massachusetts municipalities including Boston, Worcester, Quincy, and others banned married women from the portals of the classroom. In 1935 in Lynn, Massachusetts, the school board by a vote of five male to two female votes decreed that Rita Coates could not marry and continue as a teacher. In response, Miss Coates commented that the decision "definitely condemns me to the life of the spinster. I have no choice now except to remain single the rest of my life unless I wish to desert my father and mother, who are absolutely dependent upon me for their support." South in Connecticut, four married teachers in 1935 were not rehired by the Windsor Locks school board. One woman had 21 years of teaching experience. Other women were more fortunate. In 1937, the Connecticut Supreme Court ordered 17 married women dismissed by the Bridgeport public schools reinstated. The four had been dismissed four years earlier "as an economy measure."[26]

In the smaller communities of New York State the picture was mixed. Croton adopted a policy in 1935 of not hiring married women and chose not to rehire three married teachers. In Ossining, the location of Sing Sing, the state prison, the school board in the winter of 1936 modified the marriage ban and then lifted the ban completely on hiring women teachers. In the spring of 1937, however, the Auburn school board adopted the proviso for its teacher's contracts that any women who married would be subject to dismissal. On the other hand, the Port Chester school board lifted its marriage ban on the expedient ground that a number of women had concealed their marriages. In Elmira, Mrs. A. Kabatt sought judicial relief from her school board's mandatory two-year leave following her pregnancy. Mrs. Kabatt asserted that "New York City alone keeps out 1,100 of its 3,000 teachers annually by removing them arbitrarily for two years of maternity leave and replacing them with cheaper substitutes." In short, Elmira and New York City both used the mandatory leave as a cost-cutting device. As late as 1939, the community of Hamburg notified eight women teachers with experience ranging from 5 to 20 years that they would not be rehired. The board asserted, as its prerogative, that no married women teacher would merit tenure. Finally, by 1940 a state law had passed granting tenure to teachers after three years of probation.[27]

In a survey of 35,000 New York City and of 48,000 upstate New York teachers, Dr. Arvid J. Burke, research director of the New York State Teachers Association, revealed in December of 1939 that approximately 9 percent of the teachers in his study earned salaries below what the state department of labor considered a minimal salary of $1,059 for a single woman living with a family or $1,160 living alone. Commenting on Dr. Burke's findings, the *Times* was gratified "to note in a survey of classroom salaries . . . proper attention was paid to differentials." While noting that the state average salary was $2,200, that the average rural salary was $1,650, and that the average New York City salary was $3,300, the editors concluded that Dr. Burke's finding of the 9 percent was, as a result, less harsh than it seemed. The *Times* was correct in not considering all teachers as homogeneous. If rural teachers were high school graduates, then their salaries would be lower.[28]

And if women chose to moonlight? Wayne County took such a dim view of Mrs. Evelyn Horosko working after school hours in her husband's beer parlor that she was summarily dismissed for conduct unbecoming a teacher. However, a Pennsylvania State Superior Court judge ruled that a barmaid "may not be conduct becoming a school teacher" but under the law it was insufficient cause for dismissal. Nor, the court added, was an occasional glass of beer a sign of intemperance. He ordered Mrs. Horosko reinstated.[29]

Elsewhere Professor Raymond Fisher of Oberlin College found as much sex discrimination in Texas as elsewhere. But he went further than a mere recitation of woes and struck at the Achilles heel of teaching—the petticoat legacy of Horace Mann. Fisher insisted in 1938 that "teaching is not at present a profession for women; it is a job." Sharply he noted that "'trousseau teachers' cannot reasonably be expected to concern themselves with long-range improvements or even with any very thorough preparation for the immediate job. . . . Their jobs are secured not by improving conditions but by remaining spinsters." Continuing his trenchant observations, Fisher stated, "The typical classroom teacher in this country neither enjoys the satisfaction of a nun nor the privileges of a human being. She is saved only by the consciousness that her humiliation is as temporary as her job." Pointedly he concluded that if educators "really want to improve public education . . . they will insist on the emancipation of the classroom teacher." If these comments were close to the mark, then how far away were the editors of the *Social Frontier* when they called upon the teachers of the land to assist in the birth of a new social order. Ironically, Fisher's article appeared in the *Social Frontier*.[30]

But where were the educational equivalents of Lincoln's proclamation? In the absence of such good news, the teachers could fall back on the National Education Association or more unlikely gamble with the American Federation of Teachers. Eschewing both organizations, the teachers of America could choose by default to sit out the Depression. Or attend the annual show of the NEA. Forsaking mundane success, the NEA provided a temple and high priests replete with ritual and the balm of "professionalism." Presided over by the elders of education—university and college presidents, professors of education, and superintendents—the teachers took "part in the applause." In chapter 3 we saw how the NEA had met the emergency in education by dutifully recounting the plunge in school budgets during the Depression. More often than not the annual roll call of speakers at the convention and countless studies ratified the status of the teacher as a "hired hand." Despite Dean Russell's strictures on materialistic wanderlust among teachers, the NEA offered a substitute for worldly success, a psychological good—the *ceremony of professionalism*.

Despite their "hired hands" status, many teachers since Mann had become true believers in the efficacy of this ceremony of professionalism. Professor J.M. Stephens has reminded us that "lavish verbal support is often the rule for activities that have chiefly remote survival value." Thus the history of teaching reveals that the ceremony of professionalism has been *inversely* related to pecuniary and true professional standards.[31]

But one historian would have no truck with this balm of ceremony. At the close of the Depression the foremost scholar on the sorry state of teaching in America, Howard K. Beale, could conclude his study noting that "comparisons of detail make a teacher look much freer in 1939 than in 1900. . . . The significant fact is that the teacher is still subjected to all sorts of regulations and prohibitions that are not applied to members of the community in other callings." Unfortunately, "the teacher is still the 'hired man' of the community that feels privileged to dictate what he shall and shall not do whenever his activity involves a question on which it cares what anybody does."[32]

While the Depression waned across the land by 1939, retrenchment of school budgets remained the order of the day. As noted in chapter 4, the battle in New York City to replace higher paid teachers with novices persisted. Two groups of teachers were recommended for early retirement. Of 15 teachers in one group who were ordered to report to Dr. Altman's office for a medical examination, only Miss Mary Byrne, a veteran of 33 years in the classroom, refused to do so. She surmised that the medical examination was but a prelude to involuntary retirement. For her refusal she was suspended in October 1939. Tried in a departmental hearing a month later, she was summarily dismissed. Miss Byrne immediately appealed to State Commissioner of Education Frank Graves. Four months later, Dr. Graves ordered Miss Byrne reinstated with back pay, holding that teachers could be compelled to appear only before the Teacher Retirement Board, but not before the school system's medical staff. Without delay, the Board of Education appealed the reinstatement. Rare as this appeal was, the *New York Times* reported that the board felt that its prerogatives to hire and fire had been diminished. In addition, four civic and professional organizations filed with the court *amicus curiae* briefs in support of the board's decision. A year after Miss Byrne's dismissal, Judge Pierce H. Russell of the New York State Supreme Court sustained the state commissioner's decision.[33]

Victories for teachers, however, were few and far between. Early in 1939, in New York City a Teachers Union spokesman objected to the existence of dual lists of men and women teachers by the central office. Defending the lists, James Marshall, president of the Board of Education, insisted that the state Court of Appeals had upheld the procedure, but he agreed to take the issue under advisement for further study.[34]

Discrimination against teachers, especially women teachers, by whatever measure was one issue, but the attempt to limit family incomes was another matter. Mayor La Guardia ordered the Board of Education to survey city teachers as to their sources of income and to determine if both husband and wife were in public employment. Immediately, a joint committee of teachers' organizations opposed the call for the survey. In the committee's view, the survey was but a prelude to possible state legislation nullifying the tenure of married women teachers whose spouses were also on the public payroll. Filling out her survey under protest, Netty L. Grief appealed to the state commissioner. But Dr. Ernest E. Cole, acting commissioner of education, upheld the school board's right to seek information as to a teacher's martial status and sources of family income from public employment. In this atmosphere, James J. Lyon, a county official of the city, proposed that married women teachers voluntarily resign to make room for single women.[35]

Reviewing the decade, Benjamin Fine, the *New York Times* education writer, noted that only 2 states protected women teachers while 18 states had pending bills to bar married women. Across the land one out of four women teachers were wed, officially. How many concealed their marriages is unknown. Of nearly 1,500 cities surveyed, Professor Dennis H. Cooke discovered in 1939 that only 23.4 percent had hired married women teachers as new teachers. Cooke found Married Teachers Not Wanted signs more and more evident.[36]

Married Teachers Not Wanted signs vanished during World War II when millions of men and women entered the armed forces. The resulting wartime labor shortages on the home front made women, married or not, worth their weight in the classroom or as "Rosie the Riveter" in war plants. It is an extraordinary social trajectory from Mann's noble teacher clad "in garments of virtue. . . . of pure tastes, of good manners, [and] of exemplary morals." to Rosie clad in overalls and bandanna on her head. For women in wartime it was opportunity and justice of sorts, although by happenstance rather than by design.

8 THE WPA IN THE SCHOOLS

If fingerprinting is done at school age, we could follow the child all through life and by the time the children [sic] were adults we would have complete records of all mental defectives, perverts and psychopathic cases.
—*John J. O'Connell, Deputy Chief Inspector of the New York Police Department, 1937*[1]

Turning from the high drama of the Depression, President Roosevelt in an address before the annual convention of the NEA spoke in 1938 of the need not to be bound by the narrow keeping of financial books. There was a need, he instructed, for future as well as immediate balancing of the books. Secondly, FDR asserted that the two most important elements of a democratic society were the wise husbanding of natural and human resources. Using language that anticipated later economists' concerns with the effects of schooling on economic growth, Roosevelt noted that "man's present-day control of the affairs of nature is the very direct result of *investment in education.*" Thus in FDR's view, prudent use of both natural and human resources would redound to the nation's benefit. This chapter reviews the contrast between political rhetoric on aid to education and federal programs that rendered direct aid to schools, notably the Works Progress Administration.[2]

In his address, FDR pointed out the wide variation of income per capita among the states. Just as Eunice Barnard had done five years earlier, the president observed, "We all know that the best schools are, in most cases, located in those communities which can afford to spend the most money" on teachers' salaries, buildings and equipment. Whereas the communities with the lowest taxable rates had the least of these educational inputs." Since federal dollars like all other dollars were in short supply, FDR proposed that assistance be given to the poorer communities in order to lift "the level at the bottom" rather than giving aid to "the top."[3]

Given the president's support, would general federal aid to education be forthcoming? The question was pertinent since the administration the preceding year had decided to reduce federal expenditures, thereby ushering in the economic recession of 1937. To a number of historians, this decision brought the domestic side of the New Deal to a close. With federal expenditures reduced, unemployment had unfortunately increased, thereby aborting the administration's goal of restoring the economy to 1929 levels. As to the fate of the particular Harrison educational bill in Congress, Turner Catledge of the *New York Times* wrote that the budget decisions of the New Deal "implied that the President had set his face against certain extraordinary projects, such as federal aid to education" and other domestic programs. Accordingly, the bill was sidetracked while the president continued to espouse the cause of education. Political rhetoric and reality diverged.[4]

But if explicit general federal aid to education lay dormant, actual federal expenditures were numerous and substantial, even if often under the guise of "emergency" programs. Various alphabet agencies such as the CCC (Civilian Conservation Corps), NYA (National Youth Administration), WPA (Works Progress Administration) and PWA (Public Works Administration) either had educational components, or worked in conjunction with public schools. As such, necessity often overruled the debate over the "principle" of federal aid. Consider, for example, the construction of schools. Alice Barrows, of the U.S. Office of Education, pointed out that "it is not generally understood that the public schools have never caught up with the serious lag in construction [since the First] World War when thousands of children were on part-time or double sessions." As we mentioned above, New York City and Seattle's experiences testified to this recurrent lag in matching students and seats. "Public Works Administration has been a life saver," Barrows believed, "for the schools. In four years from 1934 to 1938, the PWA has made grants and loans for school buildings amounting to $452,444,344."[5]

But given the New Deal's budget decisions in 1937, a cutoff date of January 1939 had been established for further PWA funds for school projects. This meant Barrows added "no more Federal money . . . for school building construction." With modest prescience, Barrows asked that with a new war looming, would there again be "an almost complete stoppage of school construction?" Altogether federal funds for school construction between 1934 and 1939 amounted to $1.7 billion with a matching state and local component of approximately $300 million. For these expenditures by 1939, the public received 59,614 classrooms for schools and colleges. In addition, 102 public libraries had been built.[6]

Nevertheless, many school districts out of principle, or of inability to raise matching funds, refused the carrot of federal funds. In White Plains, a suburb of New York City, a $585,000 PWA grant to build two schools was turned down by the city council and the board of education since the grant entailed raising locally $715,000 which was considered a new "burden to the taxpayers." But no qualms existed during Mayor La Guardia's reign at city hall in New York City. From the outset in 1933, La Guardia had sought an initial $14.9 million grant. By 1937, 18 out of 25 newly built schools in the city were funded by the PWA. Echoing Barrows, a PWA official in New York State noted, "This PWA school and college program in New York City has come at a time when the city was far behind normal construction schedules." As Diane Ravitch has reminded us, this scarcity of adequate classrooms from the immigration waves of the 1890s onward had been an endemic situation in the city's schools.[7]

But it was the Works Progress Administration (WPA) that provided badly needed *operating* funds to the schools. While the WPA of all the alphabet agencies spawned by the New Deal suffered from the notoriety as a "boondoggle" enterprise of leaf raking, it created much of social value. From the outset, under Harry Hopkins' direction, the WPA's primary task had been to put men back to work. In the seven years of its existence from 1935 to 1942, when it was liquidated, WPA had spent about $10.5 billion. In 1938 it provided 3.8 million jobs. But given Roosevelt's decision in 1937 to retrench and cut jobs, a WPA Teachers Union, Local 453, staged protests, sit-ins, and strikes over the layoffs of 3,200 people and cuts in salaries of 16,000 other WPA job holders. Despite the protests, the cuts remained.[8]

In New York City, Superintendent Campbell announced that any WPA personnel in the school system found guilty of disturbances and demonstrations over the imposed layoffs would face disciplinary action by the schools. Campbell added that WPA teachers sentenced by the courts would be "undoubtedly fired." In New York City alone approximately 15 percent of WPA jobs had been abolished. Responding to a national strike by WPA workers two years later, the President retorted that "you cannot strike against the government." Nevertheless, WPA protests and walkouts continued over layoffs and cuts in pay.[9]

Aside from job creation and pump-priming of the economy, what impact did the WPA have on the schools? Reviewing the accomplishments in 1938, Aubrey Williams, deputy administrator of the agency, observed that the WPA had initiated new educational programs such as adult education and nursery schools. He added that under the rubric of "emergency education" that had begun under the aegis of the Federal Emergency Relief Administration and continued by his agency, the WPA had provided jobs, reduced illiteracy, and stimulated state and private agencies to set up comparable programs for the young and the old. Still further, Williams noted that 100,000 teachers had been employed to instruct 4 million men and women as well as 150,000 preschool children. For 1938 alone, 30,000 teachers had been employed and 1.25 million adults enrolled in 48 states in various programs.[10]

Anticipating the Head Start program of the 1960s, Williams stated that "the WPA nursery school program, for example, has focused the attention of many educators on the importance of the preschool years for the later physical and social development of the child. Defects in health and nutrition . . . may be corrected with comparative ease . . . whereas their correction in later years may be costly, if not impossible." The WPA had operated 1,500 nursery programs across the country, some as demonstration projects. While Williams's statement is as apropos today as then, we may not be as sanguine that personal and social defects may be changed with "comparative ease" even among the young. Human beings may be less tractable then we once supposed.[11]

If the preschool program was a WPA minor gem, its adult education program was of equal luster. For the school year 1937–1938, approximately 1.5 million adults had been enrolled nationally in classes that ran the gamut from cooking and nutrition to *family* budgeting, personal hygiene, care of the sick, and other *family* welfare concerns. Note the attention paid to the family. All the more remarkable was the fact that despite reductions in the numbers of classes and teachers, enrollment continued to climb. In addition, as wave after wave of immigrants fleeing Nazi Europe arrived, they immediately sought out classes in English and citizenship training and, above all, flocked to classes to understand the new virulent disease called propaganda.[12]

At a Teachers Union conference in New York City, Rose A. Cohan, a specialist in parent education, remarked that the WPA was "blazing the trail" in nursery and parent education. What do we have here? The recognition that it was the WPA that outlined a de facto family policy during the Depression with the schools in a supporting role. Not from the resolutions of the NEA, not from the pages of the *Social Frontier*, and not from the elder statesmen of education. Whereas school officials more often than not saw WPA funds as simple extensions or supplements to their status quo efforts. Consider the adult illiteracy program. One WPA official observed in 1938 that 1 million adults since 1933 has been taught to read—a feat of no mean political, economic, and social significance. Yet for the schools, servicing new clienteles was seen as a sometime thing. Thus, students who failed their subjects during the regular school year could avail themselves of remedial classes during the summer under WPA auspices. Could not the schools have mounted such necessary classes? Also, there were innovative summer programs, for example, that opened 40 summer play schools in New York City, which in turn permitted 8- to-14-year-olds to study what they wished, and if they wished, field trips were available. To needy children, free lunches were supplied.[13]

Institutionally, the schools appeared unwilling or incapable of extending the mantle of legitimacy beyond their traditional programs for a select age group: the young. But the blindness system motif makes explicable this institutional inertia. Yet the schools on occasion could stumble into opportunities soon to be forgotten. As always, it would be New York City schools that would have the dubious distinction of trying at least *once* a new educational experiment, then filing it into the sink hole of forgetfulness. As a result of population shifts, a junior high school on the Lower East Side of Manhattan became surplus for disposition or conversion to other purposes. Fortunately under both WPA and Board of Education sponsorship, a free *adult day and night school* had opened that was believed to be the first of its kind in the nation. In this predominantly Jewish and Italian neighborhood, immigrant mothers were offered English and citizenship courses by day while their children received nursery care. Thus this school was a microcosm of what the public schools across the land might have become had they the presence of mind singly or in concert with the WPA to reach into the family and community. This golden ring of opportunity to shore up the family with its putative ally the schools was ignored.[14]

Worthy of mention was the WPA nutrition project in New York City that supplied 119,000 free hot lunches daily to needy children. Instead of teacher philanthropy, the WPA had institutionalized since 1935 the provision of this social necessity. Of course, this did not preclude true "voluntary" giving by teachers if they chose. For the most part, the WPA lunch consisted of a sandwich and a half, a hot dish, one piece of fruit or pudding, and milk.[15]

Earlier we have mentioned Leonard Covello's use of idle store fronts as adjuncts to his high school. The WPA also utilized this device but less as a social meeting place than truly to supplement the work of the schools. In Brooklyn one store front offered a 10-week course in retail training. In another direction, the WPA opened the first boarding school for girls in Chicago accommodating about 130 youngsters between the ages of 16 and 25 for a 3-month course in "community leadership." At this school the candidates were restricted to youngsters whose parents were either on relief or worked for the WPA.

However, at times WPA decisions aroused opposition. David Dubinsky and Sidney Hillman, labor leaders in the garment trades, objected to Colonel B.B. Somervell's order as New York WPA director merging the workers education program with the adult education program. The two labor leaders claimed that this merger represented an attack upon labor. Somervell denied the charge by pointing out that centralized facilities would permit greater supervision. Finally, other WPA programs included a youth employment service, advice to shopkeepers on how to avoid robberies, and courses on fingerprinting, to which we shall return below.[16]

As we have seen, while President Roosevelt chose the high ground of principle on the role of federal aid, the pragmatic side of the New Deal was pronounced through the expediency of "emergency expenditures." On the other hand, the NEA, as we have noted, was content to issue a mishmash of slogans on "Meeting the Emergency in Education." Yet there were those eager to bestow bouquets and brickbats over the "principle" of federal aid to education. As had the President, Professor John K. Norton of Teachers College cited the disparity of educational expenditures across the land. Given these sobering facts, Norton concluded that some state deficiencies "cannot be corrected by the States themselves." Accordingly in his view, federal aid would be the countervailing force to assure educational opportunity. Much ink and chalk had been dispensed since Mann had asserted that the school itself was "the balance wheel of the social machinery." Now the schools required a *federal balance wheel*. Finally the President's Advisory Committee on Education released its report in 1938 suggesting federal grants to the states totaling $70 million commencing in 1939 and gradually rising to $199 million by 1944. Once allotted, federal funds would be used for a number of purposes, including teacher preparation, school construction, aid for rural libraries, the strengthening of state departments of education, and, last, a provision for southern states to distribute funds between white and black schools.[17]

At the NEA's convention in 1938, the focus of attention centered on the aforesaid report. Opinions differed on the central and collateral issues. Long a prominent member of the educational establishment, Professor George Strayer opposed federal aid lest it lead to controls of the schools or to "a national system of education for the youth of the nation." F. Rederfer, the secretary of the Progressive Education Association, opposed aid lest nonpublic schools also become recipients. In his view, "It is not proper to have public funds expended for schools which cannot be publicly controlled."[18]

In similar fashion, the American Association of School Administrators went on record in 1939 opposed to federal controls or to the existing "emergency" educational agencies with the likelihood of "two public school systems." Yet while the school administrators backhandedly admitted that federal agencies had performed "indispensable service," they were in no mood for national controls. Even the New Jersey Federation of Women's Clubs entered the debate by also opposing federal aid as destructive of local control of schools.[19]

Two years earlier, the governors at their annual conference disagreed too over the virtues and vices of federal assistance to education. But southern governors were unanimous in rejecting the principle. As an illustration, Governor Olin D. Johnston of South Carolina echoed the prevailing sentiment: "In federal control there would necessarily be rigid uniformity which would not reckon with the admitted wide differences in local communities or geographical areas. The free school population of South Carolina is made up of 46 per cent Negroes. . . . South Carolina will always demand its right to segregate the whites and blacks, a policy deemed essential not only to our welfare, but to that of Negroes as well." Thus racial politics in education lingered for another 17 years until *Brown v. Topeka School Board* overturned Jim Crow. While the governors of the South played conventional politics in education, 40 southern leaders two years later called for vigorous federal assistance in agriculture, health, education, labor, the abolition of the poll tax, and assistance in altering transportation rates.[20]

From time to time within the confines of the NEA's annual conventions there arose a voice championing federal aid to education. In 1936, Charles Judd of the University of Chicago introduced a resolution favoring permanent federal aid instead of the hodgepodge of emergency measures. Two years later, Willard Givens, secretary of the NEA, believed that teachers would come to favor the principle, too. Even though Roosevelt had turned his back on domestic reforms at this juncture, educators seemed to be afflicted by time lags as to the direction of political winds of fashion. Nevertheless, Dr. Dawson, an NEA specialist on rural education, called, as had others, for federal aid to remedy the rustic backwaters of education. Another educator, Dr. Frank Graham, president of the University of North Carolina, called for federal aid to remedy inequality of educational opportunity.[21]

On the political front, while taking a leaf from the President's Advisory Committee on Education, Representative Emanuel Cellar of New York proposed in his bill that the WPA educational services be made permanent. Second, he proposed the establishment of a national advisory committee of five to assist the U.S. commissioner of education in administering the proposed act. Finally, he proposed funding levels of $70 million for 1939 and rising to $250 million by 1943. Apparently this was the sole attempt to bestow the mantle of legitimacy on the wide range of WPA programs in education and to use these programs as the vehicle for permanent federal aid. Although the Second World War intervened to make the issue moot, it is doubtful in the absence of strong support from the president that the resistance of the purists in education would have been overcome with their odd bedfellows, the southern governors. To many superintendents, school board officials, and others like George Strayer, the public schools were not a social agency but simply a school dispensing instruction. That the schools had strayed far from the three Rs since Horace Mann's time did not give pause to the purists.[22]

If the WPA educational programs came close to implicitly articulating a family and school social policy, there was one program that appeared to be a curiosity. In conjunction with the New York City schools, the WPA operated 10 educational centers in which free courses on the subject of fingerprinting were available to anyone over the age of 17. Was this simply a wish to permit citizens the pleasures of Sherlock Holmes? Hardly. After the kidnapping of the Lindbergh baby in 1932, J. Edgar Hoover, director of the Federal Bureau of Investigation (FBI), mounted a campaign to have all schoolchildren in the United States fingerprinted. Why? Ostensibly to aid law enforcement officials in identifying the victims of future kidnappers. With the president's blessing and with much fanfare, Vice President John N. Garner was fingerprinted at a capitol luncheon in 1939 by Hoover. As the photographers flashed away, the vice president quipped "I might just as well plead guilty in the future."[23]

A few school systems joined Hoover's bandwagon. Earlier the city of St. Cloud, Minnesota, at the suggestion of the FBI, claimed, in a project sponsored by the junior chamber of commerce, the distinction of having fingerprinted its entire public and parochial school population of 6,600 students. On the east coast in Ventnor, New Jersey, parents were asked by the chairman of the local school board to cooperate with the police in providing three sets of fingerprints of their children. Of the three sets of prints, one would be kept locally, another set sent to the state police, and the third one deposited with the FBI. In fact, all but 11 children out of 1,312 elementary school students were fingerprinted. The reasons given included the above mentioned one of aiding the police to locate a kidnapped victim and to aid in the recovery of children with amnesia.[24]

In New York City, Superintendent Campbell skirted the issue. Of a plan to fingerprint all pupils leaving elementary school, Campbell chose not to implement the proposal, less with due regard for civil liberties questions than on a wish to avoid public controversy. Nonetheless, he did suggest an extended campaign to inform the public of the virtues of fingerprinting children as an aid to civil identification. Three years later, Campbell vetoed a request to hire a fingerprint expert by the Board of Examiners and a further request to have all new teacher candidates fingerprinted. He objected this time on the basis of economy. Finally, statewide attempts in New Hampshire and New Jersey to fingerprint all children were defeated in both legislatures.[25]

As to public sentiments on the issue, a number of letters to the *Times* provided a clue. To a New York State senator, William L. Love, the case seemed straightforward if not compelling when he asked, "Why should any modern parent object to this routine measure of 'individual identification'? There is no disgrace attached to it, any more than there is to the routine medical inspection of children to which the previous generation of parents objected." Another correspondent, K. Kingston, chastised Love for his implicit surprise that parents might object to "wholesale fingerprinting in the schools." To Kingston, fingerprinting was an "obvious symbol of autocratic government" on the march toward "universal registration." Still another writer from Minneapolis, J.W. Hamilton, raised the issue of civil liberties in that fingerprinting gave the authorities a control that made students "hostages to their future good behavior." Illustrating Hamilton's concern with civil liberties more sharply, another correspondent from New Jersey stated that while he wished to check crime, he was unalterably opposed to fingerprinting of students. To this writer, such action by local government or school systems was but a prelude to universal ID cards that might lead the police to indiscriminate stop and inspection of the citizenry. In the time of Hitler, Mussolini, and Stalin, this was not an unreasonable fear. And had not Sinclair Lewis in 1935 raised the specter of an American dictatorship in his novel *It Can't Happen Here?*[26]

On the other hand, law enforcement officials from the FBI to the local police viewed fingerprinting as a normal extension of their repertoire of crime fighting tools. Testifying before a New York State legislative committee on the need for universal fingerprinting, Deputy Chief Inspector John J. O'Connell, director of the New York City Police Academy, and of its crime laboratory, began by dismissing critics brusquely. Like Senator Love, O'Connell saw fingerprinting as neither an invasion of privacy nor more onerous than a medical examination. Moreover, the benefits to the public in detecting criminals was substantial. Going further, O'Connell declared that "if fingerprinting is done at school age, we could follow the child all through life and by the time children [*sic*] were adults we would have complete records of all mental defectives, perverts and psychopathic cases." Such zealous statements as O'Connell's fanned the fears of those who sincerely believed that the police "following anyone through life" went beyond the particular issue of crime. It touched upon the right to be secure and free of surveillance.[27]

Finally we turn from the impact of the WPA on education to the presidential elections of 1936. In that year the playlet of the schools was raised if only peripherally and fleetingly to the drama of presidential politics. In the spring of the year, a whispering campaign had begun that the likely Republican presidential candidate, Governor Alf Landon of Kansas, had been calloused in balancing the state budget at the expense of the public schools. To this allegation by the president of the American Federation of Teachers, George Davis, the secretary of the Kansas Teachers Association, affiliated with the NEA, countered that contrary to rumor, Governor Landon had been a true friend of education. Landon had opposed a state tax limitation on the schools. To be sure, Landon had adopted as early as 1933 a "pay-as-you-go" state budget, which had necessitated reductions in rural schools.[28]

Reviewing the controversy for the *New York Times*, Eunice Barnard found that half of the state's elementary school teachers were employed in one-room schoolhouses. Rural teachers earned annually $453 while their city brethren earned $1,267. All in all, Kansas ranked forty-eighth on state aid to education. Clearly, the people of Kansas believed in locally funded and controlled schools.[29]

Above, Avis Carlson had written of the plight of Kansas rural teachers. But locally funded education relied on the roller coaster of property taxes. Carlson recalled, "It may be true, as I recently heard a tax expert insist, that we must wreck our educational system in order to get an intelligent tax system and a decent social order." Plaintively, she added, "It may be true. But it is a crying shame that the children have to foot the bill."[30]

Even a Republican voter took up the whispering campaign against Landon. He felt that Landon owed him an explanation of why he had closed so many schools in Kansas. Another writer felt that Kansas' low salaries were better than no pay. More pointedly, two professors, Sophonisba Breckenridge of the University of Chicago and Blanche C. Williams of Hunter College, questioned Landon's fitness for the highest office. They wondered if the "treatment of teachers in Kansas [is] an indication of your wish to return to the old" round robin of teachers boarding out among parents in the community. By September 1936, the Republican National Committee took note of this tempest in the pedagogical inkpot by denouncing the whispering campaign that Landon had closed 700 schools. The committee noted that while some schools had been closed, transportation had been provided in order to secure "better educational opportunities for their pupils." Further they noted that since education was a completely local matter in the state, the governor had had no hand in closing the schools. Lastly, Landon had been a true friend of education in defeating a tax limitation amendment to the state constitution detrimental to the schools.[31]

William Allen White's *Emporia Gazette* was more than a trifle miffed at the national ruckus over Kansas schools. In pride the *Gazette* noted two interesting facts, to wit, that the illiteracy rate for Kansas was 1.2 percent compared to New York's 3.7 percent and the national average of 4.3 percent. Furthermore, Kansas had twice as many boys and girls in high school in proportion to its population as New York. In short, whatever the squabble over closed schools, the quality of education in Kansas was a source of satisfaction. In the closing days of the presidential race, FDR visited Kansas City and declared that the last expenditure upon which the country should scrimp was that for the schools. On election day the voters retained the New Deal as Roosevelt swept 46 out of 48 states and thereby relegated Alf Landon, and the *Literary Digest*, which had predicted his election, to the dustbins of history.[32]

Roosevelt's sweep of the nation was aided in large measure by the support of John L. Lewis and the Congress of Industrial Organizations (CIO). Labor provided canvassers, money, and votes. After the election, sporadic sit-down strikes erupted by December 1936 in the auto industry. "The press and the courts denounced the sit-down strikers," Saul Alinsky has written, "for illegal seizure, confiscation of private property, and general insurrection." While various sit-down strikers advanced the rationale that they possessed a "property interest" in their jobs, John L. Lewis simplified the economics of the issue by asserting that "Americans have a right to work and a right to a job." But the skirmishes by the workers gave way in the new year as a massive sit-down strike took place at General Motors that eventually won union recognition for labor. The sit-down strike joined the arsenal of union weapons. In the White House, Roosevelt preoccupied with the backlash to his attempt to "pack" the U.S. Supreme Court with six additional judges, washed his hands of the labor/industrial conflict, with a dismissive plague on both of their houses. Lewis became embittered by this alleged turncoating of FDR. "Friends of Lewis," Alinsky has written, "reported that his face resembled a black thundercloud when informed of Roosevelt's remark."[33]

At the time, Arthur Krock of the *New York Times* held that if the U.S. Supreme Court upheld the Wagner National Labor Relations Act of 1935, the sit-down strike as a tactic would spread. Yet on the advice of "good" lawyers, Krock concluded that the court would not sustain the Wagner Act. In short order, the Court upheld the constitutionality of the labor act. Krock then wrote that "the effect of the momentous decision was electric." But the legality of the sit-down strike remained unclear. A young professor of law at Yale University, Abraham Fortas, observed before the annual Institute of Labor at Rutgers University that the numerous 5 to 4 court decisions led him to conclude that the law was "merely a guidepost, a set of ambiguous principles which can be adjusted to meet particular situations." In this context, he averred that the sit-down strike might be declared a legal labor tool. Two years later, the Court declared the tool illegal. Nevertheless, the device had served its purposes for the CIO. For Lewis, 1937 had been a year of harvest in union membership and of bitter estrangement from that "man in the White House."[34]

Receiving its benediction from the U.S. Supreme Court, after its green light under the Wagner Act, labor moved rapidly to organize the mass production industries of the land. Legitimacy coupled with the whirling dynamo of John L. Lewis proved an irresistible force. But Lewis' intelligence, driving ambition, and ruthlessness never permitted him to pause before unfinished business. "Not only are the unorganized often in a condition of virtual serfdom," Lewis observed, "but their very existence in a state of helplessness acts as a cancer draining the well-being of others." He added that the unorganized workers of the land "must be given a voice with which to bargain and an organization strong enough to protect themselves." For the Fannie Biggs of the country, Lewis had his eyes elsewhere.[35]

9 CUT SCHOOL BUDGETS FIRST

Never before, save perhaps during the [First] World War, has Middletown's business life been so centrally controlled as at present, and never before has this control system been in a mood to tolerate so little dissent.
—*Robert and Helen Lynd, 1937*[1]

By 1937 the New Deal–induced plunge in economic activity gripped the nation. How fared the schools? The economic arithmetic of the nation baffled the schools. While the Gross National Product had inched upward, governmental tax receipts continued to lag. Of course, the unemployed paid no income or property taxes. Also, home owners and business firms were often in default of their property taxes, thus affecting the collection of school taxes. Therefore for those school systems that chose out of principle to refuse federal funds, political virtue demanded that slashed budgets were squeezed still further.

In this chapter the reprise of retrenchment will be followed by parental concerns over curricula changes with a closing segment on the state of black education. Once again, as in the winter of 1933, mother nature added its dividend of misery to social and human dislocations. Between January and April 1937, schools were closed in Denver, Boston, and Salisbury, Connecticut, in the wake of an influenza outbreak. Farther south in Texas and New Mexico, schools closed because of nightlike dust storms. To this display of nature was added the thunder of labor strikes across the land including the aforementioned sit-down strikes. The year also marked the New Deal's transition from a preoccupation with domestic to foreign affairs.[2]

It was one thing to keep federal funds at bay on principle, but it was another matter to ignore poverty in the classroom. Surplus food from the federal government, for example, was ordered suspended by the Elgin, Illinois, school board. The president of the board stated that some members of the board "thought it wasn't proper to accept surplus food . . . as un-American and would give the children the idea that the government owed them a living." It was a viewpoint, as we saw above, shared by Superintendent O'Shea of New York City. So the month-long experiment of serving free school lunches to approximately 150 youngsters initiated by the PTA in Elgin came to an end. Placing this issue of poverty in perspective, Aubrey Williams, director of the National Youth Administration, had testified before a U.S. Senate labor subcommittee that approximately 3.5 million youths were unable to attend their high school classes because of poverty.[3]

In a survey of eight states in 1938, the American Federation of Teachers reported further retrenchment, not restoration of school budgets, as local revenues declined. In fact, a few rural schools in Illinois had already shut down, whereas Minneapolis and Cincinnati simply increased their winter "vacations" for teachers and taught. In Newark, New Jersey, teachers were asked to sign waivers reducing their salaries. Elsewhere, the Woburn, Massachusetts, schools closed in November and December 1938 for lack of funds. Pending state aid, the schools were reopened as teachers received their first pay checks in eight weeks while local firemen and policemen had received theirs only five weeks in arrears.[4]

As in other states, New Jersey had passed a 1933 statute permitting municipalities to slash salaries of school teachers on a sliding scale. Three years later, 95 teachers of West New York, New Jersey, appealed a lower court decision sustaining the pay reduction statute to the U.S. Supreme Court. In Patterson, New Jersey, as the mayor saw it in 1937, despite pressure and "vile un-American methods" employed by teachers, he announced that the 5 percent pay cut of September 1936 would be immediately restored. Pleading lack of funds, the controller of Jersey City urged the 450 teachers to sign waivers continuing their 10 percent pay cuts for city employees. It was one thing for teachers to suffer the same fate as other public employees, but at times they appeared to be less deserving of fair treatment. In Carteret, New Jersey, a teacher delegation representing 100 teachers who had been unpaid for six weeks sought to confer with the mayor. Teachers sought parity with other city employees who had been paid. Unpaid or slashed, annual salary increments had been suspended from 1930 to 1937 in Elizabeth, New Jersey. Resumed in 1938 by the city, they were again suspended the following year. As to drive home the impotence of teachers to defend their interests, the New Jersey Supreme Court upheld the state's right to divert $2 million from the Teachers Pension and Annuity Fund to general relief.[5]

In adjacent Pennsylvania, approximately 200 teachers went on strike in the spring of 1939 in the town of Coal Township over unpaid salaries of eight months in arrears. Short of state funds, school officials stated that there was little likelihood of paying teachers. In the peach state, Governor E.D. Rivers of Georgia informed the state Senate that he "would immediately borrow $2,181,000 to pay long overdue school salaries and avert a threatened closing of virtually all public" schools.[6]

To the north in Port Chester, New York, 200 teachers and 50 school employees accepted for the 1939–1940 school year a 3 percent pay cut. Nearby in White Plains, the school board in Westchester County voted to restore the full salaries of all teachers in its proposed 1938 budget. But the mayor of White Plains took exception insisting that teachers' salaries should be restored only when other city employees received this boon. Interestingly enough, this had been the first time since White Plains' incorporation in 1916 that a school board had been overruled by the mayor and city council.[7]

Two years later, the mayor of White Plains appointed a citizen's committee to survey the fiscal health of the city. The committee recommended that the salaries of 435 teachers and clerical workers be cut while urging that PWA funds be sought for school construction. For business groups the Depression was an entering wedge in reducing the scope of government. Seeking the adoption of a flat 25 percent reduction in New York State expenditures, the Westchester County Taxpayers Association, for example, had taken the lead in launching a statewide movement. A spokesman for the group, oblivious of the question begging in the association's goal, disingenuously declaimed, "We intend to be fact-finders and not fault-finders. We would employ research experts and approach state financial problems in a scientific manner." Cutting the cloth to fit the 25 percent cut was hardly a dispassionate search in the "scientific manner."[8]

Retrenchment in Ohio's schools in 1938 and 1939 confirmed a familiar scenario—but with an added fillip. Like Washington state, the state of Ohio utilized annual and biennial votes of the people to pass extra-millage rates which in essence bestowed *annual tests of legitimacy* for the schools. Neither the police nor fire departments nor other public services were subject to such a test. Thus Horace Mann's legacy of the schools as one of the wonders of the world remained unfulfilled. Wonder or not, the schools were kept on short fiscal leashes. After seven years of austerity budgets, the Dayton, Ohio, school board in the fall of 1938 voted to close the schools for six weeks. Similarly, Parma, a suburb of Cleveland, closed its schools early in November for an extended winter vacation. But the governor stood aloof insisting that school closures were local problems.[9]

Taking exception to the school closures in Ohio, the *New York Times* noted that "when something like 35,000 children are thrown out on the streets, it means preparing the way for a harvest of idleness and even crime that may cost the future more than it saves in interest on school loans." The *Times* added that the Dayton teachers had voted for the closures since they were "tired of having their pay held up." As another school levy election neared, Richard Withrow, a Dayton school board member, claimed that Dayton teachers would be willing to work without pay on assurance that back pay would be forthcoming. He asserted that "teachers *owe it to their community* to continue their services in this emergency." Once again, moral obligation and philanthropy was foisted upon the teachers.[10]

And so the "services" of the teachers were obtained by court order. On the first of November in 1938 a court injunction and contempt citations against Dayton teachers were dissolved pending the teachers' acceptance of a court order to work for three weeks of deferred pay and for *five weeks without pay*. The following day, the Dayton teachers voted 1,010 to 3 to keep the schools closed. After the vote, the teachers issued a statement that "six times in the past six years the citizens have had a chance to show concern over the school problem." For the seventh time the citizens of Dayton voted negatively. However, with the promise of state aid, the Dayton schools reopened three weeks later. Similarly, the same state of affairs prevailed in Toledo in the winter of 1939 as the schools closed for six weeks from Thanksgiving to the first of the new year. As in Dayton, the citizens of Toledo had rejected a school levy. If the state of Washington required super majorities of 60 percent to pass extra-millage levies, the state of Ohio required an affirmative 65 percent.[11]

If the lack of tax dollars proved the primary issue for the schools during the Depression, there arose from time to time concern by parents over what constituted proper schooling. The tenets, much less the practice, of "progressive education" came slowly to the public schools. Some 25 miles from Times Square in New York City, a minor imbroglio occurred in the Roslyn, Long Island, school district. A group of parents had circulated a petition demanding a return to the three Rs. They objected to the lack of student homework and questioned the utility of the many school "activities and projects." Particularly irksome to the parents was the making of nut bread in school. All together, 491 parents signed a petition. To counter the criticisms, the school superintendent replied that the nut bread lesson was a good way of teaching arithmetic. To defuse the situation, he invited the protesting parents to visit the schools.[12]

However, the parents received confirmation of their concerns a year later when a state education report was released assessing the school district. To a packed audience presided over by the school board, the report was read. While noting that the Roslyn children were eager to go to school, that truancy was minimal, and that children were working up to their intellectual capabilities, the report faulted the schools for their limited use of basal textbooks and, more tellingly, the absence of a systematic evaluation of student work. The report also noted the *absence of parent/school conferences.* But many parents were shocked by one key passage in the 57-page document. The report observed that "it is evident that on the whole the children of Roslyn are performing up to their intellectual ability, but it is also evident when comparing the median achievement . . . with the norm that they are considerably below the average of expectation." The report went on, "Obviously greater average achievement should not be reasonably expected."[13]

Why did the report draw this pessimistic conclusion? Perhaps a clue can be gleaned from the cover letter to the report by Dr. Frank Graves, the state commissioner of education. Graves spoke approvingly of the "progressive methods" utilized and their adaptation to the needs of the children. He thought this practice significant "in a community where so large a percentage of children come from homes with limited social and economic resources." Was Graves confirming, too, that progressive education had roots largely in private schools supported by middle and upper middle classes. Hence Graves' surprise that the children of working-class parents had been exposed to the new pedagogical ideas. But the protesting parents were not mollified over the report's observation that competition had been de-emphasized in the classrooms without the rewards of "marks, prizes, stars," or "comparison of child with child." To many of these parents this was not "progressive" but mis-education of their children.[14]

Was misspelling a proper concern of parents and educators? In culling New York statewide Regents examinations of 1937, examiners found that many students could not spell the president's name correctly, instead providing variations among others such as Rosevelt, Roosavelt, Rosevalt, Roosevalt, and Rosavalt.[15]

Similarly in Seattle, parents concerned with departures from basic education objected at a high school open house. One parent asked of school administrators, "Why not teach fundamentals and cut out the frills and fads." Another parent wondered if high school students enjoyed too much liberty.[16]

Criticism of the current practices of the schools came as well from professional educators. The St. Louis public schools commissioned a survey of its schools by Professor George Strayer and his associates. The report recommended in 1939 that high school seniors should assume a major responsibility for their schooling and the running of the school. Another recommendation was that literature be de-emphasized in favor of newspaper and magazine reading. Still further, Strayer and his colleagues urged that IQ tests be restricted since they failed to measure artistic and mechanical skills. Given the de-emphasis on the formal curriculum, the report called for an expansion of the extracurriculum and for the adoption of vocational guidance. Laudable as some of these planks were, the danger lay in moving the schools toward a present-mindedness with vocational education as the center of schooling.

If retrenchment remained in 1939 the order of the day for school and society as earlier in the decade, then for black students in particular it seemed a bottomless pit. Drawing upon a New York City Board of Education report, Franklin J. Keller at a conference on the economic status of the Negro noted that the "Negro problem" was the "white man's problem." Keller added that it was a problem to be solved by a cooperation between the races with sympathetic understanding and a "frank facing of the facts." As to an agenda of action, the Board of Education's report had recommended ten items of change, including black admission to vocational schools, an effort by school counsellors to secure a "more liberal attitude toward Negro workers," and that school attendance laws for black students between the ages of 15 and 17 be strictly enforced.[17]

If black education and opportunities in New York City left much to be desired, the situation elsewhere was grim by comparison. After completing a survey of educational conditions in the South, Mabel Carney of Teachers College, perhaps the leading authority on rural schools at the time, concluded that the only way to improve black education was through federal aid. For the year 1930, the disparities in per capita expenditures underlined the stark realities of inequality of educational opportunity. Carney found that whereas the national per capita average per child was approximately $87, the figure per white child in the South was $44 and for the black child in that region the figure was $12. To be sure, this disparity was due partly to the legacy of Jim Crow, partly to rural neglect, and partly to the South's reliance on primary economic activity such as agriculture.[18]

In 1936 Dr. Homer P. Rainey, director of the American Youth Commission, observed that black education was woefully neglected in at least seven states and that less than 10 percent of black youths of high school age were actually in school. For the most part, black and white leaders continued to view education despite the Depression as a stepping stone to social and economic betterment. In this context, Eugene N. Jones, executive secretary of the National Urban League, suggested that the "difficulties which face Negroes are directly related to those which the entire nation must meet." Jones therefore welcomed economic recovery as in the best interests of blacks if not all people. A healthy economy would provide jobs for all. In addition, Jones urged the establishment, as had others, of better vocational education and guidance in the schools for blacks and the adoption of a child labor amendment. The latter would remove children as competitors in the job market. Underlining Rainey's observations, the superintendent of schools in Washington, D.C., reported to the NEA convention in 1938 that 230 counties in 15 states did not have high school facilities for black students who numbered approximately 160,000. It was another reminder that the doctrine of *Plessy v. Ferguson* had meant neither separate nor equal but simply nonexistent facilities.[19]

At a dinner sponsored by Fisk University in New York City, James R. Angell, president of Yale University, declared that the nation, both the North and the South, had failed to provide for adequate black education. The *Times* applauded Angell's views and commended Fisk University for eschewing black education in favor of "an education of the highest type." Approvingly, the *Times* quoted this prophetic passage from Angell's address that "if history has taught us one thing more conclusively than any other, it is that one cannot permit any segment of the population to be snubbed, ill-treated and deprived of opportunity, without having the bill come back home to be paid a thousand fold, at the hands of the group which indulges in that kind of ungenerous treatment."[20]

With a population of 350,000, it was Harlem that served as a bellwether of black progress. Curiously, Mayor Fiorello La Guardia felt compelled to defend the "true" Harlem as opposed to the tourist trap that attracted white tourists to its night spots. La Guardia warned that "it is all staged for you as an exhibition. It is not the life of the normal New York Negro." Following the mayor's lead, the *Times* similarly distinguished between the "normal Harlem which represents striking economic and social changes in Negro life in the United States, changes registering notable progress on a wide front." The editorial recounted the progress in the growth of black actors. More significant was the increase in numbers of "lawyers, engineers, editors, authors, business men, cooperatives, [and] insurance companies," whereas the other Harlem catered to a "bored white public in search of new night-life thrills."[21]

Following a Harlem riot in the spring of 1935, Mayor La Guardia appointed a Commission on Conditions in Harlem. The commission elicited numerous black complaints of discrimination by the utilities, of the denial of professional openings in Harlem Hospital as well as in the public schools. If the *Times* had been self-congratulatory as to black progress, the residents of Harlem thought otherwise. In a city-wide survey of schools, the United Parents Association (UPA) had found, as noted above, overcrowding in general, but in the Harlem public schools the conditions were worse. The UPA found short sessions in the guise of double and triple sessions for students; "of classes meeting in stock rooms, corridors, lunch rooms, backstage and in the indoor yards." While federal funds had alleviated some critical shortages in the city, the UPA concluded that "steps taken so far will supply but a fraction of [total school] needs." To illustrate its contentions, the UPA cited PS 89 whose enrollment "is almost entirely Negro" with one wing built 40 and another wing built 46 years earlier. While the capacity of the school was 41 classrooms, 56 classes met daily in makeshift arrangements cited above.[22]

Assailing La Guardia for not expeditiously implementing his commission's report on Harlem's conditions, Charles J. Hendley, president of the Teachers Union, further charged that not one new school had been built during the preceding 10 years in Harlem. Taking the initiative, the Teachers Union proposed a seven-point program to improve the schools of Harlem. They recommended (1) a reduction in class size, (2) construction of new schools, (3) the extension of kindergarten activities, (4) the establishment of classes for overaged students, (5) an increase in the number of manual and physical training classes, (6) a program of free food and clothing to children of parents on relief, and (7) the implementation of the mayor's commission report. A few months later, Mrs. Gertrude E. Ayers became the first black woman appointed as principal in the city schools.[23]

A year after the riot of 1935, the mayor met again with his commission on Harlem and then summoned the press to announce his program. He stated that transit porters, who were largely black, would receive pay increases, that Harlem Hospital would obtain a new wing to ease overcrowding, that police procedures would be reviewed, and, last, that sites for two schools would be acquired in which each school would be "exceptionally large."[24]

Although PWA funds had been welcome by the New York City schools, normal maintenance had been neglected, a common occurrence. Both Superintendent Campbell and the Board of Education had on numerous occasions pleaded for additional funds from the La Guardia administration. One school board member noted that some of the schools were old, some dating back to the 1860s. Some building had structural failings. As to

Harlem High School, the fifth and sixth floors had been severely damaged in 1937 by heavy summer rains. Why had this transpired? Because the school had no roof. Earlier the roof had been condemned, removed, but not replaced, hence the rain and new damage to the school. Similarly, the high school's boiler tubes had been condemned, removed, and again not replaced, until after the winter cold had arrived. In the interim the school had received a coat of paint.[25]

On a related matter, the New York State Department of Education on an inquiry from a Kingston judge ruled that disciples of Father Divine, a black evangelist, could not use "heavenly" names for children of the sect. Earlier the judge had ruled that heavenly names threatened school discipline. "One can imagine what will happen," he wrote, "to discipline in a school where a teacher is required to address a boy as 'Great Baer' or a girl as 'Bright Beautiful.'" The children attended the Ulster County schools. On another issue, Governor Herbert Lehman signed into law in 1938 the Feld bill, which repealed provisions of the education law that had permitted school officials in New York to establish separate schools for black children.[26]

Yet there was another issue of importance that the future would have to grapple with. The question: should students be taught by someone of their own sex, race, or religion? At a New York City Board of Education meeting in 1938, a delegation of Harlem teachers and representatives of the Teachers Union protested the replacement of 25 black substitute licensed teachers by white permanently licensed teachers. It will be recalled that substitutes were long-term teachers who had either failed the permanent license examination or who had never had an opportunity to take one. As noted, since the examinations were given at irregular intervals, this practice constituted a cost-cutting device.[27]

A black teacher, Miss D.E. Watson, a substitute since 1920, spoke feelingly of her replacement and termed the school board's action "a regular Negro purge." (With the Moscow show trials on public display, the word "purge" entered the lexicon of the time.) Going further, Miss Watson asserted that "Harlem is the only place where the Negro substitute can teach. We understand the boys. . . . Those of us who have been there the longest should be given consideration." In turn, a black minister asked the board president to tell the "people of Harlem" why "these teachers were displaced." Side-stepping the question, the board president, James Marshall, referred the matter to Johanna Lindlof's Committee on Instruction in the hope of finding a way "out of the dilemma." Marshall felt perplexed since if the board did not act on this question, it would be accused of giving Harlem only substitute teachers. It was a disingenuous reply at best since in New York City, substitute teachers such as Miss Watson were not necessarily inferior ones.[28]

Elsewhere in the land there were numerous examples of social, institutional, and legal obstacles to equality of opportunity. The Maryland Court of Appeals, for example, refused to order the Baltimore County schools to admit a black girl to the Catonsville High School after the student, Margaret Williams, had failed the entrance examination. In court, her father contended that the examination was not required by law and was not given equally to both races. Brushing aside both contentions, the court disagreed by observing that the examination was of long standing and given to both blacks and whites. Differences in the examinations were, the court added, "of only a minor importance and would not justify issuance of the *writ of mandamus*." But if the law and the courts were slow to change, it remained for the alphabet federal agencies such as the NYA, CCC, PWA, and WPA that gave blacks some measure of fair play and opportunity. In conjunction with the Brooklyn Urban League, for example, the National Youth Administration established an experimental job-training unit to assist black girls to "discover their aptitudes for junior executive positions and for general employment in private jobs." As a result, it was the reach of federal programs that led blacks to abandon the party of Lincoln in 1936 and to vote Democratic ever since.[29]

Another harbinger of things to come occurred in 1939 when New York State Senator Jacob Schwartzwald, chairman of the Temporary Commission on the Condition of the Urban Colored Population, sharply criticized the Mt. Vernon superintendent of schools for a public comment. W.H. Holmes, the superintendent, had made an observation that the appointment of a black teacher in his school system would cause what amounted to white flight. For uttering these views, Senator Schwartzwald directed that the state commissioner of education be apprised of these statements. The following day the Mt. Vernon school board president supported the superintendent's ban on hiring black teachers except for classes in which blacks were a majority. He noted that Nathan Hale School with a student black population of 40 percent with a new school building was "staffed by as competent a group of teachers as any school in the city." He agreed with Superintendent Holmes that some white parents would leave the city if black teachers taught predominantly white classes. Furthermore, he welcomed a state investigation because he was certain that the report would end up "complimenting us on our treatment of the Negro situation in Mt. Vernon."[30]

On another aspect of racial discrimination, in perhaps the first test case of its kind to reach a federal court, Judge W. Calvin Chestnut in 1939 issued an injunction against a Maryland county school board for paying black teachers and administrators less than white ones. The suit in question had been brought by Walter Mills, a black principal, charging discrimination in that he received an annual salary of $1,050 compared to a white principal of $1,800. Ruling in Mills' favor, Judge Chestnut found that the evidence revealed "unlawful discrimination" in violation of the fourteenth Amendment's equal protection clause. A similar case was brought by Melvin O. Alston, a black teacher in Norfolk, Virginia, against the school board for pay discrimination. Although the federal district court rejected the suit, the Fourth Circuit Court of Appeals found in Alston's favor and reversed. The U.S. Supreme Court's refusal to review the case sustained the appellate level's decision.[31]

As had New York, the New Jersey legislature created a commission to study the economic, cultural, health and living conditions among the black population of the Garden State. The commission discovered the presence of discrimination in employment, housing, and education and noted that "the attempts of Negro families to train their children properly are hampered by unequal educational opportunities especially manifested in many of the *separate schools established for Negroes* in Southern counties of the State." Again, this was New Jersey in 1939—not Mississippi. Needless to say, the report added that "attempts of Negro family heads to provide security for their families in event of death, illness or accident" were compounded by discriminatory practices by insurance companies. Not surprisingly, as in New York City, blacks disproportionately were on the relief rolls.[32]

To this bleak profile of black discrimination, there was an exception worth noting. A New York City Welfare Council committee sought to discover why 39 Negro families were *not* on relief in communities where the proportion of black relief cases was four times the city average. The investigating committee discovered that the families in question had avoided relief through a combination of steady work, maintaining good health, having fewer children, careful budgeting, and taking in boarders, thereby augmenting family income. Above all, the committee report singled out the "will to manage" among the families, half of whom were childless. As to occupations, unskilled and domestic work predominated. But instead of applauding the "will to manage" among the 39 families, the report concluded diffidently by questioning "how socially desirable some of these factors are in solving community problems is a question to be taken under serious advisement."[33]

Finally at a national conference on the problems of black youth in 1939, Eleanor Roosevelt addressed the gathering in the nation's capital by calling for the passage of an anti-lynching bill through Congress "as soon as possible."[34]

In the international climate of propaganda, a Berlin newspaper chided the First Lady for speaking out on black rights but scolded her for remaining silent on the blockade of Germany which "would have resulted in the deaths of many German women and children—[but] not a word of condemnation was heard from Mrs. Roosevelt."[35]

Among the many twists and turns on the road to the "Final Solution," the German Nationalist Socialist Teachers League demanded in 1935 the exclusion of Jewish children from the German public schools on the ground that no Jew was capable of comprehending the Third Reich and its purposes. A month later, Reich Minister for Culture Bernhard Rust decreed the establishment of separate schools for Jews. Thereafter subsidizing private schools for Jews was to be abandoned in favor of compulsory albeit separate Jewish public schools—for a while. In due course, all Jews in German clutches came to comprehend only too well the "purposes" of the Third Reich.[36]

10 WORLD'S FAIR OF 1939

The city's children are still the city's chief concern, whatever we may say about the revolution in family life and in general mores. The child is still the nucleus of the family *and the main item in the municipal budget.*
—*Editorial,* New York Times, *1939*[1]

The year 1939 was a year of promises. Domestically the year opened with the hope that the Depression had entered its waning phase. For the schools this waning might prove a boon. Nationally, unemployment had declined, and home construction for the first quarter of the year had shown the largest gain in seven years. On April 30, New York City played host to a World's Fair bright with promise of world peace and a window on the "world of tomorrow." As to another promise, the first blinkings of a workable television had led NBC officials to predict that the new instrument would be a "powerful medium for teaching." The officials asserted confidently that television would be an ideal means for musical demonstrations as well as for such fields as bridge, golf, fencing, dancing, tennis, and foreign languages as "naturals." Naively, an NBC official added that "students can see and hear by television and that is all that is needed in wholesale education." This piece of foolishness soon joined others issued upon the birth of the telephone, typewriter, the airplane, and the radio.[2]

Belying the promise of world peace, in mid-August Germany and the USSR signed a 10-year nonaggression pact to the chagrin of countless fellow travelers from Union Square in New York City to Union Square in San Francisco. For numerous Americans who had joined the Communist Party or had remained on its fringes, the pact with the archenemy of communism created apoplexy. In turn, some left the party quietly; others later would tell of *"The God that had Failed."* Within weeks of the pact, the two nations invaded and then divided the spoils of Poland. On the first of September 1939 as the lights again dimmed in Europe, another world war commenced. While war rumbled in Europe, a year later the United States began a peacetime draft and a Lend Lease program to aid Great Britain. For a while longer the United States remained at "peace." While it lasted, Americans spent the last year of the decade trekking to the World's Fair, to the national pastime, and to the movies to see *Gone With the Wind*.[3]

While bombs fell on Warsaw, political rhetoric in New York City fell as easily. What follows below is the anatomy of a school war in the summer and fall of 1939 in New York City. Finally, a review of a state conference on the family brings the chapter and the narrative to a close.

To refugees fleeing the terror of Nazi Europe, America beckoned as the land of promise. But these newcomers along with home-grown radicals raised questions in the minds of some as to the limits of dissent. Never mind that refugees for the most part, as we have seen, were anxious to work, to learn the language, and to become good citizens, hardly the hallmarks of revolutionaries. But as the Lynds had noted of Middletown, in times of stress beliefs tended to stiffen.

In New York City, for example, at a packed meeting of the Board of Education to consider a board member's resolution to bar controversial speakers and groups from using school property, the responses were quick. Groups opposed to Walter Carlin's resolution were relentlessly booed and heckled by various Catholic groups (St. John's University Chapter of Catholic Action, Christian American Committee Against Communism, and Minute Man Confraternity).[4]

The following day, Johanna Lindlof, another school board member and colleague of Carlin, charged at a luncheon that intolerance and anti-Semitism were creeping into the school system. Further, she was miffed that some of the vocal demonstrators at the board meeting had been products of the public school system. To Lindlof, this denial of free speech revealed that "we evidently have not gone to work the right way in developing a constructive program of democracy." Like others, Mrs. Lindlof believed that the remedy for civic misbehavior lay in a proper pedagogical package of civics classes or perhaps in decorum of "How a Gentleman Practices Democracy."[5]

Decorum aside, the American Association of School Administrators also assailed the Carlin resolution as inimical to democratic life. Finally, a formal vote on Carlin's resolution resulted in a three to three tie-vote with one member absent because of illness. Hence the resolution failed. A few days later at a dinner honoring the retiring Walter Carlin from the school board, Miss Martha Byrne, registrar of New York County, called upon the city's teachers to cleanse their ranks of all disloyal members who did not subscribe to 100 percent Americanism. In part, Byrne's denunciations was a thinly veiled call to arms against the Teachers Union, which had long been under communist influence.[6]

Patriotism or propaganda aside, the principal issue for most Americans remained the retention of, or the lack of, a job. For government agencies, lackluster tax receipts continued. In the absence of a new social policy, the schools were simply one among many public institutions competing for scarce funds. As we have seen in Ohio and Washington, the schools were subjected to de facto annual tests of legitimacy along with pleas for funds. To be sure, the implicit rationale for unlimited access to the public treasury among schoolmen from Mann to Cubberley to Campbell rested on the self-serving assumption that schools were above politics and the corollary that children had first claim on our sympathy, if not on our purse. By repetition, these assertions became incantations to the true believers and to the cheer leaders of the schools such as the Progressive Education Association and in New York City the United Parents Association and the Public Education Association.[7]

As the year opened for the schools in the city, the auguries seemed if not hopeful, at least benign. For the 1939–1940 school year, for example, a Board of Education committee on finance adopted a school budget of $160 million, up $7.75 million from the preceding year. Of the total budget, $25 million had come from the WPA to cover, as noted above, a host of programs. As to the capital budget, $25 million had been earmarked, including PWA funds for school construction with an additional $5 million for sorely needed maintenance.[8]

Contributing to the sanguine view of the schools were the results of a reading test given to 46,000 fifth graders in the city's schools. The test scores indicated that the city average was two months *above* the national norm. Whereas, four years earlier in 1935, a similar survey had revealed that 22,000 youngsters had scored three months *below* the national norm. Why the turnaround? Dr. Stephen Bayne, an associate superintendent of the schools, gave due credit to the establishment of special remedial reading classes in the schools. More tellingly, Bayne admitted that techniques and procedures tested by the WPA reading program had been so successful as to be adopted by regular classroom teachers. Enjoying tenuous legitimacy within the schools, it was but another example that various WPA school programs and personnel on the periphery were oases of pedagogical innovation. Their story, as Sol Cohen has observed, as pedagogical pioneers is yet to be told.[9]

But the honeymoon of institutional pride was to be short-lived.

Launching a major attack on the city schools, the Citizens Budget Commission (CBC) charged that while elementary school pupil enrollments had declined, the number of teachers had not correspondingly fallen. Presenting a table of 13 school systems that had reduced the number of teachers, the CBC, which had been a perennial critic of the schools, called for sharp retrenchments in personnel. Responding to such criticism, the Board of Education stated that the existing number of teachers had been used to reduce overcrowded classrooms and to implement new programs. But this explanation did not mollify the CBC and other civic groups which had also called for economy in the operations of the school. The New York Realty Board, for example, urged an immediate 10 percent cut in salaries.[10]

In addition, the New York Taxpayers Federation called upon Governor Lehman to appoint a citizens committee to investigate the "excessive cost of education in this state as compared with other leading Eastern States." At this juncture, the Republican-controlled state legislature reduced the statewide allocation to education by $9.7 million with approximately $5 million of the sum earmarked for New York City schools. Accordingly, the counter blasts of propaganda commenced in the school war of 1939. Approving of this legislative cut, one writer asserted that "a swollen educational budget is in need of a sizable trimming in days like these." To implement such a view, he suggested graduated salary cuts and the pensioning of "those who have outlived their usefulness as instructors." Once again the stalking shadow of Dr. Emil Altman's little list surfaced.[11]

Rallying to the support of the schools, George Meany, president of the New York State Federation of Labor, pledged the support of over a million AFL members in seeking restoration of the state cuts. Furthermore, Meany accused the Taxpayers Federation of being indifferent to the plight of children denied an education. Despite the counter criticisms, the Taxpayers Federation urged the legislature to "stand firm." The civic group argued that, given the rise in government expenditures, the need for economy was imperative and that minor reductions would "place no great hardships on either the government or the legislators, if there is a sincere desire to reduce the cost of government."[12]

At the center of the political maelstrom was the ebullient, feisty Mayor Fiorello La Guardia. To his satisfaction, La Guardia "balanced" the city's 1939–1940 school budget by cutting 106 out of the 154 line items of the budget including a proposed $8 million increase for the schools over the preceding year. In short La Guardia proposed a new school budget that was $383,000 less than the previous one. To provide leadership, the mayor cut his own annual salary from $25,000 to $22,500. His predecessor had enjoyed a salary of $40,000 in 1931. Thus school supporters had to contend not only with a reluctant legislature and hostile civic groups, but also a mayor sensitive to the political winds of economy. In response, the Board of Education chose in April 1939 simply to recite the dangers of the state cuts upon its central task of instructing the young, as well as the effects on community activities, evening schools, and school maintenance. In Albany, the state capital, Democratic legislators addressed a gathering of parents and teachers while the Republican leaders remained unruffled by the public clamor.[13]

On the other hand, the Public Education Association (PEA) questioned the propriety of the proposed budget cuts which, in the PEA's view, would, increase class sizes, defer teaching appointments, and perhaps lead to teacher layoffs. Or salaries might be slashed across the board. Whatever the course of events, the PEA concluded that "we are at a loss to see" how the schools could absorb the cuts by the legislature and the mayor. Taking pen in hand, James Marshall, the president of the Board of Education, wrote to the respective legislative chairmen of the finance and the ways and means committees to predict that unless the state cuts were restored, the schools would be virtually wrecked. Marshall indicated, for example, that adult day and evening schools, after-school recreational activities, and summer play sessions would be shut down. More ominously, he mentioned that 6,189 positions would be abolished. Was this public posturing, or brutal intention?[14]

Undeterred, the New York Merchants Association suggested that the school budget deficit could be wiped out simply by teachers accepting a 4.1 percent salary cut. Marshall was quick to respond to the Merchants Association for "thinking more of tax cuts than of the welfare of our children" and added that the businessmen lacked the "guts" to call for a general reduction in all city employees' salaries and not just teachers. Despite Marshall's reply, the business group in a letter to all members of the legislature advised that "we sincerely hope that you will not be influenced by the hysterical pleas for restoration of the cut in State aid for education."[15]

Interestingly enough, two Republicans, City Council president Newbold Morris and Manhattan Borough president Stanley M. Isaacs both denounced the Republican-controlled state legislature for slashing school expenditures as the "falsest type of economy" and in direct contradiction to the "new conception of our party as a modern, streamlined, socially conscious instrument of progress." Following Alf Landon's crushing electoral defeat in 1936, Morris and Isaacs sought to remind their Republican brethren of their political arithmetic. Editorially, the *New York Times* similarly spoke of the legislators' possible gain in prestige "if they took notice of the widespread protests from educators, parents and disinterested citizens" by restoring 50 to 75 percent of the stipulated reductions. Pointedly, the *Times* noted, "Starve the schools in this generation and we feed the demagogues . . . in the next generation." Weighing in, too, the United Neighborhood Houses, an umbrella organization of 46 settlement houses, also urged full restoration of the state cut so as to permit the schools to offer the full social services of summer schools, public baths, and swimming pools.[16]

But educational ping-ponging continued as the Board of Education in June reshaped its January budget. The board proposed a list of cuts that included the dismissal of 984 kindergarten teachers, the closure of evening schools and community centers, the curtailment of citizenship classes, and cutbacks in daily high school activities. As waves of public protests increased, Governor Lehman sought to fix the blame, or responsibility, for the school cuts solely on the Republican legislature. In New York City, Superintendent Campbell explained the subtleties of tenure by insisting that if job positions were abolished, then teacher tenure similarly took flight. At this point, the CBC applauded the cuts and scolded school administrators for not exhibiting leadership in taking salary cuts. In addition, the CBC claimed that average teacher's salaries of $3,524 in 1939 were $383 higher than in 1929. Once again the CBC called for a reduction in the number of elementary teachers.[17]

After citing the proposed cuts in the city's school budget, the *Times* dolefully asserted that "this melancholy experience ought not to discredit *true economy*. For many reasons . . . our schools have increased tremendously in cost. . . . [T]he Regents' Inquiry found that expenditures per pupil between 1917 and 1935 . . . rose 88 per cent in New York City, 108 per cent in the rest of the State." Instead of bestowing bouquets on the city for its lower expenditures, especially given its history of political corruption that led to escalation of city costs, the editorial concluded by demanding "a new audit of all our agencies . . . to find out how many tax dollars we can afford to invest."[18]

To be sure, what a community "can afford" for public purposes may be suggested by experts, but ultimately the public through the ballot box determines what portion of its personal income it wishes to allocate to collective ends. Complicating our perceptions is the fact that most public goods, such as police and fire protection services, are of short-term duration and are akin to private consumption items such as food, clothing, and entertainment. On the other hand, public education contains components of short- and long-term benefits to the individual and to the community—the latter akin to a capital investment yielding a stream of future benefits. Thus the crucial question for the electorate at the local level is how much private income should be discounted in favor of the community or the future? [19]

With thunderclouds forming on the international horizon, the clouds in New York for teachers lowered and darkened. After signing petitions to the Board of Education to rescind the proposed cuts, in early June some 1,500 teachers milled around the central headquarters of the school and then marched to PS 59. In Times Square, another contingent made up mostly of students picketed the offices of the Republican State Committee.[20]

In a bellicose manner, the president of the Taxpayers Federation insisted that the state cuts were "only the beginning of economies" possible. He then urged that $48 million additionally could be saved from the state budget by reducing the average teacher's salary to the level of neighboring New Jersey's teachers. To support his contention, he cited the fact that "New York State's cost per pupil is $41.66 higher than the average of the four progressive and enlightened" states of Pennsylvania, New Jersey, Massachusetts, and Connecticut. Was this an escalation in the war of numbers? At a meeting of 15 civic, business, and community agencies the call for economy in government was sounded. Representing the Merchants Association, George McCaffrey urged teachers that it was better to "reduce salaries rather than suspend services. The morale of the school teachers will not break down over a 2 or 4 per cent cut." Frank Peer of the Community Councils suggested that the legislature pass enabling laws to permit salary cuts aside from direct budget cuts. On the other hand, the United Parents Association preferred that the schools operated a full program until April 1940 or until funds evaporated. Implicit in this position, unlike in Ohio, was the expectation that the legislature would restore a full school year.[21]

In its continuing commentary on the revolving stage of players in this school war, the *Times* editorially reflected the random and confusing positions that educators were wont to take. In this mental set, all school programs were of equal worth, all children were deserving of equal resources, except that not all teachers were of equal utility given sex, age, or weight. Tying to clarify this conflict, the *Times* stated that confusion had occurred over a "situation which is at bottom reasonably simple." To the *Times*, a 3.5 percent state cut that reduced school budgets by 10 percent was disproportionate unless salaries were slashed. Gently the editorial chastised the legislature for making cuts "clumsily and blindly" whereas savings could have been achieved "without hurting the efficiency of the schools." Without naming them, the *Times* asserted that "we cannot afford to abolish or cripple essential school services." Nor was it clear that the *Times* was not confusing, as had others, effectiveness in discharging the school's goals with the efficiency of utilizing human and physical inputs to produce within a given time period an outcome: student learning.[22]

Shifting to the court rooms, our schoolish drama found New York Supreme Court Justice John F. Carew acceding to a request by the Kindergarten Teachers Association to bar the adoption of the Board of Education's proposed budget. A week later, Judge Carew issued a final restraining order on the board's budgetary actions. But still later, the appellate courts reversed Judge Carew and argued that the Board of Education was well within its powers to make budgetary reductions. On another suit challenging the adoption of the state budget, the New York Court of Appeals (the highest state court) ruled unanimously that the Republican legislative budget was unconstitutional. Chief Justice Frederick Crane declared that the substitution of lump-sum items for line items was a reversion "to the old system which years of endeavor and agitation have sought to abolish." And so the school war of 1939 received a judicial fillip.[23]

Immediately, school forces regrouped. James Marshall called for a conference of 59 heads of school boards throughout the state to meet in New York City to map common strategy. A few days later only 17 school board presidents convened at the city schools' central office. Of the group, 14 school board heads sought full restoration while the three others defended the cuts. While agreeing with the minority view, the president of the Elmira school board called for statutory changes to reduce teacher retirement age from 70 to 65, thereby enacting substantial economies.[24]

Meanwhile 54 prominent citizens in the city formed an Emergency Committee to Save Our Children's Schools. Their first order of business was to denounce the state cuts and to send a telegram to the governor seeking his support. The telegram stated, in part, that the cuts "outrage the common sense of all who recognize that the maintenance and extension of social services is the surest defense of democracy." Two days later, James Marshall led 10 school board presidents in ineffectual eleventh-hour attempts to confer with legislative leaders. Toward the end of June, Governor Lehman in a special legislative session called for full restoration of state aid to education. But the Republican legislative leaders remained cool to the governor's pleading. Also, labor leaders, including Thomas J. Lyons, president of the New York Central Trades and Labor Council, called, as had others, for full restoration of the cuts; otherwise, he averred, the reductions were "economies taken out of the hides of the children of workers," which were "monstrous."[25]

Relentlessly, the petit-drama rolled on. In intricate political maneuvering, the legislature recessed, but did not adjourn, on the last day of June without enacting or restoring the educational cuts. Governor Lehman, in addition, had refused to issue emergency messages in the special session. In part, the governor had refused to use this tactic for fear that Abbot Low Moffat, chairman of the Assembly's Ways and Means Committee, would counter with a bill to slash teachers salaries from 2 to 5.5 percent, thereby permitting perhaps the retention of kindergarten and evening schools. Also there was concern that state supervision might encroach on the daily operations of the schools via these budget dictations. Fearing the worst, the New York City Board of Superintendents began to discuss a contingency plan to implement salary cuts (with the first $2,000 of salary exempt) ranging from 4.2 to 23 percent. Since the average teacher salary was in the $3,000 to $4,000 salary range, the average cut amounted to 5 percent. Only the superintendent earning $25,000 would be subject to the top rate.[26]

Never one to acquiesce in a good fight, La Guardia in a letter to the presiding officers of both houses of the legislature proposed that if the state would abolish all mandatory salaries and positions in the county offices and courts located within the city, he felt that since the city already paid 100 per cent of the budgeted items, the amount saved could accordingly be shifted to education. In short, La Guardia sought to disturb entrenched political practices and officeholders "who render absolutely no service at all." The mayor's ploy and letter died in the Senate Finance Committee without a reading.[27]

Shortly thereafter, the New York Court of Appeals sustained the prerogative of the New York City School Board in eliminating kindergartens and teachers. In an opinion written by Chief Justice Frederick E. Crane, the justice held that "if there be one public policy well established in this State, it is that public education shall be beyond control by municipalities and politics." In quick turn, Fred Kuper, law secretary to the Board of Education, hailed the decision as "a milestone in educational law. It reaffirms the independent power of the school system." Truly, beyond "politics" and the reach of the mayor? Reacting too, La Guardia recommended to the board of education that 4,318 teachers eligible for retirement be pensioned off thereby effecting a savings of $8 million. Thus in one fell swoop, that is, by La Guardia's wave of retirement, the schools crisis could be resolved. In fact, while 1,013 teachers were over 65, only 94 were at the mandatory retirement age of 70. Reactions to the mayor's "suggestion" were not long in coming. James Marshall replied that only the board of education could compel retirement at age 70.[28]

Once again, teachers were dunned. And dunned in the midst of the crisis of budgetary cuts. Superintendent Campbell reminded teachers that in 1931 they had *contributed* $4 million to a relief fund, yet despite criticisms, he insisted in July 1939 that "knowing our teachers, I anticipate the same generous loyal response. New York City teachers," he went on, "have never failed in an appeal affecting their profession." Affecting their jobs? Or the notion that teachers were philanthropic agents? But an angry letter writer, presumably a teacher, cited pay cuts, payless furloughs, and "contributions" of 35 million over the decade "toward easing the burden of the taxpayer." The writer added, "There is no particular reason why teachers, above all others, should be called up to prove their patriotism . . . by accepting periodic reductions in their pay."[29]

Aside from dunning of teachers, the Teachers Union (TU) representing 5,000 teachers, opposed the school cuts and the attempt to take "the politicians out of a hole." Instead the TU urged the mayor simply to transfer funds from other city departments to the school budget! On the other hand, the Board of Superintendents voted to accept a voluntary salary cut ranging from 2.5 to 15 percent, thereby saving about $4 million and thus negating the need, in their view, to abolish any teaching positions. But representatives of teacher and parent groups quickly opposed the recommended salary cuts until alternative avenues had been explored. With the exception of the TU, the Joint Committee of Teachers Organizations similarly went on record as opposed to the salary cuts until the board had utilized all financial devices such as loans, shifting of accounts, and other bookkeeping wizardry to keep the deficit at bay. More militant than others, the TU repeated its opposition to "voluntary" pay cuts that were compulsory. Nor did the TU consider it politic "to relieve politicians of the embarrassment they have brought upon themselves by their hit-and-run methods of achieving economy."[30]

Giving point to teacher weakness, Superintendent Campbell despite the opposition of teacher groups to pay cuts of any sort remained confident that most of the 40,000 teachers and supervisors would accept "voluntary" cuts from 2.5 to 15 percent. Yet unlike teachers in other parts of the country, with the school and city budgets entwined, there was the question of the virtuoso politician at the helm. What would be the mayor's next move in this game of thrust and counterthrust? With the legislative cuts hanging over the city, La Guardia urged teachers not to agree "to any voluntary cut in salary in order to cover the perfidy of politicians." He added that teachers are "not required to 'kick-in' to keep in idleness loafing politicians drawing fat salaries." Warming the cockles of teachers' hearts, La Guardia advised teachers that reductions in school administration alone would permit all school classes to operate till January 1940, at which time the legislature would be forced to tackle the potential closure of the nation's largest school system. It was fine theater for the Little Flower.[31]

Following the mayor's lead, the Board of Superintendents withdrew their demand for voluntary cuts by teachers. Undaunted, Superintendent Campbell announced that administrators and supervisory personnel would still suffer a "voluntary" pay cut. But the Principals Association immediately went on record as opposed to the pay cut of 5 percent for supervisors earning $5,000 and of a 10 percent cut on salaries above $10,000. Cozily, the principals objected to the attempt to separate them from classroom teachers and thereby create "class differences." The principals regretted the attempt at class division "at a time when the profession is more in need of solidarity than ever before." In the spirit of newly won unity with teachers, the principals recommended salary cuts for all school personnel.[32]

Whatever the degree of persuasion or coercion, 30 administrators at school headquarters agreed to salary reductions. But the practical effect of these cuts amounted to $20,000 while the deficit remained at $8 million. Nevertheless, Campbell approvingly noted, "It is gratifying that we got this virtually unanimous response from the administrative employees earning $5,000 or more. They went along with a full appreciation of the city's financial plight." Even administrators, much less teachers, were "employees" to Campbell.[33]

Late in July the school budget was revised still once more as a host of special services, from day classes in citizenship to all-day care centers, were simply eliminated. Also, by not filling 145 vacant teaching positions and by maintaining kindergarten and regular teachers until January 1940, the Board of Education's finance committee reported that although the total cuts came to $6.1 million, they were still $2 million short of a balanced budget. Faced with this fiscal need, the board accepted oversized classes and austerity until the first of the new year. Needless to say, various interested groups objected to these fiscal cuts. At a board meeting, James Marshall jibed at real estate interests by noting that one of the economies proposed was the elimination of $1 million to replace antiquated sanitary facilities on school grounds. With intended irony, Marshall noted that the smelly school yards in "the finest residential districts cannot now be made more attractive [perhaps] injur[ing] renting in many of these neighborhoods."[34]

Taking stock of the schoolish skirmishes so far, the *Times* editorial trenchantly observed that some of the dire predictions by the school people and their supporters had not come to pass. Caustically, the editorial added that the "bungling ways" to economize might prove in the end a useful civic lesson. And the themes of the lesson? That closing citizenship classes, depriving children of swimming pools in the summer, and delaying the removal of smelly latrines "are not the best way." However, the *Times* provided no yardstick to ascertain which school program was of greater student or social benefit much less to announce a criterion that pointed to the "best way." In the absence of these benchmarks, the board could only muddle through. With a temporary appointee to the Board of Education by La Guardia, the board voted 3 to 1 to accept the oft revised budget.[35]

However, Mrs. Johanna Lindlof, while urging the retention of evening schools, nevertheless cast the sole vote against the new budget. Responding to this new budget, the *Times* praised the retention of kindergarten classes and insisted that "the city's children are still the city's chief concern, whatever we may say about the revolution in family life and in general mores. The *child is still the nucleus of the family* and the main item in the municipal budget." The *Times* joined Dr. Sexson, mentioned above, and the efforts of various programs by the WPA in touching upon an implicit family policy that might have enveloped the public schools.[36]

Once again the spotlight shifted to the courts. Early in August 1939 the TU initiated a suit in New York Supreme Court to direct the Board of Education under Section 877, subdivision 8 of the Education Law to declare the existence of an emergency. Once declared, the board could apply to the city's Board of Estimate for additional funds. A month later the suit was dismissed by Judge Ferdinand Pecora. Still another suit was brought by a private citizen to test the legality of the Board of Education's adoption of the revised budget. The suit claimed that the three affirmative votes constituted less than a quorum. Undermanned, aside from the temporary appointee, the board had two vacancies and two absent members.[37]

Four days before Germany and the USSR signed their mutual "non-aggression" pact, New York Supreme Court Justice J. Sidney Bernstein declared the adopted revised budget of July 27 as illegal in the absence of a permanent majority or quorum in session. In addition, Judge Bernstein ordered that evening elementary schools be maintained. To this decision, the *Times* as well applauded the reinstatement of night school classes. Triumphantly, Mrs. Lindloff commented, "I was opposed to the adoption of the budget" and to earlier budgets with cuts. Accordingly, she urged that the May budget be used and all services operated until January 1940. Once again the Board of Education harkened to its budgetary lessons. Late in August with fatigue at work, the board sailed through 90 items and then adjourned without adopting a new version of the budget. The board's actions implied that the preliminary budget as modified by La Guardia was still the one of record. However, many board members were mystified as to the status of the budget as September and a new school year beckoned.[38]

Minor economies were forthcoming as 68 high school teachers lost their stipends of $1,188 for administering high school annexes. By returning the teachers to full-time teaching, the school system savings amounted to $185,000. In September, Superintendent Campbell once again urged voluntary salary cuts by administrators. In response, the principals and their assistants flatly rejected the call by Campbell. Midway through September, Campbell deplored the fact that only 194 out of 1,307 school administrators had volunteered for the cuts. With this poor showing, he concluded that opponents of the schools would join a bandwagon for general salary reductions. In this setting, the Board of Superintendents recommended the retirement of 10 veteran teachers. Two weeks later, as noted in chapter 7, an additional 15 women teachers were called to the office of Dr. Emil Altman for a medical examination as a prelude to retirement.[39]

While taking note of teachers' opposition to pay cuts, Campbell insisted that he "would still have to scrape the bottom of the pot." As an example of scraping the bottom of the pot, Frederick Ernest, an associate superintendent, suggested that daily substitutes for ailing high school teachers be banned for absences of less than five days. Thus during a colleague's illness, other members of the faculty would have to double up classes or forgo their daily preparation periods. Despite the opposition of teachers, this measure was put into practice. In another area, while evening schools were reopened, the $10 per night paid to day time principals moonlighting as evening principals was dropped as another economy measure. More fundamentally, 300 evening teachers were laid off. A contingent of 60 irate teachers protested their layoff at school headquarters but to no avail. Many of the dismissed teachers had had more than 20 years of teaching experience but lacked tenure and pension rights.[40]

At a luncheon in late September, Mayor La Guardia pledged to renew his fight for state aid to education at the January 1940 legislative session. And so with each passing day, James Marshall's earlier hint that the schools would operate without a formal budget came to pass. However, the lassitude of September in the verbal school wars gave way as Abbot Low Moffat resumed the wars in October. He charged that the New York City Board of Education was "pretty incompetent" individually and collectively. Having challenged their competence, Moffat now chastised the school system for not accepting the state reductions and for choosing to "play politics with the situation." On another matter, Moffat was equally incensed that the City Council had not removed its cigarette tax when the state had imposed its own. Returning blast for blast, La Guardia denounced Moffat as the "wizard of finances" while "working with the opponents of good, clean government in the city."[41]

Responding to Moffat's charge of incompetency, La Guardia retorted at a luncheon of the New York Young Republican Club that "there isn't a politician on it and they can all read and write." It was surely a giddy sight to behold a Republican mayor roasting a Republic state legislative chairman before the eager faces of young Republicans. Quick to counter, Moffat replied that La Guardia, not he, was "playing politics." He accused La Guardia of reneging on a "gentleman's agreement" to remove the cigarette tax. Given the facts of falling state revenues and the unpalatability of raising taxes, Moffat declared that "only in New York City has the board utterly failed to appreciate its responsibilities in a democracy." Continuing his civic lesson, Moffat stated that if school and city officials had the political will "savings of about 3 per cent" could be implemented without "serious effect" on services. Cutting closer to home, he argued that La Guardia by attacking him had diverted attention from a $3 million budgetary cut by the mayor. Compelled to join the exchange of brickbats, James Marshall rejoined that "with the technique of an ostrich, Moffat locked himself in his office so that he could not see the schools." But the school system, Marshall insisted, could not afford the "luxury of an ostrich, nor cooperate by burying its head."[42]

While the wars of prose and legal actions flourished, teachers continued to lose their jobs. Taking heed of the Citizens Budget Commission's earlier recommendations, the Board of Education dismissed 138 elementary substitute teachers and 13 clerks. Altogether, 564 teaching posts had been abolished. Commenting on the economies, Rufus Vance, an assistant superintendent, called the curtailments an "unfortunate trend" with the result that class size would increase, but he cautioned as to "whether the efficiency of the teaching staff" would be affected. If class size increased, then, ipso facto, since teachers served more students per hour or per day, efficiency had improved but whether effectiveness had improved was a question that depended on teacher morale, health, and attitude. Again, educators, including Raymond Callahan as noted above, rarely distinguished among the three Es of education: economy, efficiency, and effectiveness.[43]

Speaking at a Brooklyn luncheon, Campbell reverted to the nineteenth-century role of superintendent as patriarchal figure bestowing his blessing on the faithful. At best he offered the cherished maxims of Mann, to wit, that only an unrepentant and obstinate public chose to ignore the beneficent role of public education. Echoing Joseph Mayer Rice's complaint of the 1890s, for example, Campbell asserted that if the public, and parents in particular, took a greater interest in the schools, ergo greater financial support of the schools would be forthcoming. For schoolmen like Campbell, keeping "politics" out of the schools meant a blank check on the public's purse. Campbell's mind set revealed in part a traditional stance of educators and in part reflected an unwillingness to accept that in the real world beyond the classroom private and public choices had to be made daily, monthly, and annually. The choices were often between competing desirable ends or goods or the converse among the choices of lesser evils or "bads." Daily, as children often discover without the aid of parents or teachers, mundane trade-off of more of this means less of that take place. Unfortunately, no one spoke of retiring shopworn superintendents full of bromides and trained incapacities minted at the knees of Horace Mann.[44]

Never at a loss for an idea or riposte, La Guardia proposed that the New York State operate the city's school system with the city providing basic revenue while the state made up the shortfall. This ploy fell too on deaf ears. (But it was an idea that would return thirty years later during another fiscal crisis in the city when the state assumed the funding of the city's public colleges.)[45]

On a minor matter, La Guardia prevailed over Campbell's refusal to allow the city's schoolchildren to attend the World's Fair in the closing days of October. Campbell had initially refused, claiming that state apportionment funds would be lost for a day of absence. Campbell relented and permitted the release, however, of seventh and upper graders from schools on October 22.[46]

After Hitler's blitzkrieg of Poland on September 1939, "there ensued a period of inaction which was fatuously denominated a 'phoney' war." By the following spring of 1940, Commager and Morison added that "early in April the 'phoney' war came dramatically to an end." The Battle of Britain had begun. In the backstage drama of education in New York City, the schools muddled through the school year. In a continuing series of economies, the Board of Superintendents by June 1940 had voted to abolish 612 elementary teaching posts. The upshot was that by various pruning devices the school budget deficit of $8.3 million had been wiped out. Thus Moffat had not been far from the mark. During the summer of 1940, the Board of Education took up residence in their new headquarters at 110 Livingston Street. The "phoney" school war of 1939–1940 had come to an end.[47]

Before we bring our tale to a close, another singular event that touched upon the family deserves mention. Buried in the back pages of the *New York Times* in April 1939 was a significant request from a New York State Conference on Marriage and the Family. The Conference urged Governor Lehman to call for an interdepartmental agency to study and coordinate *all state services bearing upon the family*. The conference took cognizance of the fact that while numerous services were oriented to individuals, most services were "organized with little relation to the family as a unit of human living." Ironically, the conference reported that government services "tend in many ways to divide citizens into categories, cutting across family lines. They miss the opportunity to strengthen family loyalties and to use the latent strength of the family as a resource for social security." Finally, the conference called for a "closer working relation" between the schools and social welfare agencies.[48]

A year earlier in New York City, 50 private social and 4 public agencies along with the schools had met to discuss closer cooperation. In his address, Superintendent Campbell observed that many problems such as poor health, inadequate housing, and "unsatisfactory home conditions" were factors beyond the control of the schools. "It has long been apparent," Campbell continued, "that many of the most serious problems confronting the schools are those that arise out of conditions the educational authorities either have no power at all to remedy, or cannot remedy without the help of other city departments and private agencies." Once again, it was rare and refreshing to hear an educator admit that there were student problems beyond the reach of the schools, that school and outside agencies were needed in joint endeavors no matter how "unsatisfactory home conditions" might be. But educators sometimes hid behind bureaucratic rules as the Tusher case above illustrated, thus cutting off vital home/school support.[49]

At the close of the Depression, of these two meetings of social agencies, it was the Conference on Marriage and the Family that suggested a new rationale implicitly for the public schools in its fight to stave off budget cuts and to avoid being the first among municipal services to walk the public plank. Instead of citing the shortchanging of children, or the penurious status of teachers, here lay an entering wedge to shore up the family and school and in its wake the community. Only the WPA in its various programs from preschool to day care centers and summer play centers was the sole practitioner of child, parent, school, and community interactions. What was needed was a paradigm that placed home and school closer to the center of society rather than on the periphery. Of educators, only Dr. Sexson had touched upon the relationship, and the *Times* too had touched upon the theme. But the educational establishment—from the NEA to the *Social Frontier* and from the professors of education to the school superintendents—remained obtuse.

Nor did John Dewey, full of years and honors, arise to the challenge of his career. He failed to fashion the social and institutional equivalent to what Keynes had done to rescue the imperfections of market capitalism. A new paradigm for school and family was not forthcoming from the arch proponent of social reconstruction in thought.

EPILOGUE

THE CASE FOR INTELLIGENCE

In the conditions of modern life the rule is absolute, the race which does not value trained intelligence is doomed. Not all your heroism, not all your social charm, can move back the finger of fate. Today we maintain ourselves. Tomorrow science will have moved forward yet one more step, and there will no appeal from the judgment which will then be pronounced on the uneducated.

—*Alfred North Whitehead*[1]

In the summer of 1945 the Second World War came to an end. With alacrity, the nation demobilized its armed forces with cries of "bring the boys back home." And so they came home—the soldiers, sailors, marines, and airmen as well as the women in uniform. While individuals and institutions turned to the task of conversion from war to peace, an "iron curtain" fell over Eastern Europe. But most Americans turned their attention toward matters of family, jobs, and the pursuit of happiness. For many ex-servicemen and women, the pursuit of happiness was aided by the benefits of the GI Bill that provided opportunities for training and college education as well as assistance in buying a home.

Without the predicted postwar depression, peacetime prosperity rolled on. Twenty years of pent-up demand for housing, furniture, appliances, and cars exploded. Also the exodus from the cities to suburbia had begun as car and highway altered the social and political landscape.

The Great Depression, a time of shortages and stunted hopes, had given way to one of unparalleled affluence. Oddly enough, the generation of the Depression came to an end with the flower children of the 1960s. The former knew material deprivation, the latter spiritual want. A "social curtain" descended separating generations. Yet where the children of the 1930s had dressed poorly of necessity, the grandchildren of the 1960s chose rags of poverty along with the obligatory touches of the time: unkempt hair, body odors, Salvation Army clothing, and pot smells. Costumes were oddlot. At times, the grandchildren turned the 1960s into an ongoing casting party of thousands at Woodstock and elsewhere.

If there had been intellectual truants in the Depression, in the 1960s there were adults on and off campuses masquerading as children and children only too happy to play truant from any obligation to pursue studies, enter the labor force, or serve in the armed services. The rationalizations for truancy were numerous and easily voiced: "Relevance"; "NOW"; and "Tune out, turn on." As another sign of the times, contrast the faces of youth of the 1960s with the haunted looks of their grandparents in family Kodak snaps or in the professional photos of Walker Evans, Russell Lee, and Dorothea Lange.

Rather than admit to a lack of talent, the ultimate playacting consisted in tearing down the theater. Ironically, while opposed to the Vietnam War, the young rebels adopted the militant stance that in order to save the nation, one must destroy it. And so the tearing and social lacerations of authority and institutions by the young continued. On their very own search-and-destroy missions, these idealist youth accused the very families and the land that had nurtured them of *social imperfection*. Not content with this charge, they then proceeded blindly to assert that both family and society were living hells, no different from the Soviet Union and its Gulags by not one whit or degree. Neither common sense nor basic knowledge of history, economics, and thought deterred these "mis-educated" idealists.

But what transpired in education? With the end of the war, the schools responded to the baby boom by hiring new teachers and building schools to accommodate burgeoning enrollments. College campuses welcomed sober and serious-minded veterans. As with so many other things, this bubble of growth came to an end late in the 1960s as enrollments peaked and budgetary constraints made their appearance once again as they had done in the 1930s. By this time, the social interventions of the Great Society too had come to an end. For all its merriment, Woodstock was the apogee and the signal that the party of perpetual youth at last was over.

More prosaically, teachers were asked to do many things other than teach the basics in the 1950s and 1960s. More and more their roles merged into social worker, surrogate parent, sometime baby-sitter and cheerleader for the passing winds of fashion. As the decades wore on, teachers were asked to fight the cold war, then the wars against poverty and racism, and further enlisted in the simultaneous skirmishes against chauvinism, sexism, genetic disorders, and venereal diseases. The war on drugs and the hunt for an AIDS cure received special political and media attention.

As to New York City's public schools, a long-time education writer observed that the schools were "in crisis. The number of dropouts is alarming, but the authorities don't even know what the actual numbers are. Charges of bureaucratic lethargy are leveled against the Board of Examiners, which licenses teachers. School construction is a shambles." Fred Hechinger went on to observe that "so little has changed in the problems facing the schools over the last 25 years, or in the proposals to deal with them that have repeatedly made and repeatedly rejected." The 1930s revisited? No, the year was 1987. Clearly, Hechinger was too modest; the problems he cited harked back at least to the turn of the century when Mayor Red Hylan had been followed by James Walker and his retinue with "tincups."[2]

But there was a significant change in education from the 1930s. For example, instead of 74 teacher organizations in New York City, the number after World War Two had dwindled to 3 and by 1960 there was only 1, the United Federation of Teachers under the mantle of Albert Shanker. Tactically, one-day strikes were succeeded by strikes of several weeks and months in 1966 and 1968, respectively. Today, the UFT can bargain with the best of public unions and can exercise a veto over the appointment of a new chancellor of schools. Clearly, the teachers are no longer the doormats of education. *The ceremony of professionalism* has finally been abandoned in favor of collective bargaining.[3]

In time external forces prodded the schools from the Soviet launching of the Sputnik, court-ordered desegregation of the schools, and the long decline of SAT scores. In the 1980s and 1990s, the reform of the schools, again, became a favorite indoor sport from the president and governors on down to the local PTA. While school and nonschool benchmarks such as teen pregnancies, rising dropout rates, crime and violence within the schools disturbed the tranquility of learning, from the supporters of the schools came the familiar cry for more money as the cure-all.

Yet as one economist noted between 1950 and 1986, the cost of educating the same cohort of students increased from 2 percent to 3.5 percent of GNP. "In constant-dollar terms," Richard Vedder has written, "expenditures per pupil more than tripled."

To challenge the Balkanized local monopolies of public education, the voucher system had been proposed to give parents the right to choose schooling as they would choose any other good and service. But it was an idea whose time had yet to come. Meanwhile, the state of Minnesota launched an experiment in *statewide open enrollment* in which parents could send their child to any public school in the state, thereby bringing a measure of competition to the schools.[4]

In April 1975, the Vietnam War came to an end. The veterans came home not to parades and public welcome but to silence and personal abuse. For some veterans the public neglect, wartime memories, injuries, and personality quirks combined to make the adjustment to peacetime life a difficult and painful one. The erection of the Vietnam Memorial was a long overdue gesture of reconciliation. Perhaps that spirit of healing contributed in part to the extraordinary receptions that greeted our men and women home from the Persian Gulf war.

Domestically, despite the constraints of nature and resources, the war metaphor in dealing with social issues persisted. Yet one war finally came to an end by 1989 signaled by the crumbling of the Berlin Wall. A year later the Soviet experiment of 70 years came to a close. As such, the cold war gave way to conventional power politics. For American society, in turn, the new challenges were global competition and the emergence of the information superhighway. Clearly, the new challenges of the age placed a premium on "trained intelligence" and a penalty on the uneducated.

Appendix

Table A1

Enrollments in Public and Private Schools

	1929–1930	*1933–1934*	*1937–1938*	*1939–1940*
Kindergarten				
Public	723,443	601,775	607,034	594,647
Private	54,456	37,506	37,806	57,341
Elementary				
Public	20,555,150	20,228,014	19,183,392	18,286,906
Private	2,255,430	2,333,191	2,214,670	2,106,030
Secondary				
Public	4,399,422	5,669,156	6,226,934	6,601,444
Private	341,158	360,092	446,833	457,768

Source: U.S. Office of Education, Biennial Survey of Education, *Statistical Summary of Education, II*, 1939–1940 (Washington, D.C.: Government Printing Office, 1943), Ch. 1, p. 7.

Table A2

Number of Teachers, Supervisors, and Principals and Combined and Average Annual Salaries

1929–1930	1931–1932	1933–1934	1935–1936	1937–1938	1939–1940
854,263	871,607	847,120	870,963	877,266	875,477
$1,420	$1,417	$1,227	$1,283	$1,374	$1,441

Source: U.S. Office of Education, Biennial Survey of Education, *Statistics of State School Systems, 1939–1940, and 1941–1942* (Washington, D.C.: Government Printing Office, 1944), p. 16, for income data and p. 15 for number of educators.

Table A3

National Income and School Data

Calendar Year	National Income ($ billion)	School Expenditure ($ billion)	Education as % of NI	Education Index (1930 = 100)
1929	87.8	2.3	3.0	100
1930	75.7			
1931	59.7			
1932	42.5	2.1	4.9	91
1933	40.2			
1934	49.0	1.7	3.4	73
1935	57.1			
1936	64.9	1.9	2.9	82
1937	73.6			
1938	67.6	2.2	3.2	95
1939	72.8			
1940	81.6	2.3	2.8	100

Source: U.S. Bureau of the Census, *Historical Statistics of the United States, Colonial Times to 1957* (Washington, D.C.: Government Printing Office, 1960), p. 139, for columns 1 and 2.

Consumer Price Index and Education Index

Calendar Year	Consumer Price Index (1935–1939 = 100)	Educator's Index (1929–1930 = 100)
1929	122.5	
1930	119.5	100
1931	108.7	
1932	97.6	99
1933	92.4	
1934	95.7	86
1935	98.1	
1936	99.1	90
1937	102.7	
1938	100.8	96
1939		99.4
1940	100.2	101

Source: U.S. Bureau of the Census, *Statistical Abstracts of the United States, 1942*, 64th ed., (Washington, D.C.: Government Printing Office, 1943), pp. 377–378, and column 3 recomputed from Table A2's average salaries.

TABLE A5

Aggregate Public School Outlays for Capital Construction, Plant Operation, and Maintenance

School Year	Capital Outlay ($1,000)	Operation and Maintenance ($1,000)
1929–1930	370,878	294,882
1931–1932	210,996	257,424
1933–1934	59,277	203,477
1935–1936	171,322	233,264
1937–1938	238,853	260,168
1939–1940	257,974	267,687

Source: U.S. Bureau of the Census, *Historical Statistics of the United States, Colonial Times to 1957* (Washington, D.C.: Government Printing Office, 1960), p. 209.

Seattle Public Schools 10–Year Trends

	1929	1931	1933	1935	1937–1938
Total Enrollment	66,545	70,189	70,215	66,306	64,665
Average Daily Attendance	54,119	57,551	57,974	55,109	53,882
Number of Teachers	1,703	1,763	1,707	1,646	1,695
Average Teacher Salary	$2,080	$2,215	$1,901	$1,685	$2,111
Per Pupil Costs	$103	$106	$86	$81	$112

Source: *Seattle Municipal News*, V, XXIX, No. 9, March 4, 1939, p. 4.

TABLE A7

Seattle Public Schools Expenditures on Textbooks and Library Books

School Year	Elementary	Junior High	Senior High
1930–1931	$67,644	$6,384P	$41,191
1931–1932	15,644	3,614	30,716
1932–1933	9,378	2,522	15,271
1933–1934	2,196		25,656
1934–1935	3,720		43,187
1935–1936	3,017		75,609
1936–1937	3,869		89,529
1937–1938	4,382		57,772
1938–1939	6,969		44,785

Source: Compiled from Seattle School District No.1, *Annual Financial Reports*, June 30, 1931, to June 1939 inclusive.

Note: Through the school year of 1933, the dollar figures for senior and junior highs include textbooks and library books, but for elementary schools, textbooks only. At the bottom of the Depression in 1933, the school district combined the dollar figures for textbooks into one with the second figure for library books and periodicals. As can be seen, the recession of 1937 was felt immediately, at least in textbook expenditures.

New York City Schools: Average Daily Attendance,
School Years: 1930–1931 to 1944–1945

School Year	A	B	C	D	E
1930–1931	981,590	33,969	686,648	94,580	158,231
1931–1932	999,590	33,326	682,442	98,673	176,497
1932–1933	1,017,808	34,426	677,369	101,475	195,351
1933–1934	1,022,810	34,090	671,578	104,174	205,895
1934–1935	1,018,154	33,364	651,116	111,775	214,960
1935–1936	1,030,818	32,096	637,522	115,846	219,516
1936–1937	1,023,165	32,773	620,405	118,711	220,830
1937–1938	1,015,220	32,948	598,872	122,663	224,471
1938–1939	993,734	32,365	572,229	123,070	223,627
1939–1940	968,143	33,587	544,337	123,709	220,482
1940–1941	933,491	32,840	519,141	120,619	212,821
1941–1942	887,937	33,521	495,301	116,067	194,707
1942–1943	812,968	32,188	456,769	109,171	170,753
1943–1944	761,814	30,499	427,881	101,808	160,487
1944–1945	748,979	32,267	417,036	97,962	162,230

A = Total Schools   D = Junior High
B = Kindergarten   E = Academic High
C = Elementary

Source: *Fifty-Sixth Annual Report of the Superintendent of Schools*, City of New York Board of Education, School Year 1953–1954, p. 115.

NOTES

Opening Quotations

1. Sidney Hook, *Out of Step* (New York: Harper & Row, 1987), p. 195.

2. William Barrett, *The Truants* (Garden City, N.Y.: Anchor Press/Doubleday, 1982), p. 13.

3. Irving Kristol, "US Foreign Policy Has Outlived Its Time," *Wall Street Journal*, January 21, 1988, p. 30.

Preface

1. Reuven and Gabrielle A. Brenner, *Gambling and Speculation* (New York: Cambridge University Press, 1990), pp. 83–88.

2. William Stott, *Documentary Expression and Thirties America* (New York: Oxford University Press, 1973), p. 143. Russell Lee et al., *Far From Main Street: Three Photographers in Depression-Era New Mexico* (Santa Fe: Museum of New Mexico, 1994).

Introduction

1. *Inaugural Addresses of the Presidents of the United States* (Washington, D.C.: Government Printing Office, 1961) pp. 236, 237, 238 (stress added). Intuitively, FDR understood the relationship between the media and the metaphors of war and the emergency. Paul Weaver in a recent study of the media concluded that "what Pulitzer & Company created around the turn of the century wasn't merely a new journalism, but a new and powerful permanent *emergency mode of operation* that constitutional government was routinely urged to resort to and routinely rewarded for doing so," in *News and the Culture of Lying* (New York: Free Press, 1994), p. 67 (stress added).

2. John M. Keynes, *The General Theory of Employment, Interest and Money* (New York: Harcourt, Brace, 1936). Roy F. Harrod, *The Life of John Maynard Keynes* (New York: Harcourt, Brace, 1951). On the uses of *paradigms*, see the seminal work of Thomas Kuhn, *The Structure of Scientific Revolutions* (Chicago: University of Chicago Press, 1970), Ch. 5.

3. Arthur Mann, *La Guardia Comes to Power* (Philadelphia: J.B. Lippincott, 1965).

4. Saul Alinsky, *John L. Lewis* (New York: G.P. Putnam's Sons, 1949), Chs. 4–6.

5. John Dewey, *Reconstruction in Philosophy* (New York: New American Library, [1920] 1950). Note also Dewey's view that the bankers' dictation of school

finances represented "a pathetic and tragic commentary on the lack of social power possessed by the teaching profession." *New York Times*, March 2, 1933, p. 18.

6. William E. Leuchtenburg, "The New Deal and the Analogue of War," in John Braeman et al., *Change and Continuity in Twentieth Century America* (New York: Harper Colophon Books, Harper & Row, 1966), pp. 81–143; S.E. Morison and H.S. Commager, *The Growth of the American Republic*, Vol. 2 (New York: Oxford University Press, 1950), p. 516, for the influence of the First World War upon the New Deal.

7. For Keynes' open letter to FDR, see *New York Times*, December 31, 1933, VIII, p. 2; (stress added) for Keynes' call for international action on loans to start public works, see *New York Times*, March 13, 1933, p. 2; for Arthur Krock's comment on Keynes' visit to the White House, see *New York Times*, June 5, 1934, p. 23; Harrod, *Keynes*, pp. 448–450.

8. For an interesting ironic parallel, note that echoing Jefferson's 1801 inaugural call that "we are all republicans—we are all federalists," President Richard M. Nixon could say that "we are all Keynesians," *New York Times*, January 5, 1971, p. 20; January 7, 1971, p. 19; and January 10, 1971, IV, p. 1.

9. J.K. Galbraith, *The Great Crash* (Boston: Houghton, Mifflin, 1961), pp. 188–189.

10. Howard K. Beale, *Are American Teachers Free?* (New York: Charles Scribner's Sons, 1936) and his *A History of Freedom of Teaching in American Schools* (New York: Charles Scribner's Sons, 1941), where Beale observes in the latter work that "the teacher is still a 'hired man' of the community that feels privileged to dictate what he shall and shall not do whenever his activity involves a question on which it cares what anybody does," on p. 245. While his insight is astute, Beale erred on the gender of his teacher.

11. The preceding themes on school structure, bureaucratic ethos, and the life of the teacher draw on my "Public Schools in Search of Legitimacy: Mandarin Schools and Fok Teachers, 1900–1929" (Ph. D. dissertation, University of Washington, 1971), Chs. 2, 3, and 8.

12. For a discussion of the effects of third parties upon the provision of schooling and the schools' misuse of resources, see Kenneth Boulding, "The Schooling Industry as a Possibly Pathological Section of the American Economy," *Review of Educational Research*, 42, 1 (Winter 1972), 129–143.

13. Donald A. Schon, "The Social System and Social Change," in *Social Change*, Robert Nisbet, ed. (New York: Harper Torchbooks, Harper & Row, 1973), p. 90 (stress in original).

14. Kenneth Burke, *Permanence and Change* (Indianapolis: Bobbs-Merrill, 1935), pp. 5–9, for an amplification of the concept of "trained incapacity" (stress added).

15. Max Lerner, ed., *The Portable Veblen* (New York: Viking Press, 1948), p. 449.

16. For a discussion of the contours of adaptation and adaptability by individuals and institutions, see Kenneth Boulding, *The Meaning of the Twentieth Century* (New York: Harper Colophon Books, Harper & Row, 1964), pp. 147–148.

Chapter 1

1. Robert and Helen Lynd, *Middletown in Transition* (New York: Harcourt, Brace, 1937), p. 225.

2. John Dewey, *Liberalism in Social Action* (New York: Capricorn Books, 1963), pp. 15–16, 45–46. For reappraisals of Dewey's influence on education, see Reginald D. Archambault, ed., *Dewey on Education* (New York: Random House, 1966), and the Spring 1975 issue of *History of Education Quarterly*, 15, 1 devoted to Dewey, 3–92.

3. *HEQ, ibid.*, pp. 16–17.

4. Roy F. Harrod, *The Life of John Maynard Keynes* (New York: Harcourt, Brace, 1951), pp. 453–462, 451. To be sure, not all economists and politicians were of a like mind. See Charles P. Kindleberger, *The World in the Depression, 1929–1939* (Berkeley: University of California Press, 1973), for a thorough examination of governmental, institutional, and individual efforts and thoughts in explaining the cause(s) of the Great Depression.

5. *Ibid.*, p. 452.

6. John M. Keynes, *The General Theory of Employment, Interest and Money* (New York: Harcourt, Brace, 1936), pp. 383–384.

7. *New York Times*, March 1, 1933, p. 18.

8. *New York Times*, November 9, 1935, p. 17.

9. *New York Times*, November 9, 1935, p. 17; December 20, 1935, p. 2; November 15, 1935, p. 19; see Edward A. Krug, *The Shaping of the American High School, II* (Madison: University of Wisconsin Press, 1972), pp. 221–224.

10. See Saul Alinsky, *John L. Lewis* (New York: G.P. Putnam's Sons, 1949), pp. 73–85, on the birth of the CIO. For the sitdown strike at General Motors, see pp. 94–147; also *New York Times,* July 24, 1936, p. 19.

11. *New York Times*, November 14, 1935, p. 24.

12. *Social Frontier*, 3, 27 (June 1937), 291.

13. *New York Times*, May 4, 1939, p. 10.

14. *New York Times*, May 4, 1939, p. 24; May 6, 1935, p. 21.

15. *New York Times*, August 6, 1935, p. 4. For a further discussion of the impact of the "social efficiency" doctrine in the schools, see Edward A. Krug, *The Shaping of the American High School, 1880–1920* (Madison: University of Wisconsin Press, 1964), Ch. 11.

16. *New York Times*, September 11, 1935, p. 9: October 25, 1938, p. 17 (stress added).

17. *New York Times*, August 13, 1939, IV, p. 9.

18. *New York Times*, December 16, 1939, p. 16.

19. *New York Times*, September 11, 1939, p. 21.

20. *New York Times*, December 31, 1939, II, p. 5.

21. *Ibid.*

22. *New York Times*, October 26, 1938, p. 12.

23. *New York Times Magazine*, April 15, 1934, pp. 3, 20.

24. *Ibid.* (stress added).

25. *New York Times*, January 8, 1939, II, p. 10.

26. C.A. Bowers, *The Progressive Educator and the Depression* (New York: Random House, 1969), Chs. 1–4; Gerald Gutek, *The Educational Theory of George S. Counts* (Columbus: Ohio State University Press, 1970), pp. 62–77, 99–106; Lawrence Cremin, *The Transformation of the Schools* (New York: Vintage Books, Random House, 1961), pp. 225–234; see also David Tyack, Robert Lowe, and Elisabeth Hansot, *Public Schools in Hard Times: The Great Depression and Recent Years* (Cambridge: Harvard University Press, 1984), pp. 18–20, 24–27.

27. *Social Frontier*, 1, 9 (June 1935), 40 (stress added).

28. John Dewey, "The Teacher and His World," *Social Frontier*, 1, 4 (January 1935), 7. Note as with Howard Beale, Dewey used the masculine pronoun in the title.

29. *Social Frontier*, 1, 1 (October 1934), 3, 4. Goodwin Watson, "Education is the Social Frontier," *Social Frontier*, 1, 1 (October 1934), 22.

30. John Dewey, "Can Education Share in Social Reconstruction?" *Social Frontier*, 2, 1 (October 1934), 12.

31. William H. Kilpatrick, "Educational Ideals and the Profit Motive," *Social Frontier*, 1, 2 (November 1934), 13.

32. *Social Frontier*, 1, 2 (November 1934), 3, 4.

33. *Social Frontier*, 1, 4 (January 1935), 31, 33 (stress added).

34. Charles A. Beard, "Property and Democracy," *Social Frontier*, 1, 1 (October 1934), 14, 15.

35. Ernest E. Bayles, "Merits of the Democratic Way," *Social Frontier*, 1, 5 (February 1935), 35 (stress added).

36. *Social Frontier*, 1, 4 (January 1935), 30; *Social Frontier*, 1, 7 (April 1935), 8.

37. Henry P. Fairchild, "A Sociologist Views the New Deal," *Social Frontier*, 1, 1 (October 1934), 16, 18.

38. Broadus Mitchell, "The Choice Before Us," *Social Frontier*, 1, 2 (November 1934), 15.

39. *Ibid.*, 16.

40. *Social Frontier*, 1, 3 (December 1934), 7, 8.

41. *Social Frontier*, 1, 1 (October 1934), 9.

42. *Social Frontier*, 1, 8 (May 1935), 14.

43. *Social Frontier*, 1, 2 (November 1934), 8; *Social Frontier*, 1, 3 (December 1934), 5 (stress added).

44. *Social Frontier*, 1, 6 (March 1935), 4, 5, 6 (stress added).

45. John Dewey, "Toward Administrative Statesmanship," *Social Frontier*, 1, 6 (March 1935), 9.

46. Jesse Newlon, "The Great Educational Illusion," *Social Frontier*, 1, 6 (March 1935), 16, 17.

47. *Social Frontier*, 1, 7 (April 1935), 7.

48. *Ibid.*; *Social Frontier*, 1, 9 (June 1935), 4.

Chapter 2

1. Forrest Allen, "A Layman Speaks His Mind," *Social Frontier*, 3, 23 (February 1937), 143, 144 (stress added).

2. *Social Frontier*, 1, 2 (November 1934), 5.

3. *Social Frontier*, 1, 4 (January 1935), 4.

4. *Ibid.*

5. Benjamin Ginzburg, "The Scientist in a Crumbling Civilization," *Social Frontier*, 1, 3 (December 1934), 15. See H.C. Engelbrecht and F.C. Hanighen, *The Merchants of Death* (New York: Dodd, Mead, 1934).

6. *Social Frontier*, 1, 3 (December 1934), 9.

7. *Social Frontier*, 1, 7 (April 1935), 8; Goodwin Watson, "Initiative in Our New America," *Social Frontier*, 1, 3 (December 1934), 21.

8. *Social Frontier*, 1, 4 (January 1935), 6. See also David Tyack, Robert Lowe, and Elisabeth Hosset, *Public Schools in Hard Times: The Great Depression and Recent Years* (Cambridge: Harvard University Press, 1984), pp. 60–61.

9. See Anonymous, "Why White Collar Workers Can't Be Organized," *Harper's Magazine* (August 1957). Of course, this changed in the 1960s along with other social and economic issues. The organization of teachers and other public employees has been significant and may modify the above conclusion while the numbers of blue-collar workers organized continues to decline relatively and absolutely.

10. *Social Frontier*, 1, 5 (February 1935), 3, 5; *Social Frontier*, 1, 6 (March 1935), 4.

11. *Social Frontier*, 1, 6 (March 1935), 4; Charles Beard, "Freedom of Teaching," *Social Frontier*, 1, 6 (March 1935), 18, 20; George S. Counts, *The Social Composition of Boards of Education* (Chicago: University of Chicago Press, 1927). Was Counts' work an unintentional parody of Charles Beard's thesis that our U.S. Constitution had been drafted by, and reflected the interests of, men of property?

12. *Social Frontier*, 1, 3 (December 1934), 8. John Dewey, "Can Education Share in Social Reconstruction?" *Social Frontier*, 1, 1 (October 1934), 12.

13. Charles A. Beard, "Freedom of Teaching," *Social Frontier*, 1, 6 (March 1935), 18, 20.

14. *Social Frontier*, 1, 6 (March 1935), 7–8 (stress added).

15. *Social Frontier*, 1, 7 (April 1935), 10.

16. Lawrence Martin, "William R. Hearst—Epitome of Capitalist Civilization," *Social Frontier*, 1, 5 (February 1935), 14.

17. Forrest Allen, "Control of the Press or Education of the Reader?" *Social Frontier*, 1, 7 (April 1935), 27, 28.

18. Bruce Bliven, "Free for What?" *Social Frontier*, 1, 5 (February 1935) 24; Harry D. Gideonese, "Non-Partisan Education for Political Intelligence," *Social Frontier*, 1, 4 (January 1936), 16.

19. Selden Rodman, "Why There Is No Youth Movement," *Social Frontier*, 1, 8 (May 1935), 21.

20. *Social Frontier*, 2, 1 (October 1935), 7, 8, 23 (stress added).

21. George Hartman, "A Professor Runs for Office," *Social Frontier*, 1, 7 (April 1935), 26; Harry Fleischman, *Norman Thomas* (New York: W.W. Norton, 1964), Chs. 10–12.

22. Norman Boardman, "Are We Moving Towards a New Social Order?" *Social Frontier*, 1, 9 (June 1935), 21.

23. *Ibid.*, 24.

24. Norman Woefel, "The World We Live In," *Social Frontier*, 1, 9 (June 1935), 31.

25. Henry P. Fairchild, "The Job Insurance Red Herring," *Social Frontier*, 1, 9 (June 1935), 19, 21.

26. Editorial in the *New Republic*, 85, 1099 (December 1935), 183.

27. Florence Becker, "No Matter," *Social Frontier*, 2, 1 (October 1935), 21.

28. *Social Frontier*, 2, 4 (January 1936), 99; see Edward A. Krug, *The Shaping of the American High School, II* (Madison: University of Wisconsin Press, 1972), pp. 252–254.

29. *Social Frontier*, 3, 19 (October 1936), 7 (stress added).

30. *Social Frontier*, 2, 7 (April 1936), 208.

31. Forrest Allen, "A Layman Speaks His Mind," *Social Frontier*, 3, 23 (February 1937), 143, 144 (stress added).

32. *Social Frontier*, 3, 24 (March 1937), 166; *Social Frontier*, 4, 31 (January 1938), 102.

33. *Social Frontier*, 4, 30 (December 1937), 73.

34. *Social Frontier*, 2, 4 (January 1936), 103.

35. Harold Rugg, "Immediate Proposals," *Social Frontier*, 3, 19 (October 1936), 13.

36. *Ibid.*, 14.

37. Russell, Counts, and the superintendent are quoted by Edward A. Krug in *American High School, II*, p. 239; and for a critical look at pedagogical doctrines in the 1930s, see in same, pp. 285–306.

38. Kandel is quoted by Gerald Gutek, *The Educational Theory of George S. Counts* (Columbus: Ohio State University, 1970), pp. 57, 76 (stress added).

39. John Tildsley, "Why I Object to Some Proposals of the Frontier Thinkers," *Social Frontier*, 4, 37 (July 1938), 322.

40. John Dewey, *Democracy in Education* (New York: Free Press, [1916] 1966), p. 144. Counts is quoted by Lawrence Cremin in *The Transformation of the Schools*, (New York: Vintage Books, Random House, 1961), p. 227.

41. Bowers, *The Progressive Educators and the Depression* (New York: Random House, 1969), pp. 164–198.

42. Sidney Hook, *Out of Step* (New York: Harper & Row, 1987), p. 195.

43. Keynes and his *General Theory* need no further comment. Karl Mannheim's seminal work on the sociology of knowledge was implicitly grasped by a single writer in the pages of the *Social Frontier*, Joseph K. Hart, "City Dwellers with Small-Town Minds," *Social Frontier*, 3, 21 (December 1936), 73–75; see Karl Mannheim, *Ideology and Utopia* (New York: Harvest Books, [1936] 1967), especially part 5. See also Kenneth Burke, *Permanence and Change* (Indianapolis: Bobbs-Merrill, 1935), which

touched upon Veblen's "trained incapacity," which obscured our ability to see the unfamiliar. Also see Peter Marris, *Loss and Change* (New York: Pantheon Books, 1974), for an exposition on the inflexible nature of personal change that is rooted in biology and psychology.

44. Quoted in Ray Ginger's *Altgeld's America* (Chicago: Quadrangle Books, 1965), p. 1.

Chapter 3

1. James Agee and Walker Evans, *Let Us Now Praise Famous Men* (Boston: Houghton Mifflin, [1941] 1960), p. 44.

2. For Prohibition's repeal, see *New York Times*, April 6, 1933, p. 1. On Alabama's schools, see *New York Times*, April 23, 1933, II, p. 1.

3. *Ibid.*

4. *Ibid.*

5. *New York Times*, April 16, 1933, IV, p. 7.

6. *New York Times*, May 14, 1933, IV, p. 6; March 26, 1933, IV, p. 7.

7. *New York Times*, January 3, 1934, p. 6; August 2, 1933, p. 13; March 15, 1933, p. 15.

8. *New York Times*, January 26, 1934, p. 19.

9. *New York Times*, December 20, 1933, p. 18; March 16, 1933, p. 20; November 2, 1933, p. 23; November 23, 1933, p. 3.

10. *New York Times*, October 12, 1933, p. 21; January 5, 1934, p. 3.

11. *New York Times*, June 6, 1933, p. 25. In the spirit of dual unionism, communists and Lovestoneites sponsored unemployed and unappointed teachers' organizations to embarrass the Teachers Union. See Robert W. Iversen, *The Communists and the Schools* (New York: Harcourt, Brace, 1959), p. 34.

12. Robert A. Caro, *The Power Broker* (New York: Alfred A. Knopf, 1974), pp. 325–327. For the 1970s New York City fiscal debacle, also predicated on fiscal sleights-of-hands, see Steven R. Weisman, "How New York Became a Fiscal Junkie," *New York Times Magazine*, August 17, 1975, pp. 8–9ff., and for a collateral article, see Damon Stetson, "Pensions by City Rated Generous," *New York Times*, July 6, 1975, p. 1.

13. *New York Times*, April 15, 1934, II, p. 3; January 6, 1934, p. 1; January 13, 1934, p. 27; Sol Cohen, *Progressives and Urban School Reform* (New York: Teachers College, 1963), p. 171.

14. *New York Times*, January 18, 1934, p. 20; February 2, 1934, p. 16 (Fannie Biggs' letter to the *Times*).

15. *New York Times*, January 5, 1933, p. 14; January 6, 1933, p. 18.

16. *New York Times*, November 1, 1934, p. 1, for the Hopkins quotation; "The Teachers School Relief Fund of New York City and the Hofstadter Committee," *School and Society*, 35 (March 12, 1932), 358–359; "Gifts by Teachers," *School and Society*, 35 (February 6, 1932), 181–182. For the Seabury investigation of the Jimmy Walker administration, see Arthur Mann, *La Guardia Comes to Power* (Philadelphia: J.B. Lippincott, 1965), pp. 51–62.

17. *New York Times*, March 8, 1933, p. 15.

18. *New York Times*, April 1, 1933, p. 17.

19. *New York Times*, January 6, 1933, p. 18; March 2, 1933, p. 16 (stress added).

20. Givens quoted in Howard K. Beale, *A History of Freedom of Teaching* (New York: Charles Scribner's Sons, 1936), p. 273.

21. W.H. McKeever, "The Forgotten Classroom Teacher," *Journal of Education*, 116 (May 1, 1933), 224–225.

22. Replies to McKeever, *Journal of Education*, 116 (May 15, 1933), 255, 271.

23. *New York Times*, February 17, 1933, p. 21 (stress added).

24. *New York Times*, July 2, 1933, p. 6 (stress added); January 6, 1933, p. 21.

25. *New York Times*, January 22, 1934, p. 17.

26. *Ibid.*; *New York Times*, August 8, 1934, p. 12.

27. *New York Times*, January 22, 1934, p. 17.

28. *New York Times*, February 6, 1934, p. 20; January 30, 1934, p. 18.

29. *New York Times*, February 18, 1934, II, p. 2.

30. *New York Times*, November 23, 1933, p. 1. See Diane Ravitch, *The Great School Wars* (New York: Basic Books, 1974), pp. 107–158, 189–230.

31. *New York Times*, November 26, 1933, VIII, p. 4; also November 27, 1933, p. 16.

32. See Ray Ginger, *Altgeld's America* (Chicago: Quadrangle Books, 1965), pp. 89–112; Richard Hofstadter, *The Age of Reform* (New York: Alfred A. Knopf, 1955), pp. 180–184; *New York Times*, November 16, 1933, p. 25; Diane Ravitch, *School Wars*, pp. 181–186; David Tyack, "Centralization of Control in City Schools at the Turn of the Century" (1971); and Joseph M. Cronin, "The Centralization of the Boston Public Schools" (1971), both papers delivered at the American Educational Research Association, New York City (February 5, 1971). On the uses and gradations of graft, see James Q. Wilson, "Corruption Need Not Be Scandalous," *New York Times Magazine*, April 28, 1968.

33. *New York Times*, May 28, 1933, II, p. 2; February 2, 1934, p. 16.

34. *New York Times*, May 28, 1933, II, p. 2; May 16, 1933, p. 3. See Albert Halper, "Comrade Rivera Gets the Business," *Good-bye, Union Square* (Chicago: Quadrangle Books, 1970), pp. 89–97.

35. *New York Times*, April 25, 1933, p. 19; *Seattle Times*, September 24, 1934, p. 1, and September 25, 1934, p. 1.

36. *New York Times*, October 9, 1934, p. 2.

37. *New York Times*, April 25, 1933, p. 1. See also David Tyack et al., *Public Schools in Hard Times* (Cambridge: Harvard University Press, 1984), pp. 43–45, 86–88.

38. J. Stephen Hazlett, "NEA and NCA Involvement in a School Controversy: Chicago, 1944–47," *School Review*, 78, 2 (February 1970), 202–205.

39. *New York Times*, August 26, 1934, II, p. 6; August 29, 1934, p. 16.

40. *New York Times*, September 9, 1934, IV, p. 6.

41. *Ibid.*

42. Avis D. Carlson, "Deflating the Schools," *Harper's*, 167 (November 1933), 709 (stress added).

43. Interview with Carl Foulk in Seattle, February 25, 1969, recalling his teaching days in Kansas during the Depression.

44. *New York Times*, October 2, 1933, p. 21; for an exploration of black and white schools at the turn of the century, see Louis R. Harlan, *Separate and Unequal* (New York: Atheneum, 1968), Chs. 1 and 3; Cremin, *Transformation of the School*, pp. 82–85, 145–146.

45. Quoted in *Seattle Educational Bulletin* [Seattle Public Schools], 8, 3 (May 1932).

46. *New York Times*, January 6, 1933, p. 21.

47. *Ibid.*; *New York Times*, February 27, 1933, p. 16.

48. *New York Times*, April 6, 1933, p. 4. In Denmark the school leaving age was raised by one year to check the increase in national unemployment, *New York Times*, January 19, 1933, p. 8.

49. *New York Times*, March 2, 1933, p. 18.

50. *New York Times*, May 28, 1933, p. 2; February 26, 1933, II, p. 1. On the WPA Federal Writers' Project, see Jerre Mangione, *The Dream and the Deal* (Boston: Little, Brown, 1973).

51. *New York Times*, July 2, 1933, p. 6.

52. *New York Times*, August 23, 1933, p. 4; August 16, 1934, p. 1.

53. *New York Times*, October 14, 1933, p. 3 (stress added).

54. *New York Times*, May 28, 1933, p. 2; February 26, 1933, II, p. 1; February 5, 1933, VIII, p. 4.

55. *New York Times*, January 6, 1933, p. 21; "The Growing Cost of Education," *Nation's Business*, 20, No. 3 (March 1932), 15 (stress added).

56. *New York Times*, April 28, 1933, p. 19. For Hearst's campaign to rid the schools of "reds," see Robert W. Iversen, *Communists and the Schools*, pp. 184–188; and Alfred Kazin, *Starting Out in the Thirties* (Boston: Little, Brown, 1965), especially Ch. 3.

57. *New York Times*, April 22, 1933, p. 14.

58. *New York Times*, August 23, 1933, p. 4; August 25, 1933, p. 2; August 27, 1933, IV, p. 7. See Robert W. Iversen, *Communists and the Schools*, for the fractional politics among teacher groups in New York City, pp. 34–56.

59. "Meeting the Emergency in Education," National Education Association, Department of Secondary School Principals, *Bulletin*, 46 (April 1933), 13.

60. *Ibid.*, 3.

61. *Ibid.*, 16, 25.

62. Robert and Helen Lynd, *Middletown in Transition* (New York: Harcourt, Brace, 1937), p. 229 (stress added).

63. *Ibid.*, pp. 228, 230, 206 (stress added).

64. *Ibid.*, p. 225.

65. *New York Times*, December 25, 1933, p. 1.

Chapter 4

1. *New York Times*, March 30, 1934, p. 20.

2. *New York Times*, January 13, 1935, II, p. 3; February 3, 1935, II, p. 3.

3. Sol Cohen, *Progressives and Urban School Reform* (New York: Teachers College, 1963), p. 160.

4. *New York Times*, May 27, 1937, p. 25.

5. *New York Times*, November 15, 1940, p. 23.

6. *Ibid.*

7. Quoted by Howard K. Beale, in *Are American Teachers Free?* (New York: Charles Scribner's Sons, 1936), p. 685.

8. *New York Times*, January 11, 1937, p. 12. For a discussion of the changing role of the superintendent, see my "Public Schools in Search of Legitimacy, 1900–1929" (Ph.D. dissertation, University of Washington, 1971), Ch. 2.

9. *New York Times*, December 6, 1937, p. 6 (stress added).

10. Robert Lynd and Helen Lynd, *Middletown in Transition* (New York: Harcourt, Brace, 1937), p. 222.

11. Sol Cohen, *Progressives and Urban School Reform*, pp. 123–126.

12. Quoted by Howard K. Beale in, *Are American Teachers Free?* (New York: Charles Scribner's Sons, 1936), p. 685.

13. *New York Times*, February 25, 1937, p. 25.

14. *New York Times*, May 21, 1935, p. 14; May 9, 1937, II, p. 7; September 27, 1937, p. 23.

15. *New York Times*, January 17, 1936, p. 21; January 20, 1936, p. 20; January 22, 1936, p. 12; July 1, 1937, p. 29; and a *Times* editorial on July 2, 1937, p. 20.

16. Quoted by Sol Cohen in *Progressives and Urban School Reform*, p. 165.

17. *New York Times*, August 1, 1937, II, p. 5.

18. Edward A. Krug, *The Shaping of the American High School, II* (Madison: University of Wisconsin Press, 1964), p. 280.

19. *New York Times*, October 24, 1937, II, p. 6.

20. *New York Times*, March 26, 1939, III, p. 2.

21. See Jane Addams, *The Spirit of Youth and the City Streets* (New York:

Macmillan, 1909); Robert Hunter, *Poverty* (New York: Harper Torchbooks, Harper & Row, [1904] 1965), p. 208. See also Leonard Covello, *The Heart is a Teacher* (New York: McGraw-Hill, 1958) for a sprightly account of his years as a teacher and principal in New York City.

22. *New York Times*, November 28, 1937, II, p. 5; February 2, 1934, p. 16.

23. *New York Times*, December 20, 1937, p. 2; November 26, 1938, p. 17; May 28, 1939, III, p.3.

24. *New York Times*, June 8, 1938, p. 25; June 20, 1938, p. 17; July 6, 1939, p. 25. For a discussion of the birth of the junior high school, see my "Public Schools in Search of Legitimacy," pp. 111–114.

25. *New York Times*, October 25, 1939, p. 23.

26. *New York Times*, February 8, 1938, p. 23; May 20, 1938, p. 21; January 30, 1938, II, p. 1; for a biographical sketch of Mrs. Johanna M. Lindlof, see January 8, 1939, IV, p. 2.

27. *New York Times*, January 6, 1938, p. 21; Leonard Covello recalled how the city schools' speech examination given during the Depression served to deny entry of otherwise talented individuals into teaching, *Urban Review*, 3 (January 1969), 18.

28. *New York Times*, February 9, 1938, p. 15 (stress added).

29. *New York Times*, October 18, 1937, p. 19; May 19, 1934, p. 7.

30. *New York Times*, January 7, 1935, p. 16 (stress added).

31. *New York Times*, June 19, 1935, p. 17; January 11, 1936, p. 1; February 14, 1936, p. 21; September 25, 1936, p. 19; February 4, 1937, p. 2.

32. *New York Times*, May 25, 1933, p. 3; July 12, 1933, p. 2; June 1, 1933. p. 19; June 29, 1933, p. 21.

33. *New York Times*, March 14, 1935, p. 21. For the political affiliations of Begun and Burroughs, see Robert W. Iversen, *The Communists and the Schools* (New York: Harcourt, Brace, 1959), pp. 27, 46; for another view, see Celia L. Zitron, *The New York City Teachers Union* (New York: Humanities Press, 1968), pp. 177–180.

34. *New York Times*, August 23, 1935, p. 4; August 24, 1935, p. 17; August 29, 1935, p. 23.

35. *New York Times*, August 30, 1935, p. 18; September 6, 1935, p. 19; October 10, 1935, p. 7.

36. *New York Times*, July 25, 1935, p. 15.

37. *New York Times*, April 3, 1928, p. 18; April 19, 1928, p. 51; May 15, 1929, p. 34; for biographical information on Dr. Emil Altman, see September 12, 1942, p. 13.

38. *New York Times*, March 27, 1934, p. 3; March 28, 1934, pp. 25, 21; March 29, 1934, p. 3.

39. *New York Times*, March 29, 1934, p. 22; March 30, 1934, p. 20.

40. *New York Times*, May 12, 1936, p. 25.

41. *New York Times*, May 27, 1936, p. 25.

42. *New York Times*, June 5, 1936, p. 6: January 4, 1938, p. 3.

43. *New York Times*, February 7, 1939, p. 21; February 19, 1939, p. 10; March 31, 1939, p. 23.

44. *New York Times*, June 17, 1939, p. 17; July 23, 1939, II, p. 5.

45. *New York Times*, August 12, 1939, p. 15.

46. *New York Times*, September 28, 1939, p. 27.

47. *New York Times*, October 15, 1939, II, p. 6.

48. *New York Times*, November 27, 1939, p. 18; November 30, 1939, p. 44; March 20, 1940, p. 24.

49. See Eric Goldman, *The Crucial Decade—And After, 1945–1960* (New York: Vintage Books, Random House, 1960), p. 142; see *New York Times*, September 12, 1942, p. 13, for Dr. Emil Altman's obituary.

Chapter 5

1. *Seattle Times*, March 13, 1939, p 1.

2. Raymond E. Callahan, *Education and the Cult of Efficiency* (Chicago: Phoenix Books, University of Chicago Press, 1962); see James Hoetker and William P. Ahlbrand, Jr., "The Persistence of the Recitation," *American Educational Research Journal*, 6 (March 1969), 163.

3. Francis M. Morris, "A History of Teacher Unionism in the State of Washington, 1920–1945" (Masters' thesis, University of Washington, 1968), pp. 36, 38–39, 40, 38.

4. *Ibid.*, p. 43.

5. *Ibid.*, p. 47.

6. *Ibid.*, p. 59.

7. Robert L. Friedheim, *The Seattle General Strike* (Seattle: University of Washington Press, 1964), pp. 180, 153; Francis M. Morris, "Teacher Unionism," p. 72. In the throes of the Depression and with the Teachers Union disbanded, the school board rescinded the "yellow-dog" contract stipulation on January 2, 1931, without comment, in Morris, *idem*, p. 73.

8. *Seattle Educational Bulletin*, [Seattle Public Schools], 7, No. 1 (September 1930); for biographical information on Worth McClure see *Seattle Times*, August 21, 1962, p. 41.

9. *Seattle Educational Bulletin*, 8, No. 1 (September 1931).

10. *Seattle Educational Bulletin*, 9, No. 1 (September 1932).

11. *Seattle Educational Bulletin*, 6, No. 1 (September 1929) (stress added). For a discussion of the Gary Plan see my "Public Schools in Search of Legitimacy" (Ph.D. dissertation, University of Washington, 1971), Ch. 5; see also Diane Ravitch, *The Great School Wars*, pp. 197–228, for Superintendent Wirt's attempt to implement his ideas in New York City schools; for contemporary accounts, see John Dewey and Evelyn Dewey, *Schools of Tomorrow* (New York: E.P. Dutton, [1915] 1962), Ch. 7; Randolph Bourne, *The Gary Schools* (Boston: Houghton Mifflin, 1916). For a critical look at the Gary Plan, see Abraham Flexner and Frank P. Bachman, *The Gary Schools* (New York: General Education Board, 1918).

12. *Seattle Educational Bulletin*, 6, No. 4 (December 1929).

13. *Seattle Educational Bulletin*, 6, No. 6 (February 1930).

14. *Seattle Educational Bulletin*, 8, No. 2 (February 1932).

15. *Seattle Educational Bulletin*, 9, No. 1 (September 1932) (stress added).

16. Francis M. Morris, "Teacher Unionism," p. 75.

17. Interview with Parker Cook on February 4, 1969, on his recollections of the Depression and its effects upon his life and teaching at Garfield High School, Seattle.

18. *Seattle Educational Bulletin*, 9, No. 1 (September 1932). Francis M. Morris, "Teacher Unionism," p. 76; *Seattle Post-Intelligencer*, May 27, 1933, p. 5, and May 25, 1933, p. 15.

19. *Seattle Educational Bulletin*, 10, No. 1 (March 1934).

20. *Seattle Times*, September 1, 1934, p. 1; September 24, 1934, p. 3.

21. *Seattle Times*, September 26, 1934, p. 1 (stress added); *Seattle Educational Bulletin*, 11, No. 2 (December 1934).

22. *Seattle Educational Bulletin*, 10, No. 3 (June 1934).

23. *Ibid.*; *Seattle Educational Bulletin*, 10, No. 1 (March 1934).

24. *Seattle Educational Bulletin*, 11, No. 4 (June 1935) (stress added).

25. *Ibid.*

26. *Seattle Educational Bulletin*, 12, No. 2 (December 1935).

27. *Annual Report of the Public Schools*, Seattle School District No. 1, June 30, 1938, p. 24.

28. *Seattle Educational Bulletin*, 12, No. 4 (June 1936).

29. *New York Times*, August 17, 1933, p. 17; *Annual Financial Reports, 1931–1939*, Seattle School District No. 1 (1939); see Table A7 for the Seattle Public Schools expenditures on textbooks. For New York City schools' restoration of its textbook budget, see *New York Times*, September 13, 1940, p. 18.

30. Michael B. Katz, "American History Textbooks and Social Reform in the 1930s," *Paedagogica Historica*, 6, 1 (1966), 158, 160; see also David Tyack et al., *Public Schools in Hard Times*, p. 65. Also, David Tyack, *The One Best System* (Cambridge: Harvard University Press, 1974). *Social Frontier* 2, No. 8 (May 1936), 257.

31. *Triennial Report of the Seattle Public Schools, 1924–1927* (1927) Seattle, p. ix.

32. *Seattle Educational Bulletin*, 6, No. 9 (June 1929); 7, No. 1 (September 1930).

33. *Seattle Educational Bulletin*, 13, No. 3 (January 1937); 13, 5 (March 1937).

34. *Seattle Municipal League News*, 29, 9 (March 1939), 4.

35. *Seattle Times*, March 13, 1939, p. 1.

36. *Annual Reports of the Public Schools*, Seattle School District No. 1, June 30, 1938, p. 25, and June 30, 1939, p. 4.

Chapter 6

1. *New York Times*, February 2, 1939, p. 21.

2. Quoted by Howard K. Beale in *Are American Teachers Free?* (New York: Charles Scribner's Sons, 1941), p. 685.

3. *New York Times*, November 9, 1935, p. 17.

4. *New York Times*, June 13, 1935, p. 25; April 2, 1936, p. 15.

5. *New York Times*, October 29, 1935, p. 23.

6. *New York Times*, January 31, 1935, p. 18; February 14, 1936, p. 21; July 24, 1936, p. 19.

7. *New York Times*, April 14, 1937, II, p. 7; May 23, 1937, II, p. 10; April 4, 1937, II, p. 7; June 17, 1938, p. 23; June 9, 1938, p. 1; June 11, 1938, p. 17; July 23, 1938, p. 15.

8. *New York Times*, October 1, 1936, p. 21.

9. *New York Times*, February 2, 1939, p. 21.

10. *Ibid.* (stress added).

11. New York Times, February 3, 1939, p. 17. During the winter/spring of 1939, the author attended PS 123.

12. *Ibid.*; *New York Times*, February 4, 1939, p. 17.

13. *Ibid.* (stress added).

14. *New York Times*, February 8, 1939, p. 25 (stress added).

15. *New York Times*, February 9, 1939, p. 13; February 10, 1939, p. 25.

16. *New York Times*, February 11, 1939, p. 17.

17. *New York Times*, February 15, 1939, p. 25; February 16, 1939, p. 23; February 17, 1939, p. 20.

18. *New York Times*, February 18, 1939, p. 17; February 22, 1939, p. 23.

19. *New York Times*, March 4, 1939, p. 1. Perhaps public officials in New York City were influenced less by the lessons of Hitler and Mussolini than by the remarkable presence of Robert Moses, master builder of parks, roads, bridges and beaches, who surely "got things done" his way. See Robert Caro, "The Power Broker: Robert Moses," *The New Yorker*, August 12, 1974, pp. 40ff., and Caro's *The Power Broker* (New York: Alfred A. Knopf, 1974).

20. *New York Times*, March 4, 1939, p. 1; March 5, 1939, p. 5.

21. *New York Times*, March 6, 1939, p. 16; March 7, 1939, p. 8.

22. *New York Times*, March 7, 1939, p. 8; March 8, 1939, p. 13; March 9, 1939, p. 23; March 11, 1939, p. 19.

23. *New York Times*, March 14, 1939, p. 23; March 15, 1939, p. 25.

24. *New York Times*, September 22, 1936, p. 3; September 27, 1936, p. 13.

25. *New York Times*, September 29, 1936, p. 29; October 1, 1936, p.28; October 2, 1936, p. 20.

26. *New York Times*, April 2, 1936, p. 5; May 7, 1935, p. 9; September 26, 1936, p. 7; September 29, 1936, p. 29; October 2, 1936, p. 23.

27. *New York Times*, April 17, 1936, p. 23; April 22, 1936, p. 20.

28. *New York Times*, May 12, 1938, p. 13; May 13, 1938, p. 3; May 14, 1938, p. 32.

29. *New York Times*, April 2, 1936, p. 5; April 9, 1936, p. 9; April 17, 1936, p. 23; April 21, 1936, p. 48; May 26, 1938, p. 27.

30. *New York Times*, May 27, 1938, p. 16.

31. For the classic work on progressive schools, see Ann Shumaker and Harold Rugg, *The Child Centered School* (New York: World Book, 1928); Lawrence Cremin, *The Transformation of the School* (New York: Vintage Books, Random House, 1961), pp. 276–290. Cremin on pp. 276–277 questions the "popular misconception" that private schools were the principal source of progressive curricula, but he does not persuade.

32. *New York Times*, November 1, 1938, p. 13.

33. *New York Times*, April 3, 1934, p. 20.

34. *New York Times*, June 11, 1933, IV, p. 5; April 18, 1934, p. 2; April 11, 1934, p. 20.

35. *New York Times*, July 23, 1935, p. 21; January 23, 1938, II, p. 4; January 19, 1939, p. 10.

36. *New York Times*, February 27, 1939, p. 17 (stress added).

37. *New York Times*, March 6, 1939, p. 14.

38. *New York Times*, March 26, 1937, p. 11; October 4, 1937, p. 14; November 30, 1937, p. 19; June 28, 1938, p. 22.

39. *New York Times*, July 21, 1938, p. 23; September 5, 1938, p. 15; September 21, 1938, p. 26.

40. *New York Times*, November 10, 1938, p. 3.

41. *New York Times*, November 29, 1938, p. 25.

42. *New York Times*, editorial, November 30, 1938, p. 22.

Chapter 7

1. Raymond Fisher, "It's My Turn," *Social Frontier*, 4, No. 35 (May 1938), 249.

2. Horace Mann quoted by Charles Burgess and Merle Borrowman in *What Doctrines to Embrace* (Glenview, Ill.: Scott, Foresman, 1969), p. 33 (stress added).

3. Lawrence Cremin, ed., *The Republic and the School: Horace Mann on the Education of Free Men* (New York: Teachers College Press, 1957), pp. 87, 52 (stress added).

4. Mary Mann, ed., *Annual Reports on Education by Horace Mann, III* (Boston: Horace B. Fuller, 1868), p. 57 (stress added).

5. Ellwood P. Cubberley, *Changing Conceptions of Education* (Boston: Houghton Mifflin, 1909), p. 68.

6. J.M. Stephens, *The Process of Schooling* (New York: Holt, Rinehart and Winston, 1967), p. 140; F.W. Hewes, "The Public Schools of the United States," *Harper's Weekly*, 39 (October 26, 1895), 1020; *Harper's Weekly*, 39 (November 2, 1895), 1041.

7. David Felmley, "Is the Employment of Untrained Teachers the Cause or Result of Low Salaries?" National Education Association, *Proceedings*, 47 (1909), 307, 308 (stress added).

8. Federal Security Agency, Office of Education, *Statistics of State School Systems*, 1945–1946 (Washington: Government Printing Office, 1949), p. 36; *New York Times*, October 22, 1939, II, p. 6; July 29, 1933, p. 13.

9. *New York Times*, July 16, 1934, p. 12.

10. *New York Times*, February 28, 1936, p. 17: February 25, 1936, p. 10; April 1, 1934, p. 1.

11. *New York Times*, April 8, 1934, IV, p. 5; May 9, 1934, p. 18 (stress added).

12. *New York Times*, May 7, 1934, p. 19.

13. *New York Times*, May 17, 1934, p. 22; May 13, 1934, IV, p. 5; May 8, 1934, p. 25.

14. *New York Times*, January 9, 1938, II, p. 1.

15. *Ibid.*

16. Horace Mann, *A Few Thoughts on the Powers and Duties of Women, Two Lectures* (Syracuse: Hall, Mills, 1853), p. 10.

17. *New York Times*, January 9, 1938, II, p. 1.

18. *New York Times*, July 17, 1935, p. 15.

19. *New York Times*, November 15, 1935, p. 25.

20. *New York Times*, December 12, 1935, p. 2; March 14, 1936, p. 13.

21. *New York Times*, March 27, 1940, p. 23; April 3, 1940, p. 25.

22. *New York Times*, July 24, 1935, p. 19.

23. *New York Times*, January 6, 1933, p. 10; July 18, 1935, p. 1; July 19, 1935, p. 16.

24. *New York Times*, October 20, 1933, p. 9; July 2, 1936, p. 23; May 20, 1938, p. 21.

25. *New York Times*, January 13, 1934, p. 2; May 20, 1935, p. 19.

26. *New York Times*, May 1, 1938, IV, p. 10; June 26, 1935, p. 12; July 31, 1935, p. 20; February 10, 1937, p. 25.

27. *New York Times*, November 24, 1935, p. 3; February 24, 1936, p. 19; April 22, 1937, p. 13; January 24, 1937, p. 29; February 25, 1937, p. 25; January 8, 1939, p. 3.

28. *New York Times*, December 6, 1939, p. 52; December 7, 1939, p. 26.

29. *New York Times*, March 5, 1939, p. 21.

30. Raymond Fisher, "It's My Turn," p. 249.

31. J.M. Stephens, *Process of Schooling*, p. 124.

32. Howard K. Beale, *A History of Freedom of Teaching in American Schools* (New York: Charles Scribner's Sons, 1941), pp. 244, 245.

33. *New York Times*, September 28, 1939, p. 27; March 20, 1940, p. 29; March 21, 1940, p. 27; March 22, 1940, p. 21; July 11, 1940, p. 19; November 13, 1940, p. 25.

34. *New York Times*, January 26, 1939, p. 40.

35. *New York Times*, June 12, 1939, p. 18; June 29, 1939, p. 24; September 19, 1939, p. 27.

36. *New York Times*, September 24, 1939, II, p. 7.

Chapter 8

1. *New York Times*, November 19, 1937, p. 25.

2. *New York Times*, July 1, 1938, p. 2.

3. *Ibid.*

4. *New York Times*, April 21, 1937, p. 1; April 28, 1937, p. 15. See also S.E. Morison and H.S. Commager, *The Growth of the American Republic, II* (New York: Oxford University Press, 1950), on p. 622, where the authors allude to the recession of 1937, but on p. 626 they suggest that by 1938 the domestic New Deal had been "rounded out." Also see Caroline Bird, *The Invisible Scar* (New York: David McKay,

1966), where she notes on p. 226 that "the Recession of 1937 ended the New Deal." For the National Education Association's attempt to secure no-string federal aid to education, see David Tyack et al., *Public Schools in Hard Times* (Cambridge: Harvard University Press, 1984), pp. 99–103.

5. *New York Times*, December 31, 1939, II, p. 5.

6. *Ibid.*; *New York Times*; October 10, 1939, p. 25.; December 26, 1939, p. 21.

7. *New York Times*, July 7, 1938, p. 21; November 23, 1933, p. 3; January 17, 1937, II, p. 1. See Diane Ravitch, *The Great School Wars* (New York: Basic Books, 1974), p. 168, where she discusses Superintendent William H. Maxwell's noble intention to secure a seat for every student.

8. For a discussion of Hopkins, see Robert E. Sherwood, *Roosevelt and Hopkins* (New York: Harper & Bros., 1948), Ch. 3; for WPA and PWA expenditures, see Harold U. Faulkner, *American Economic History*, 6th ed. (New York: Harper & Bros., 1949), p. 677; *New York Times*, February 28, 1937, II, p. 1.

9. *New York Times*, June 23, 1937, p. 1; July 10, 1937, p. 17; July 15, 1939, p. 1.

10. *New York Times*, January 16, 1938, II, p. 5.

11. *Ibid.* See also Amitai Etzioni,"Human Beings Are Not Very Easy to Change," *Saturday Review* (June 3, 1972), 45–47; also Alice M. Rivlin, *Systematic Thinking for Social Action* (Washington, D.C.: The Brookings Institution, 1971), p. 69, where she writes that "even the liberals are no longer sure they would know what to do if they had more to spend for social services, *or that it would do much good"* (stress added).

12. *New York Times*, July 5, 1938, p. 15. Aside from the innovations of the WPA, the only other educational experiment was the "Eight Year Study of Secondary Education," see Edward H. Krug, *The Shaping of the American High School, II* (Madison: University of Wisconsin Press, 1964), pp. 255–284, and Lawrence Cremin, *The Transformation of the School* (New York: Vintage Books, Random House, 1961), pp. 251–258. See also David Tyack et al., *Public Schools in Hard Times*, pp. 129–132.

13. *New York Times*, June 5, 1938, p. 2; October 30, 1938, p. 33; June 8, 1937, p. 18; June 28, 1939, p. 19; June 11, 1938, p. 17; June 5, 1938, II, p. 5; see also Sol Cohen, *Progressives and Urban School Reform* (New York: Teachers College, 1963), p. 152, where he writes tellingly that "so far as WPA is concerned, its full impact has yet to be calculated."

14. *New York Times*, March 2, 1938, p. 41.

15. *New York Times*, September 19, 1938, p. 21; May 18, 1939, p. 27.

16. *New York Times*, January 3, 1939, p. 8; December 15, 1935, p. 33; June 25, 1939, p. 15; January 23, 1938, p. 8; January 31, 1938, II, p. 5.

17. *New York Times*, February 23, 1936, p. 16; February 24, 1938, p. 1.

18. *New York Times*, March 1, 1938, p. 17; July 13, 1938, p. 44.

19. *New York Times*, March 1, 1939, p. 15; May 20, 1939, p. 16.

20. *New York Times*, September 15, 1937, p. 8; January 16, 1939, p. 1.

21. *New York Times*, February 25, 1936, p. 10; June 30, 1936, p. 20; January 2, 1938, II, p. 5; January 20, 1939, p. 16; July 6, 1939, p. 21; August 16, 1939, p. 16.

22. *New York Times*, January 7, 1939, p. 2.

23. *New York Times*, March 6, 1938, II, p. 6; March 16, 1939, p.3.

24. *New York Times*, February 14, 1937, II, p. 4; January 16, 1937, p. 36. Since the 1960s with countless teenage runaways, the question of fingerprinting young people has recurred. See David Stipp, "Many Topeka, Kans., Parents Want Police to Fingerprint Their Kids," *Wall Street Journal*, January 17, 1983, p. 19.

25. *New York Times*, November 24, 1936, p. 22; December 15, 1939, p. 18; March 17, 1937, p. 5; April 26, 1938, p. 9.

26. *New York Times*, November 26, 1936, p. 30; December 1, 1936, p. 24; December 6, 1936, IV, p. 9; November 26, 1937, p. 20.

27. *New York Times*, November 19, 1937, p. 25.

28. *New York Times*, March 1, 1936, p. 33; December 24, 1933, IV, p. 7.

29. *New York Times*, May 3, 1936, XI, p. 13.

30. Avis D.Carlson, "Deflating the Schools," *Harper's*, 167 (November 1933), 714.

31. *New York Times*, March 7, 1936, p. 14; April 12, 1936, IV, p. 9; August 26, 1936, p. 12; September 9, 1936, p. 16.

32. *New York Times*, September 10, 1936, p. 24; October 14, 1936, p. 1.

33. Saul Alinsky, *John L. Lewis* (New York: G.P. Putnam's Sons, 1949), pp. 93, 94–147, 155–156, 159, 177; C.L. Sulzberger, *Sit-Down with John L. Lewis* (New York: Random House, 1938), p. 115. As to the earlier use of the sit-down strike see Lucy Parson's advocacy of the tactic to the Wobblies in Patrick Renshaw, *The Wobblies* (New York: Doubleday, 1967), p. 85.

34. *New York Times*, February 4, 1937, p. 20; April 13, 1937, p. 1; June 15, 1937, p. 19; February 28, 1939, p. 1.

35. C.L. Sulzberger, *Sit-Down With John L. Lewis*, p. 58. Also, Saul Aliinsky, *John L. Lewis* (New York: G.P. Putnam's Sons, 1949), pp. 94–147. See *New York Times*, July 24 1936, p. 19.

Chapter 9

1. Robert Lynd and Helen Lynd, *Middletown in Transition* (New York: Harcourt, Brace, 1937), p. 225.

2. *New York Times*, January 3, 1937, II, p. 1; January 16, 1937, p. 19; January 23, 1937, p. 2; April 8, 1937, p. 1; January 1, 1937, p. 1; May 31, 1937, p. 1; July 3, 1937, p. 5. See S.E. Morison and H.S. Commager, *The Growth of the American Republic*, II (New York: Oxford University Press, 1950), on p. 622, where they observe that 1936 "was a year, too, of widespread industrial disorder and of declining wages." For FDR's preoccupation with foreign affairs, see Chapter 26 in the same work.

3. *New York Times*, November 27, 1939, p. 12; March 12, 1938, p. 19.

4. *New York Times*, January 2, 1938, II, p. 5; January 13, 1939, p. 14.

5. *New York Times*, May 15, 1936, p. 52; October 11, 1936, II, p. 2; February 2, 1937, p. 25; January 14, 1938, p. 11; May 15, 1939, p. 4; February 16, 1939, p. 23; August 2, 1939, p. 7.

6. *New York Times*, April 16, 1939, p. 2; April 17, 1939, p. 14; February 4, 1939, p. 2.

7. *New York Times*, June 3, 1939, p. 13; October 16, 1937, p. 9.

8. *New York Times*, May 3, 1939, p. 6; January 19, 1939, p. 12.

9. *New York Times*, October 28, 1938, p. 12; October 29, 1938, p. 1.

10. *New York Times*, October 29, 1938, p. 18; October 30, 1938, p. 32 (stress added).

11. *New York Times*, November 2, 1938, p. 8; November 3, 1938, p. 24; November 21, 1938, p. 11; November 16, 1939, p. 28; November 23, 1939, p. 37; January 3, 1940, p. 19. Note that the voters of Ohio in the later 1960s reenacted their experiences of the 1930s. After school levies had been defeated twice, the school board of Fremont, Ohio, ordered the schools closed for seven weeks. Also the Youngstown schools had been closed for five weeks the preceding winter after the voters had defeated the school levy *six times consecutively*, *New York Times*, October 5, 1969, p. 56. In addition, other school districts in Ohio had closed their schools in November 1969, with closures of three weeks in rural areas, New York Times, January 4, 1970, p. 50.

12. *New York Times*, March 4, 1937, p. 25; March 11, 1937, p. 25; March 14, 1937, p. 42. For an examination of progressive education and its reputed impact on the public schools see Lawrence Cremin, *The Transformation of the School* (New

York: Vintage Books Random House, 1961), Chs. 1–5; also John and Evelyn Dewey, *Schools of Tomorrow* (New York: E.P. Dutton, [1915] 1962), and the two classics by John Dewey, *The Child and the Curriculum*, and *School and Society* (Chicago: Phoenix Books, University of Chicago Press, [1900, 1902] 1956); Ann Shumaker and Harold Rugg, *The Child Centered School* (New York: World Book, 1928).

13. *New York Times*, March 9, 1938, p. 25.

14. *Ibid.*

15. *New York Times*, January 25, 1937, p. 21.

16. *Seattle Post-Intelligencer*, November 7, 1932, p. 9.

17. *New York Times*, May 12, 1938, p. 18.

18. *New York Times*, August 13, 1933, II, p. 4. On rural neglect, see Lawrence Cremin, *The Transformation of the School*, pp. 80–85. For the historical ramifications of Jim Crow, see Louis Harlan, *Separate and Unequal* (New York: Atheneum, 1968); for an overview of black urban education up to 1940, see David B. Tyack, *The One Best System* (Cambridge: Harvard University Press, 1974), pp. 217–229; and for a survey of progressive educators' responses to black education, see Ronald Goodenow, "The Progressive Educator, Race and Ethnicity in the Depression," *History of Education Quarterly*, 15, 4 (Winter 1975), 365–394.

19. *New York Times*, March 27, 1936, p. 23; February 28, 1937, p. 24; July 1, 1938, p. 2.

20. *New York Times*, April 6, 1933, p. 4

21. *New York Times*, September 8, 1934, p. 3; October 25, 1934, p. 22; see also Roi Ottley and William J. Weatherby, *The Negro in New York* (New York: Praeger, 1969), p. 265.

22. *New York Times*, March 20, 1935, p. 1; Roi Ottley and William J. Weatherby, *The Negro in New York, op. cit.*, p. 265; *New York Times*, October 29, 1935, p. 23; see also Celia Zitron, *The New York City Teachers Union* (New York: Humanities Press, 1868), pp. 85–88.

23. *New York Times*, November 22, 1935, p. 25; January 23, 1936, p. 19; Celia Zitron, *Teachers Union*, pp. 88–91.

24. *New York Times*, July 1, 1936, p. 2. A backhanded compliment was paid to La Guardia over the administration of black relief in the city. "Negroes made considerable complaints against the manner and amount of relief distributed. But discrimination is a wisp which cannot be nailed down, and investigations of it were never very fruitful, though standardized relief under Mayor La Guardia's administration reduced the number of complaints" in Roi Ottley and William J. Weatherby, *The Negro in New York*, p. 271.

25. *New York Times*, September 15, 1937, p. 25.

26. *New York Times*, June 1, 1938, p. 5; February 27, 1938, p. 6; March 30, 1938, p. 14; Diane Ravitch in *The Great School Wars*, p. 26, wrote a bit prematurely that Governor Theodore Roosevelt "had the legislature pass a law abolishing colored schools in the state."

27. *New York Times*, October 27, 1938, p. 25.

28. *Ibid.*

29. *New York Times*, May 27, 1937, p. 25; August 20, 1939, p. 24; Roi Ottley and William J. Weatherby, *The Negro in New York*, p. 281.

30. *New York Times*, January 21, 1939, p. 2; January 22, 1939, p. 18.

31. *New York Times*, November 23, 1939, p. 34; October 29, 1940, p. 51.

32. *New York Times*, March 1, 1939, p. 15 (stress added).

33. *New York Times*, March 18, 1940, p. 6.

34. *New York Times*, January 13, 1939, p. 6.

35. *New York Times*, January 25, 1939, p. 6.

36. *New York Times*, August 21, 1935, p. 7; September 11, 1935, p. 8.

Chapter 10

1. *New York Times*, July 29, 1939, p. 14 (stress added).

2. *New York Times*, April 30, 1939, pp. 6, 20, 1; March 26, 1939, X, p. 10; August 31, 1939, p. 15.

3. *New York Times*, August 22, 1939, p. 1; August 24, 1939, p. 1; September 1, 1939, p. 1; October 16, 1940, p. 1.

4. *New York Times*, January 7, 1939, p. 1.

5. *New York Times*, January 8, 1939, pp. 13, 41.

6. *New York Times*, March 2, 1939, p. 15; April 27, 1939, p. 27; April 30, 1939, p. 1.

7. For a look at the Public Education Association, see Sol Cohen, *Progressives and Urban School Reform* (New York Teachers College, 1963); for similar ground, see Diane Ravitch, *The Great School Wars* (New York: Basic Books, 1974), Chs. 11–14; for a brief discussion of "keeping politics out of the schools," see my "Public Schools in Search of Legitimacy, 1900–1929" (Ph.D. dissertation, University of Washington, 1971), pp. 14–17.

8. *New York Times*, January 16, 1939, p. 1; March 26, 1939, III, p. 2.

9. *New York Times*, May 4, 1939, p. 25.

10. *New York Times*, April 24, 1939, p. 19; June 16, 1939, p. 12.

11. *New York Times*, June 29, 1939, p. 24; May 29, 1939, p. 14.

12. *New York Times*, June 29, 1939, p. 24.

13. See Arthur Mann, *La Guardia Comes to Power* (Philadelphia: J.B. Lippincott, 1965) While Mann's second volume takes us to the inauguration of La Guardia in 1933, Robert Caro has delineated how gingerly La Guardia dealt with the "power broker" of New York City, Robert Moses. Appointed to numerous public bodies, initially by Governor Alfred Smith, Moses wielded as much, if not more, power than the mayor and did deliver public works. Thus to fire Moses would have led La Guardia, in part, to explain, as Robert Caro has written, the intricacies of "bond resolution contracts to an electorate that wanted Things Gotten Done—and that idolized the Man Who Got Them Done," Robert Caro, "The Power Broker," III, *New Yorker*, August 2, 1974, p. 52. *New York Times*, April 1, 1939, p. 1; April 3, 1939, p. 17; April 19, 1939, p. 25; April 22, 1939, p. 1; April 26, 1939, p. 1.

14. *New York Times*, April 24, 1939, p. 19; May 5, 1939, p. 1.

15. *New York Times*, May 10, 1939, p. 48; June 27, 1939, p. 18.

16. *New York Times*, May 27, 1939, p. 3; June 28, 1939, p. 20; June 16, 1939, p. 12.

17. *New York Times*, June 5, 1939, p. 1; June 6, 1939, p. 1.

18. *New York Times*, June 6, 1939, p. 22 (stress added).

19. *Ibid.*

20. *New York Times*, June 8, 1939, p. 3.

21. *New York Times*, June 12, 1939, p. 1; the respective figures per pupil were for New York, $124; Pennsylvania, $75; New Jersey, $102; Massachusetts, $96 and Connecticut, $82, *New York Times*, June 9, 1939, p. 23.

22. *New York Times*, June 15, 1939, p. 22.

23. *New York Times*, June 15, 1939, p. 1; June 22, 1939, pp. 23, 1.

24. *New York Times*, June 27, 1939, p. 18.

25. *New York Times*, June 23, 1939, p. 2; June 29, 1939, p. 24; June 24 1939, pp. 1, 6; June 23, 1939, p. 2.

26. *New York Times*, July 1, 1939, pp. 2, 1. The Citizens Budget Commission discovered in analyzing school data that of 38,030 permanent employees of the city schools, 2 per cent received less $2,000; 22 per cent received $2,001 to $3,000; 57 percent received $3,001 to $4,000; and 18 percent received more than $4,001. The average salary in 1929 had been $3,141, while in 1939 it was $3,524, *New York Times*, July 10, 1939, p. 6.

27. *New York Times*, July 9, 1939, p. 1; July 11, 1939, p. 35.

28. *New York Times*, July 12, 1939, p. 1. In a salary schedule of 15 steps in New York City schools, the pay of elementary school teachers ranged from $1,608 to $3,390; junior high teachers salaries ranged from $2,040 to $3,830; and for senior high teachers the range was from $2,148 to $4,500, *New York Times*, July 12, 1939, p. 1; July 13, 1939, p. 1.

29. *New York Times*, July 13, 1939, p. 1; June 2, 1939, p. 22.

30. *New York Times*, July 13, 1939, pp. 7, 1; July 14, 1939, p. 21.

31. *New York Times*, July 15, 1939, p. 17; July 17, 1939, p. 1.

32. *New York Times*, July 18, 1939, p. 21; July 20, 1939, p. 21.

33. *New York Times*, July 22, 1939, p. 17.

34. *New York Times*, July 26, 1939, p. 1; July 27, 1939, p. 1.

35. *New York Times*, July 27, 1939, pp. 18, 1.

36. *New York Times*, July 28, 1939, p. 1; July 29, 1939, p. 14.

37. *New York Times*, August 8, 1939, p. 37; September 23, 1939, p. 19; August 1, 1939, p. 21.

38. *New York Times*, August 18, 1939, p. 1; August 19, 1939, p. 1; August 26, 1939, p. 17.

39. *New York Times*, August 15, 1939, p. 15; September 6, 1939, p. 25; September 7, 1939, p. 27; September 8, 1939, p. 25; September 16, 1939, p. 19; September 28, 1939, p. 27.

40. *New York Times*, September 12, 1939, p. 27; September 13, 1939, p. 29; September 14, 1939, p. 24.

41. *New York Times*, September 21, 1939, p. 25; September 14, 1939, p. 1; October 12, 1939, p. 27; October 18, 1939, p. 27.

42. *New York Times*, October 19, 1939, p. 16; October 20, 1939, p. 12.

43. *New York Times*, October 14, 1939, p. 21.

44. *New York Times*, October 18, 1939, p. 29.

45. *New York Times*, November 21, 1939, p. 20. For an examination of the fiscal hi-jinks of the 1960s and the 1970s in New York City, see Steven R. Weisman, "How New York Became a Fiscal Junkie," *New York Times Magazine*, August 17, 1975, pp. 8–9ff.

46. *New York Times*, October 11, 1939, p. 18; October 12, 1939, p. 28; October 22, 1939, p. 39; October 26, 1939, p. 18.

47. S.E. Morison and H.S. Commager, *The Growth of the American Republic*, 2 (New York: Oxford University Press, 1950), pp. 648, 649: *New York Times*, June 8, 1940, p. 34, and June 22, 1940, p. 17. When Miss Ellen S. Matthews, a substitute teacher, was denied reappointment, she did not go quietly into the night as she proceeded to turn the office of Dr. Jacob Greenberg, an assistant superintendent, into a shambles, *New York Times*, February 1, 1940, p. 23. More ominously, a few months later (and reminiscent of our times) in Pasadena, California, a junior high principal, denied reappointment at a school board meeting, killed five school personnel, including the superintendent, *New York Times*, May 7, 1940, p. 1; May 10, 1940, p. 14.

48. *New York Times*, April 30, 1939, p. 42.

49. *New York Times*, June 5, 1938, II, p. 5

Epilogue

1. Alfred North Whitehead, *The Aims of Education* (New York: Mentor Books, [1929]1949), p. 26.

2. Fred Hechinger, "Schools Remain Bedeviled by Old Ills and Old Solutions," *New York Times*, December 6, 1987, IV, p. 6.

3. Fred Hechinger, "UFT Uses Its Power to Pull a Punch," *New York Times*, January 10, 1988, IV, p. 6.

4. Richard Vedder, "Small Classes Are Better for Whom?" *Wall Street Jour-*

nal, June 7, 1988, p. 34; Gary Putka, "Parents in Minnesota Are Getting to Send Kids Where They Like," *Wall Street Journal*, May 13, 1988, pp. 1, 4. Eric Hanushek, "Schools Need Incentives, Not More Money," *Wall Street Journal*, October 5, 1994, p. A18.

Selected Bibliography

Books

Addams, Jane. *The Spirit of Youth and the City Streets*. New York: Macmillan, 1909.

Agee, James, and Evans, Walker. *Let Us Now Praise Famous Men*. Boston: Houghton Mifflin, [1941] 1960.

Alinsky, Saul. *John L. Lewis*. New York: G.P. Putnam's Sons, 1949.

Archambault, Reginald D., ed. *Dewey on Education*. New York: Random House, 1966.

Barrett, William. *The Truants*. Garden City, N.Y.: Anchor Press/Doubleday, 1982.

Beale, Howard K. *Are American Teachers Free?* New York: Charles Scribner's Sons, 1936.

———. *A History of Freedom of Teaching in American Schools*. New York: Charles Scribner's Sons, 1941.

Bird, Caroline. *The Invisible Scar*. New York: David McKay, 1966.

Boulding, Kenneth. *The Meaning of the Twentieth Century*. New York: Harper Colophon Books, Harper & Row, 1964.

Bourne, Randolph. *The Gary Schools*. Boston: Hougton Mifflin, 1916.

Bowers, C.A. *The Progressive Educator and the Depression*. New York: Random House, 1969.

Brenner, Reuven, and Brenner, Gabrielle A. *Gambling and Speculation*. New York: Cambridge University Press, 1990.

Burgess, Charles, and Borrowman, Merle. *What Doctrines to Embrace*. Glenview, Ill.: Scott, Foresman, 1969.

Burke, Kenneth. *Permanence and Change*. Indianapolis: Bobbs-Merrill, 1935.

Callahan, Raymond E. *Education and the Cult of Efficiency*. Chicago: Phoenix Books, University of Chicago Press, 1962.

Caro, Robert A. *The Power Broker*. New York: Alfred A. Knopf, 1974.

Cohen, Sol. *Progressives and Urban School Reform*. New York: Teachers College, 1963.

Covello, Leonard. *The Heart Is a Teacher*. New York: McGraw-Hill, 1958.

Cubberley, Ellwood P. *Changing Conceptions of Education*. Boston: Houghton Mifflin, 1909.

Cremin, Lawrence. *The Transformation of the School*. New York: Vintage Books, Random House, 1961.

———, ed. *The Republic and the School: Horace Mann on the Education of Free Men*. New York: Teachers College Press, 1957.

Counts, George S. *The Social Composition of Boards of Education*. Chicago: University of Chicago Press, 1927.

Dewey, John. *Democracy in Education*. New York: Free Press, [1916] 1966.

———. *Liberalism in Social Action*. New York: Capricorn Books, 1963.

————. *Reconstruction in Philosophy*. New York: New American Library, [1920] 1950.

————, and Evelyn. *Schools of Tomorrow*. New York: E.P. Dutton, [1915] 1962.

Engelbrecht, H.C., and Hanighen, F.C. *The Merchants of Death*. New York: Dodd, Mead, 1934.

Faulkner, Harold U. *American Economic History*. 6th ed. New York: Harper & Bros., 1949.

Fleischman, Harry. *Norman Thomas*. New York: W.W. Norton, 1964.

Flexner, Abraham, and Bachman, Frank P. *The Gary Schools*. New York: General Education Board, 1918.

Friedheim, Robert L. *The Seattle General Strike*. Seattle: University of Washington Press, 1964.

Galbraith, J.K. *The Great Crash*. Boston: Houghton Mifflin, 1961.

Ginger, Ray. *Altgeld's America*. Chicago: Quadrangle Books, 1965.

Goldman, Eric. *The Crucial Decade—And After, 1945–1960*. New York: Vintage Books, Random House, 1960.

Gutek, Gerald. *The Educational Theory of George S. Counts*. Columbus: Ohio State University Press, 1970.

Halper, Albert. *Good-bye, Union Square*. Chicago: Quadrangle Books, 1970.

Harlan, Louis R. *Separate and Unequal*. New York: Atheneum, 1968.

Harrod, Roy F. *The Life of John Maynard Keynes*. New York: Harcourt, Brace, 1951.

Heckscher, August. *When La Guardia Was Mayor*. New York: W.W. Norton, 1978.

Hofstadter, Richard. *The Age of Reform*. New York: Alfred A. Knopf, 1955.

Hook, Sidney. *Out of Step*. New York: Harper & Row, 1987.

Hunter, Robert. *Poverty*. New York: Harper Torchbooks, Harper & Row, [1904] 1965.

Iversen, Robert W. *The Communists and the Schools*. New York: Harcourt, Brace, 1959.

Kazin, Alfred. *Starting Out in the Thirties*. Boston: Little, Brown, 1965.

Keynes, John M. *The General Theory of Employment, Interest and Money*. New York: Harcourt, Brace, 1936.

Kindleberger, Charles P. *The World in the Depression, 1929–1939*. Berkeley: University of California Press, 1973.

Krug, Edward A. *The Shaping of the American High School, 1880–1920*. Madison: University of Wisconsin Press, 1964.

————. *The Shaping of the American High School, II*. Madison: University of Wisconsin Press, 1972.

Kuhn, Thomas. *The Structure of Scientific Revolutions*. Chicago: University of Chicago Press, 1970.

Lee, Russell, et al. *Far From Main Street: Three Photographers in Depression-Era New Mexico*. Santa Fe: Museum of New Mexico, 1994.

Lerner, Max, ed. *The Portable Veblen*. New York: Viking Press, 1948.

Leuchtenburg, William E. "The New Deal and the Analogue of War." In *Change and Continuity in Twenteith Century America*. Edited by John Braeman et al. New York: Harper Colophon Books, Harper & Row, 1966.

Lynd, Robert, and Lynd, Helen. *Middletown in Transition*. New York: Harcourt, Brace, 1937.

Mangione, Jerre. *The Dream and the Deal*. Boston: Little, Brown, 1973.

Mann, Arthur. *La Guardia Comes to Power*. Philadelphia: J.B. Lippincott, 1965.

Mann, Horace. *A Few Thoughts on the Powers and Duties of Women, Two Lectures*. Syracuse: Hall, Mills, 1853.

Mann, Mary, ed. *Annual Reports on Education by Horace Mann*. Boston: Horace B. Fuller, 1868.

Marris, Peter. *Loss and Change*. New York: Pantheon Books, 1974.

Morison, S.E., and Commager, H.S. *The Growth of the American Republic*. Vol. II. New York: Oxford University Press, 1950.

Ottley, Roi, and Weatherby, William J. *The Negro in New York*. New York: Praeger, 1969.

Ravitch, Diane. *The Great School Wars*. New York: Basic Books, 1974.

Renshaw, Patrick. *The Wobblies*. New York: Doubleday, 1967.

Rivlin, Alice M. *Systematic Thinking for Social Action*. Washington, D.C.: Brookings Institution, 1971.

Schon, Donald. "The Social System and Social Change." In *Social Change*. Edited by Robert Nisbet. New York: Harper Torchbooks, Harper & Row, 1973.

Sherwood, Robert E. *Roosevelt and Hopkins*. New York: Harper & Bros., 1948.

Shumaker, Ann, and Rugg, Harold. *The Child Centered School*. New York: World Book, 1928.

Stephens, J.M. *The Process of Schooling*. New York: Holt, Rinehart and Winston, 1967.

Stott, William. *Documentary Expression and Thirties America*. New York: Oxford University Press, 1973.

Sulzberger, C.L. *Sit-Down with John L. Lewis*. New York: Random House, 1938.

Tyack, David B. *The One Best System*. Cambridge: Harvard University Press, 1974.

———, Lowe, Robert, and Hansot, Elizabeth. *Public Schools in Hard Times: The Great Depression and Recent Years*. Cambridge: Harvard University Press, 1984.

Weaver, Paul H. *News and the Culture of Lying*. New York: The Free Press, 1994.

Whitehead, Alfred North. *The Aims of Education*. New York: Mentor Book, [1929] 1949.

Zitron, Celia L. *The New York City Teachers Union*. New York: Humanities Press, 1968.

PERIODICALS

Allen, Forrest. "Control of the Press or Education of the Reader?" *Social Frontier*, 1, 7 (April 1935), 27, 28.

———. "A Layman Speaks His Mind." *Social Frontier*, 3, 23 (February 1937), 143, 144.

Anonymous. "Why White Collar Workers Can't Be Organized." *Harper's Magazine* (August 1957).

Beard, Charles A. "Freedom of Teaching." *Social Frontier*, 1, 6 (March 1935), 18, 20.

———. "Property and Democracy." *Social Frontier*, 1, 1 (October 1934), 14, 15.

Boulding, Kenneth. "The Schooling Industry as a Possibly Pathological Section of the American Economy." *Review of Educational Research*, 42, 1 (Winter 1972), 129–143.

Carlson, Avis D. "Deflating the Schools." *Harper's Magazine*, 167 (November 1933), 714.

Dewey, John. "Can Education Share in Social Reconstruction?" *Social Frontier*, 2, 1 (October 1934), 12.

———. "The Teacher and His World." *Social Frontier*, 1, 4 (January 1935), 7.

Dewey Revisited. *History of Education Quarterly*, 15, 1, (Spring 1975), issue devoted to Dewey, 3–92.

Fairchild, Henry P. "A Sociologist Views the New Deal." *Social Frontier*, 1, 1 (October 1934), 16, 18.

Felmley, David. "Is the Employment of Untrained Teachers the Cause or Result of Low Salaries?" National Education Association. *Proceedings*, 47 (1909), 307, 308.

Fisher, Raymond. "It's My Turn." *Social Frontier*, 4, 35 (May 1938), 249.

Hart, Joseph K. "City Dwellers with Small-Town Minds." *Social Frontier*, 3, 21 (December 1936) 73–75.

Hartman, George. "A Professor Runs for Office." *Social Frontier*, 1, 7 (April 1935), 26

Hazlett, J. Stephen. "NEA and NCA Involvement in a School Controversy: Chicago, 1944–47." *School Review*, 78, 2 (February 1970), 202–205.

Hewes, F.W. "The Public Schools of the United States." *Harper's Weekly*, 39 (October 26, 1895), 1020; 39 (November 2, 1895), 1041.

Hoetker, James, and Ahlbrand, William P., Jr., "The Persistence of the Recitation." *American Educational Research Journal*, 6 (March 1969).

Katz, Michael B. "American History Textbooks and Social Reform in the 1930s." *Paedogogica Historica*, 6, 1 (1966).

McKeever, W.H. "The Forgotten Classroom Teacher." *Journal of Education*, 116 (May 1, 1933), 224–225. Replies to McKeever. *Journal of Education*, 116 (May 15, 1933), 255, 271.

"Meeting the Emergency in Education." Department of Secondary School Principals, National Education Association. *Bulletin*, 46 (April 1933), 13.

Mitchell, Broadus. "The Choice Before Us." *Social Frontier*, 1, 2 (November 1934), 15.

"The Teachers School Relief Fund of New York City and the Hofstadter Committee." School and Society, 35 (March 12, 1932), 358–359.

Tildsley, John. "Why I Object to Some Proposals of the Frontier Thinkers." *Social Frontier*, 4, 37 (July 1938), 322.

Watson, Goodwin. "Education is the Social Frontier." *Social Frontier*, 1, 1 (October 1934), 22.

UNPUBLISHED MATERIALS

Moreo, D.W. "Public Schools in Search of Legitimacy: Mandarin Schools and Folk Teachers, 1900–1929." Ph.D. dissertation, University of Washington, 1971.

Morris, Francis M. "A History of Teacher Unionism in the State of Washington, 1920–1945." Master's thesis, University of Washington, 1968.

INDEX